ECOCIDE
of
NATIVE AMERICA

ECOCIDE
of
NATIVE AMERICA

Environmental Destruction
of Indian Lands and Peoples

Donald A. Grinde
Bruce E. Johansen

Foreword by Howard Zinn

CLEAR LIGHT PUBLISHERS
SANTA FE, NEW MEXICO

First Edition
10 9 8 7 6 5 4 3 2 1

Library of Congress Cataloging in Publication Data

Grinde, Donald A., 1946 –
Ecocide of Native America: environmental destruction of Indian lands and
    peoples / Donald Grinde and Bruce Johansen.
    p.   cm.
    Includes bibliographical references and index.
    ISBN 0-940666-52-9 : $24.95
    1. Indians of North America-Land tenure.   2. Indians of North
America—Economic conditions.   3. Environmental degradation-
North America.   4. Human ecology-North America.
I. Johansen, Bruce E. (Bruce Elliott), 1950-   . II. Title.
E98.L3G74   1994
333.7'097–dc20   94-17271
                                                                          CIP

In cooperation with the American Forestry Association, we have planted trees
to replace those used to manufacture these books.

We dedicate this book to generations to come.

Acknowledgments

We would like to thank our families: Don's wife Sarah and son Kee; Bruce's wife, Patricia Keiffer, son Shannon, granddaughter Samantha, and her mother Brandi. We also would like to thank University of Nebraska at Omaha Communication Department secretary Inga Ronke, as well as Jose Barreiro and the American Indian Program at Cornell University. Thanks also are due Esther Keeswood, John Redhouse, Billy Frank, Jr., Roberto Maestas, John Kahionhes Fadden, and Ray Fadden. Special thanks are due also to Jewell James and Kurt Russo of the Lummi Treaty Protection Task Force, from whose volume *Our People Our Land* (1992) we have excerpted Native testimonies in the final chapter. Many thanks, too, to Harmon Houghton, Marcia Keegan, and Sara Held of Clear Light Publishers for the long hours they put into creating this book in all its aspects, from text, to cover design, to photography.

Contents

Foreword

This book is not only a work of history—it *makes* history. It is a powerful manifestation of something recent in American culture: the revision of the historical record by African-Americans, by women, by Latino writers, by Native American scholars.

Indeed, the word *revisionist* used to describe this new history is too mild a word. What we are witnessing in the United States today is a revolutionary cultural development, a break with two centuries of history written from the point of view of the white European male elite.

The proof of how radical is this break, is the fury with which it is being viewed by defenders of the historical canon, the conservative guardians of the traditional stories of the past. Their monopoly of the marketplace of ideas is now threatened by newcomers offering information and analyses which reveal to the world that something important has been omitted from orthodox history.

Donald Grinde and Bruce Johansen are important practitioners of this new history, writing from a point of view—the Native American point of view—which has for so long been shamefully neglected by the academic establishment, and which is now just beginning to emerge as a scholarly force.

The story they tell is a grim one, of the destruction of Indian land, Indian people for five-hundred years. It is a sobering story but an instructive one, which students and teachers and ordinary citizens must understand. It compels all of us to reconsider the glorification of conquest which has been part of our cultural heritage. It asks us to rethink what we have heretofore hailed as "progress." It is a prophetic warning of what we face if we do not listen to the voices Europeans tried to smother as they invaded and took over this hemisphere.

We desperately need to hear this story if we are to save the earth, the sky, the water, the air—save ourselves. What follows in these pages has, therefore, profound meaning to us all. I thank Donald Grinde and Bruce Johansen for their eloquent and powerful contribution to our education.

Howard Zinn

Introduction

In a world full of profound and sometimes cruel ironies, one stands out: Native Americans, who held the lands of the Western Hemisphere in a living trust for thousands of years, have been afflicted by some of the worst pollution of an environmental crisis that has reached planetwide proportions. Statements from indigenous peoples around the world indicate that they perceive themselves as having been "pushed to the edge of a cliff" by environmental problems caused by industrialism.[1] Navajos and Australian Aborigines are dying of radiation poisoning after mining uranium in once-sacred areas. PCBs at toxic levels are being found in the breast milk of Inuit (Eskimo) women—and in the fish they eat. The Arctic is contaminated by radioactive waste dumped by Russia as it scraps portions of its aging nuclear submarine fleet. The mountain trails of Nepal host so many "nature trekkers" that nearby hillsides have been stripped of any vegetation that might be used for firewood.

Across North America, the peoples who traditionally made their living directly from the earth are facing environmental ruin not of their own making. Who are the primary victims of the toxic dump ranked number one on the Environmental Protection Agency's Superfund list? The Mohawks of Akwesasne (St. Regis Indian Reservation, in New York State, Ontario, and Quebec).

The effects of imported European technology have been shaping life at Akwesasne for nearly four hundred years. Are there any places now where the effects of industrialization are not felt? In the last half of the twentieth century, the ecological problems that afflicted small areas a century ago (when John Muir and others helped create the science of ecology) have become inescapable—they extend to the far reaches of the Arctic as well as to the most isolated of tropical rainforests. We may be the last generation to see tribal peoples living as they choose in a natural habitat.

In the meantime, the Henry Doorly Zoo, in Omaha, Nebraska, has opened the world's largest artificially maintained indoor rainforest, a tropical forest so convincingly real that it is almost possible to forget that it survives by the grace of humidity spray nozzles and heat supplied by the burning of fossil fuels. Just how long will it be before tourists from Brazil, Central America, and Africa visit Omaha's zoo to see what a real rainforest once looked like?

We are reminded by native testimonies that time is short and that humankind must "turn away from the industrial view of the earth as a resource to be consumed" by appreciating "the lessons of traditional cultures that have for centuries maintained a sustainable relationship to the earth."[2] In his preface to *Story Earth: Native Voices in the Environment,* a collection of native environmental statements, Pablo Piacentini, director of the Interpress Columnists Service, says that appreciation of indigenous cultures is important so that solutions to current environmental problems will not be "defined within the framework that gave rise to the problems in the first place."[3]

Gro Harlem Brundtland, prime minister of Norway, notes that "although our technological and scientific advances have created a world economy of huge dimensions, there have never been so many poor, illiterate and unemployed people in the world." This industrial economy, for the first time in human history, is "having a severe, possibly irreversible impact on nature and the living conditions of all the species on our planet."[4]

An economic model that equates economic growth with "development" has long obscured the nature and extent of ecological impacts. The new consensus, which draws from Native American environmental views, challenges traditional Western notions of development and urges a return to an attitude of reverence for the earth and a rejection of economic gain for its own sake. "We are now realizing," writes Brundtland, "that growth which causes environmental degradation is not progress but deterioration."[5]

The human and ecological costs of development have become dramatically obvious to indigenous peoples at the periphery of industrial expansion. According to Tanien (Daniel) Ashini, a Native American from Canada, life in the bush provided "the kind of spiritual tranquility that many others associate with their churches"—that is, until the architects of development built a military air base nearby. "Now," he says, "the noise of low-flying jet bombers has destroyed our peace of mind in the bush." The base also has polluted their waterways and driven away game animals, forcing many people to live in villages, where they suffer from alcoholism, family violence, and suicides which make village life "utter hell."[6] In Brazil, the population of the native people, which totaled 6 million a couple of generations ago, has been reduced to 240,000.

Hindu environmental activist Karan Singh maintains that

centuries of rapacious exploitation of the environment have finally caught up with us, and a radically changed attitude toward nature is no longer voluntary, a question of acquiring spiritual merit or condescension, but of sheer survival."[7]

Native America today provides a virtual catalog of environmental destruction. Many educated people in North America today believe that the accident at the Three Mile Island nuclear power plant resulted in the largest expulsion of radioactivity in the United States. This is accurate only if Native American lands are omitted. The biggest radioactive leak actually occurred on the Navajo Reservation in 1978. The fact that so few people have heard of this leak indicates how preoccupied the "majority society" has become with its own environmental crisis and how cheaply it still regards Native American life.

To appreciate the impact of the environmental crisis on Native Americans, it is necessary to understand the earth from a Native American perspective—as sacred space, as provider for the living, and as shrine for the dead. Ecology and land are intimately connected with Native American spirituality, which entails that land is not regarded merely as real estate, a commodity to be bought, sold, or exploited for financial gain. The contrast between Native American and European perspectives regarding the environment was never stronger than when the "frontier" encroached most quickly and painfully on Native American homelands, such as during the forced removal of the Cherokee Nation from the Southeast in the 1830s.

Tracing the roots of the differences in Native American and European worldviews through American history does not take us far enough back in time, however. The real roots go back to the Bible, with its command to subdue the earth, and to the very bases of perception utilized by Native American and European cultures. Any Western-educated reader must begin the journey toward understanding by realizing that he or she has a culturally determined way of looking at the world, one for which the basic mental metaphor is the straight line. Just as a command to subdue the earth implies there is a separation between humankind and nature, straight-line thinking implies that progress and development characterize human history.

The concept of progress is foreign to many Native American cultures, which adopt a cyclical view of reality. The Mayan calendar provides an instructive example of this difference. Mayan astronomers created a calendar that is slightly more precise than the one inherited from the Romans, but we do not use it today because it was based on measuring time as a factor of two intersecting cycles, not as a straight-line passage from the past into the future.

One's concept of landscape affects how land is used. The changes in the American landscape were described by the noted western historian Frank Waters, whose four score and ten years allowed him to witness many of the changes in the western United States:

That is exactly what the white conquerors did as they proceeded westward. They levelled whole forests under the axe, plowed under the grassland, dammed and drained the rivers, gutted the mountains for gold and silver, and divided and sold the land itself. Accompanying all this destruction was the extermination of birds and

beasts, not alone for profit or sport, but to indulge . . . a
wanton lust for killing.[8]

The attitudes of European immigrants toward the American land and its indigenous peoples have always been characterized by dualities—of love and hate, for example, of a desire to preserve and a desire to destroy. Hernán Cortés rhapsodized about the grandeur of the Aztec capital of Tenochtitlán before his soldiers sacked it out of hunger for gold. The first English immigrants in America were also divided in their view of the land they were attempting to settle. To some of them, this was "New England," a place to be subjugated by the yoke of Christianity; to others, it was "New Canaan," a refuge from English orthodoxy. In 1620, William Bradford called America a "hideous and desolate wilderness."[9] In 1629, John Winthrop enjoined recent arrivals to "multiply and subdue the earth."[10] A similar duality is evident even today: The environmental movement becomes ever more popular in the face of growing perceptions of crisis as American industrialism invades the last enclaves of ecologically independent Native America, notably in the Arctic of North America and the Amazon region of South America.

From the beginning, one impulse of European immigrants was to adopt the same attitude toward the land expressed by its native inhabitants. The other impulse was to "civilize" the wilderness, by extracting natural resources, for example, and treating not only these resources but the land itself as commodities for exchange. It is noteworthy that beavers remained plentiful in eastern North America until they were defined as a commodity by Euro-American merchants and Native American hunters.

This duality of attitude toward the land sometimes occurs in a single individual. In the eighteenth century, Benjamin Franklin evoked native examples of governance while at the same time speculating in native land. Such speculation, by Franklin and many of his prominent compatriots, laid the financial basis for the rapid colonization westward after 1800. An environmental perspective allows us to examine the westward movement in all its dimensions. As Alfred Crosby has noted, European-American expansion involved much more than the movement of people, since the settlers carried with them, intentionally or not, domesticated animals, imported plants (including weeds), and diseases.[11]

Even at the time of the first English settlements, considerable opposition developed to the Puritan ideology. Roger Williams broke off from the dominant colony and formed Rhode Island (then called Providence Plantations) with considerable Native American aid; he tried (and failed) to establish a colony in which everyone had roughly equal parcels of land. In 1622, Thomas Morton expressed a contrary view to the Puritan conception of nature as desolate wilderness:

> *And when I had more seriously considered of the bewty of the place, with all her faire endowments, I did not think that in all the knowne world it could be paralel'd. For so many goodly groves of trees, dainty fine round rising hillucks: delicate faire large plaines . . . and clear running streams . . . t'was Natures Master-peece.*[12]

At the same time that Morton was painting this idyllic picture of New England, smallpox, the most harrowing of many European pathogens, was eliminating whole native societies. William Bradford, in 1634, described the horror as he experienced it:

> *This spring, also, those Indians that lived about their trading house . . . fell sick of the small pox, and died most miserably. . . . For want of bedding & linen and other helps, they fall into a lamentable condition, as they live on their hard mats, the pox breaking and mattering, and running into one another, their skin cleaving . . . to the mats they lie on; when they turn . . . a whole side will flay off at once . . . and they will be all of a gore blood, most fearful to behold; and then very sore, what with cold and other distempers, they die like rotten sheep.*[13]

When John Winthrop evoked the biblical injunction to subdue the earth, he wrote that the Bible commanded occupancy of a continent that had lain "empty and unimproved." The selectiveness of Winthrop's perceptions is astounding, since he must have known that his colony had survived in large part because Squanto and other Native American people had taught the immigrants how to plant corn and other crops indigenous to America. Yet one common rationale for conquest of territory was that the immigrants were taking over land that had not been used—land that, by European standards, had lain uncultivated, unmined, undeveloped, unexploited. In the 1790s, a settler in upstate New York (Herkimer County) wrote to his brother in New Hampshire of the demographic and ecological transformations on the New York frontier:

> *Governor Clinton bought up most of the Indian lands west of Fort Stanwix for the State, and now we see the Oneidas and Brothertown Indians often enough, but they're little trouble, and a feeble shadow of the people who were here when the Dutch and the British forts came to the Mohawk Valley. . . . The Yankees have taken care of the wolves, bears and Indians . . . and we'll build the Lord's temple yet, build it out of these great trees.*[14]

Although some immigrants freely borrowed native farming techniques, herbal cures, and other skills and knowledge, others hardly saw Native Americans or the uses they made of the land. Although the American frontier is frequently romanticized, in reality the settlers often underwent drastic cultural changes in the process of adapting to the new environments they encountered. In Georgia, a French observer commented on the violent nature of the frontier settlers during the 1780s:

> *These Crakeurs [crackers] are very fond of . . . [whiskey]; when they drink some of it, since they are by nature quarrelsome and mean, they quarrel among themselves, and agree to fight on the day they appoint. Their fights are very much like English pugilism or*

boxing, except that they are more murderous. When the
Crakeurs have agreed on the day and the hour . . . to
fight, they gather as many spectators as they can. . . .[15]

Obviously, the changes experienced by the settlers fostered a mentality of violence. Historians of the colonial period have often ignored the social costs the colonists themselves had to pay.

Between 1800 and 1890, technology and European economic and social problems provided the impetus for an explosion of colonization. Benjamin Franklin, a product of an earlier time, had thought that it would take a thousand years for Euro-Americans to cross the continent. However, the railroad and the cotton gin, combined with the industrialization of Europe (and the eviction of many people from the land there), caused what was probably the largest-scale colonization in human history. Less than a century after Franklin's death, railroads would host "expeditions" during which aspiring buffalo hunters would shoot vast numbers of the animals from the comfort of their sleeping coaches, playing their part in the "winning of the West" by exterminating the animals that had provided an economic, ecological, and spiritual base for the Indian tribes of the Great Plains.

Through confiscation of Native American land and natural resources as well as through alteration of natural environments, the U.S. industrial and agricultural economy grew rapidly. Few economists and economic historians recognize that the confiscation of land and resources contributed significantly to the economic growth of the United States. Instead, much of the growth is attributed to "free enterprise," "Yankee ingenuity," and technological change. No doubt these factors were present, but the failure to acknowledge the role of confiscation gives the impression that the American economy grew entirely through the exploitation of virgin wilderness. This not only denies the importance of Native Americans in the growth equation but also glorifies short-term economic gains, despite the environmental degradation that tends to result.[16]

By the 1840s, the building of the railroads and the increase in industrialization created an economic and cultural matrix that forced changes in U.S. Indian policy. Fearing that American Indians would be brought to ruin by changes in land use and technologies fostered by the settlers, the U.S. government devised the reservation system as an alternative to extinction.[17] American Indians were to be removed to territory where they would no longer present an obstacle to the development of the West. Too few people realize that the destruction of wilderness and animals, such as the buffalo herds of the Great Plains, as well as the relocation of American Indians, were viewed as necessities in the development of the American West.

But even during this tidal wave of colonization, dissent continued. Appreciation of America's native peoples was still associated in the minds of some with respect for the land. In 1844, George Catlin, the frontier artist, wrote,

> *I am fully convinced, from a long familiarity with these people, that the Indians' misfortune has consisted chiefly in our ignorance of their true native character and disposition. . . . The very use of the word savage . . . is an abuse of the word. The word, in its true definition, means no more than* wild, *or* wild man, *and a wild man may have been endowed by his maker with all the humane and noble traits that inhabit the heart of a tame man. Our ignorance and dread or fear of these people, therefore, have given a new definition to the adjective.*[18]

Catlin wrote that during his many years of travel among Native Americans they had always shown him hospitality and kindness. They had fed him, clothed him, welcomed him at their fires, and had even escorted him and helped carry his awkward baggage. He remarked in 1844 that no one ever had stolen from him, even in the absence of laws against stealing.

Contrast Catlin's point of view with the position expressed by Senator Thomas Hart Benton two years later:

It would seem that the White race alone received the divine command, to subdue and replenish the earth, for it is the only race that has obeyed it—the only race that hunts out new and distant lands, and even a New World, to subdue and replenish.[19]

It was Senator Benton who used the term "Manifest Destiny" to refer to the notion that the United States was ordained to expand westward, propelled by increasing emigration from Europe, development of new transportation and agricultural technologies, and the general spread of industrialization.

In nineteenth-century America, land increasingly came to be seen as a commodity, salable, like everything else, in the appropriate marketplace. Native Americans were to be eradicated or drastically changed to make way for a new style of living and a new ethic regarding landholdings and treatment of the earth. It was said, even among some "friends of the Indian," that the most humane way to achieve this transition would be to "kill the Indian, but save the man." Indian "reformers" sometimes spoke of a "final solution" well before the Nazis used the phrase. The traditions, cultures, and worldviews of Native Americans were to be stripped away by dividing their land into farms, placing the children in boarding schools, and generally immersing them in the capitalist economy.

L. Frank Baum, who would later write *The Wizard of Oz*, penned the following words as editor of the Aberdeen, South Dakota, *Saturday Pioneer* a week and a half before the fatal confrontation at Wounded Knee in 1890:

The nobility of the Redskin is extinguished, and what few are left are a pack of whining curs who lick the hand that smites them. The Whites, by law of conquest, by justice of civilization, are masters of the American continent, and the best safety of the frontier settlements will be secured by the total annihilation of the few remaining Indians. Why not annihilation? Their glory has fled, their spirit broken, their manhood effaced; bet-

*ter that they should die than live [as] the miserable
wretches that they are.*[20]

Wounded Knee occurred at the climax of the era Mark
Twain called the Gilded Age, a time of intense government-
assisted land and resource exploitation that ironically also
witnessed the creation of the modern conservation movement. The continent had to fill up before significant numbers of Euro-Americans realized that its resources were finite.
The conservation movement did not begin to emphasize environmental stewardship until it became clear to a significant
number of non-native people that unregulated exploitation
of natural resources was threatening the entire planet.

By the late twentieth century, humankind had fulfilled
the injunction of the first chapter of Genesis so effectively
that it was beginning to drown in its own effluvia. The disper-
sion of toxins on land and in the sea, the buildup of carbon
dioxide and depletion of ozone in the atmosphere are signs
of destructive modes of production and consumption that
have become common worldwide. It is no longer possible to
escape pollution by leaving urban areas.

The growing scope of the environmental crisis has led
more and more non-Indians to develop an appreciation of
cyclical thinking and the importance of balance. Some non-
Indian environmentalists have even tended to stereotype
Native Americans as demigods, and some Madison Avenue
executives have used this stereotype to try to turn an ecobuck.
A few individuals have sought to describe honestly how
Native Americans actually viewed and used the land.

The false assumption that Native Americans did not *use*
the land was a fallacy that justified conquest in some minds
from sea to shining sea. Native Americans have not always
been environmental perfectionists. Occasionally, in pre-
Columbian times, native urban areas taxed the local environment to the point of self-destruction (e.g., by overgrazing and
razing of forests). Like all societies, those in pre-Columbian
America faced the question of how to utilize land for purposes of survival. Indians manipulated the environment to
improve their material lives. While mistakes were made, the

fact that Europeans found the Western Hemisphere to be a natural treasure house indicates that misuse of the environment was not frequent or sustained over long periods of time.

In the present-day debate regarding Native American environmentalism, some popular writers ascribe it to the alleged static nature of native societies. In his book *A Study of History*, Arnold J. Toynbee classed the culture of the Inuits (Eskimos) as an "arrested civilization," whose members attained a certain level of social and religious organization by developing ways of survival in an inhospitable environment. Toynbee wrote that Inuit culture then remained at a minimal level because it was necessary for the people to focus so much effort on wresting a living from their harsh environment.[21] Toynbee's history, like all histories, is biased by the social and scientific assumptions of his time, although the assumption that native cultures were static still survives today, despite abundant historical and anthropological evidence to the contrary. Some people are so enamored of the stereotype of Native American stagnation that they become upset when present-day native people fail to conform. Under this "authenticity fallacy," native people are assumed to lose their identity if they do not live as their ancestors did, although the same criterion is not applied to emigrants from Europe who live much differently today than their great-great-grandparents.

However, the fact is that native societies, like those of the "Old World," changed dynamically. The pace of change accelerated following contact with Europeans. Clara Sue Kidwell, professor of anthropology at the University of California, Berkeley, stated:

> *For thousands of years before European contact, Native Americans adapted to a wide range of environmental conditions throughout North America. In the Chaco Canyon region of western New Mexico, for example, a great Pueblo culture flourished from approximately 1100 A.D. to approximately 1300 A.D. Pueblo Bonito contained at least 800 rooms, and the total population of the canyon region may have been as many as 7,000*

people at the height of the culture. The development of this culture was made possible by floodwater irrigation of corn, along with river water that flowed in unpredictable volumes through the base of the canyon.[22]

Kidwell continues, illustrating the native penchant for innovative technology:

On the Northwest Coast, Makah whalers, using canoes hollowed out of single cedar logs, harpoons of yew wood, and lines of cedar fiber strung with inflated sealskin floats, hunted and killed whales weighing up to 40 tons.[23]

Indeed, the practices of many native societies contradict the popular stereotype that native cultures were static and unchanging. Instead, native peoples were adapting technologies to problems of survival over time. Another example is that of the Inuits (Eskimos), who fashioned whaling canoes so watertight that they could be overturned and righted again in near-freezing water without the occupant becoming more than slightly wet. Could we compare the Inuits' accomplishments in seafaring technology to those of the Vikings, who also lived in a taxing near-arctic environment? Neither culture was, in Arnold Toynbee's words, an "arrested civilization" but instead composed of people who successfully adapted technology to survival in an unforgiving land.

The philosophical foundation of most Native American societies is fundamentally different from that of Western, "scientific" humankind. "Science" seeks causes and effects, examining problems in minute, often isolating, detail whereas the native view assumes that the forces of the natural world are affected by spiritual forces. Many scholars have written extensively about various aspects of this worldview. A. I. Hallowell commented on the Ojibway concept of "owners" or "bosses" of the animal world—the spirits who control the movements of game animals.[24] Dorothy Lee described the Wintu notion that matter always has existed.[25]

Professor Kidwell wrote:

In native oral traditions generally figures such as Coyote, Raven, and Bear appear, die, and reappear, or change form, as wenebojo, *the trickster figure among the Chippewa changed himself into a snake to get at a particularly choice piece of meat on a moose skull.*[26] *The ability to change form is a sign of spiritual power; it attests to the immutability of essence despite mutability of form. The spirits of the world are not subject to unvarying laws of behavior. Their essence is will, volition, motion, speech. When Hallowell asked an Ojibwa man whether all stones were alive (in the linguistic category "animate") the man replied "No, but some are."*[27] *Flint is a living person in Ojibwa traditions.*[28] *In the Navajo tradition of the origins of the world, the hero twins who rid the world of monsters who were threatening human being were protected by flint armor. Flint has life and power in its ability to strike sparks.*[29]

While scientific method seeks to explain and regularize the spirit of nature, the native mind makes inquiries into the nature of spirit, finding both concepts intertwined in a natural theology that establishes a sense of sacredness in place and tradition. The "spirit world" exists outside the domain of rational science; native people believe that it sustains them, and that they may draw power from it by engaging in appropriate behavior. Attaining such power is rarely easy or swift, for tradition has created tests for those who seek to tap the spirit world. Vision quests and dreams become rigors of passage from one stage of life to another, or between the world of spirit and of flesh. The forces of nature become metaphors for aspects of the spirit world as well as a means of establishing a personal relationship with spiritual elements. Earth is often spoken of as "mother," and the sky as "father." The native hunter shares a spiritual bond with his prey, asking its permission to be killed as food.

Numerous other aspects of the American Indian worldview also differ considerably from European views. For example, Native Americans often perceived that European land-use practices and perceptions were deceptive and thought that knowledge from the written word made people into thieves. A French observer with a group of Creek Indians related the following experience at a treaty council:

> *I took ten savages with me to go to the place, where the [American treaty] commissioners were. Upon arriving at the place, one of my men stopped an American and demanded the return of a beautiful horse he was riding, claiming it had been stolen from him. The latter was not wanting to give it back, the matter was placed before the American commissioners. . . . The American left immediately and soon brought back with him twenty-five men of his nation, who gave evidence that this horse had been raised by their comrade. . . . I informed my savage then . . . of what just happened, and declared to him that he would have to give up the horse . . . suddenly [he] took a blanket from his shoulders, and threw it over the head of the horse, asking that the American state to the judges in which eye it was blind. The American, taken by surprise by this question, declared that his horse was blind in the left eye. My savage declared, on the contrary, that it was not blind in either one; which was immediately recognized, as well as the dishonesty of the American and of his witnesses. The commissioners no longer able to doubt the truth, so that the thief might be punished, [ordered] that the horse be handed over completely harnessed to the savage. I informed him of this sentence . . . he immediately took off the saddle and the bridle and threw them at the feet of the American, telling him that he would never wish to use goods which belonged to a thief; that it was no doubt the* Natchoka *[the Creek term for the written word and books] which made them so knavish and so wicked.*[30]

Violence and immorality on the American frontier did not end with the removal of American Indian people, but was redirected towards the environment.

In his book *God Is Red*, Vine Deloria, Jr., contrasts the concept of sacredness espoused by Native American religions with that of Christianity and "Near Eastern" religions, noting how native spirituality is so closely tied to the environment and thus to ecological concerns.[31] Deloria also analyzes the ways in which each culture perceives reality—Europeans seeing time as linear and history as a progressive sequence of events while native cultures do not. Further, Deloria notes that Christianity usually portrays God as a humanlike being, often meddlesome and vengeful, whereas many native religions place supreme authority in a Great Spirit, or Great Mystery, symbolizing the life-forces of nature.

The Great Mystery becomes an ecological metaphor, as Deloria explains how native religions reinforce reverence for the land, and the remains of ancestors buried in it, in contrast to Europeans' ability to move from place to place without regard for location. What results is described by Deloria as a "surplus of shamans," lost European souls trying to put down ideological roots in American soil. Deloria effectively quotes Luther Standing Bear and Chief Seal'th to describe the alienation of European religions from the land and nature and convincingly argues that abuse of the earth will kill us (and generations to come) if the concept of man's integration with nature, which is fundamental to Native American religions, is not incorporated into development plans and policies around the world. As Deloria quotes Chief Seal'th: "We may be brothers after all."[32]

Native perspective has been a key to opposition of the exploitation ethic since the beginning and remains so today. The native reverence for and interaction with the environment gains popularity as the ecological crisis becomes more acute. The environmental movement often seeks to replace an ethic of exploitation with one of reciprocity, as defined by Winona LaDuke, who is an Anishinabe: "We give something in order to get something back from the creation."[33] The native view also derives from a belief that all things—human, animal, vegetable, even rocks—share life. There is no such thing as an "inanimate object" in many Native American cosmologies. The very idea of an "ecosystem" is derived in part from this idea.

In our own time, scholarly debate has revolved around two concepts concerning the earth and Native American peoples—the concepts of reciprocity and domination. One example of this debate is provided by the exchange between Bruce Trigger, who is probably the ranking living scholar on the Hurons, and James Axtell, professor of humanities at William and Mary College. Trigger's review of Axtell's book *Beyond 1492*, in *Ethnohistory*, the journal of the American Society for Ethnohistory, indicts Axtell's moral neutrality on the American holocaust of the last five hundred years:[34]

> *Axtell asserts that cultural change is natural and morally neutral. He also maintains that we cannot indict nations for sins of the past, that modern Euro-Americans are not responsible for the sins of their ancestors, and that in any case only a small number of colonists actually committed crimes against the Indians.*[35]

The same arguments could be applied to the degradation of the American earth. Trigger continues:

> *I find much to challenge in these arguments. Few colonists personally may have killed Indians or driven them from their lands, but many were prepared to support governments that did. Most colonists also were prepared to subscribe to myths that denigrated and dehumanized Indians. . . . Moreover, to a large extent, non-native Americans continue to benefit from the encounter, while Native Americans continue to suffer from it, politically, economically, and culturally.*[36]

One might also add that Native Americans continue to suffer environmentally.

In this book we attempt to trace the evolution of a Native American environmental ethic, as we describe the ecological consequences of the "encounter" for Native Americans in our time. We begin by defining native ecological practices, as we survey the debates that follow the continuing duality of the "encounter." We then trace native ecological practices before and during early colonization in the Southeast (among the Yamasees) and in the Southwest (among the Pueblos at the time of the Pueblo Revolt of 1680). A description of the Navajos' response to ecological changes in their land during the nineteenth and early twentieth centuries follows. Roughly the last half of the book examines environmental crises in Native America during the last half of the twentieth century, from coal and uranium mining among the Navajos and in the Lakotas' sacred *Paha Sapa* (Black Hills), to disputes over fishing rights in the Pacific Northwest and Great Lakes region, to pervasive pollution on the Akwesasne Mohawk Reservation in upstate New York, Ontario, and Quebec. We end with native testimonies describing environmental destruction on the "last frontiers" of the Western Hemisphere, including the shores of James Bay, the Arctic coast of Alaska, and the tropical rainforests of Central America.

We are left, at the end, with the same moral and intellectual questions facing Trigger and Axtell. Having maintained that Axtell's views allow most non-Indians to forget history ("Axtell's arguments read too much like a placebo . . . "), Trigger argues that Axtell is in no position to forgive Euro-Americans; only America's native peoples can do that. Trigger states that, "as beneficiaries of injustice, all . . . should feel morally obligated to secure justice for the aboriginal inhabitants of this continent."[37]

At the end of this harrowing journey of environmental and human catastrophe, the duality in the American mind gives the inquiring reader two options: one is to claim forgiveness and forget; the other is to realize history as completely as possible and work to correct past and present human and environmental arrogance and plunder.

One of the most central and enduring questions is how does one construct a just and environmentally survivable society? Could one begin by replacing the materialistic ethic with one that stresses reciprocity and the satisfaction of human and natural needs? Could one construct a "hierarchy of needs" (after Abraham Maslow) which recognizes that the most basic freedom human beings can possess is freedom from hunger and from lack of other basic necessities, including shelter, clothing, and medical care? Native societies often provide examples of people who live relatively equitably with limited exploitation of resources and with a minimum of acute poverty. Next in our hierarchy of needs would be insurance of safety, which, combined with other basic needs, Benjamin Franklin and Thomas Jefferson called "happiness," the third of a triad of liberties mentioned in the Declaration of Independence. After provision for basic needs and personal safety, a just society provides membership in a group and rewards people (Maslow calls this "recognition") for work that benefits the group. Many Native American societies provide excellent examples of societies that reward group membership while allowing for personal development to attain the final step in Maslow's hierarchy of needs—autonomy, or personal freedom.

With reference to care of the earth, native societies also have lessons to teach a nomadic Euro-American society. Native notions of sacredness are nearly always intertwined with respect and reverence for the earth, especially the part of the earth defined as home. From an environmental perspective the American mind struggles with the duality between recognition of a "home," or permanent physical location, and the demands of industrial society for a mobile labor force. The displacement of native peoples has not only harmed their societies and impaired their spirituality, but has also become a rationalization for the exploitation of the earth for short-term gain. It is common knowledge these days that an emphasis on short-term gain, through industrial mechanisms such as commodization of resources, is leading the earth—and that means all of us, and generations to come—toward long-term destruction. By learning from Native American societies, we are gaining a measure of perspective on how to change consumption patterns and cultural values in order to live in reciprocity and harmony on a sustaining earth. This recognition of the need for changes in our environmental perceptions must also encompass the realization that native peoples need once again to enforce their own environmental values, unfettered by regulations and environmental management practices of the industrial state. Regaining a more harmonious environmental state means that known harmonious environmental ethics must be allowed to reemerge and become prominent as quickly as possible to facilitate the flow of ideas that will lead to a more natural relationship in all of creation.

Notes

1. Interpress Columnists Service, ed., *Story Earth: Native Voices on the Environment* (San Francisco, Calif.: Mercury House, 1993), 14.

2. Ibid., back cover.

3. Ibid., ix.

4. Ibid., xiii.

5. Ibid., xvii.

6. Ibid., 17-18.

7. Ibid., 149.

8. Frank Waters, *Brave Are My People: Indian Heroes Not Forgotten* (Santa Fe, N.M.: Clear Light Publishers, 1993), 3.

9. Carolyn Merchant, ed., *Major Problems in American Environmental History* (Lexington, Mass.: D. C. Heath, 1993), 68.

10. Ibid., 71-72.

11. Ibid., xiii-xv.

12. Ibid., 75.

13. Ibid., 71.

14. Eliphalet Stark to Ephraim Stark, June 15, 1797, quoted in Hislop Codman, *The Mohawk* (New York: Rinehart and Company, 1948), 219-22. We are indebted to Shelley Price-Jones, history graduate student, Queen's University, Kingston, Ontario, for calling this passage to our attention.

15. Louis LeClerc Milfort, *Memoirs or, A Quick Glance at My Various Travels and My Sojourn in the Creek Nation* (Savannah, Ga.: Beehive Press, 1972), 87-88.

16. See Douglass C. North, *Growth and Welfare in the American Past: A New Economic History* (Englewood Cliffs, N.J.: Prentice-Hall, 1966), for a classic example of these tendencies. North mentions American Indians twice in his analysis of colonial policies, and in both instances they are portrayed as adversaries to the expansion of the American economy. The great unanswered questions in American economic history are how did the collapsing native economy become incorporated into the colonial economy and how can we measure the native resources that were confiscated and factored into the growth of the American economy? The first step in uncovering the answers is to recognize that the transference occurred. Appropriate measurement can then follow.

17. See Robert A. Trennert, *Alternative to Extinction: Federal Indian Policy and the Beginning of the Reservation System, 1846-1851* (Philadelphia: Temple University Press, 1975) for a fuller discussion of this policy.

18. Merchant, *Major Problems in American Environmental History*, 182.

19. Ibid., 250.

20. L. Frank Baum, *Saturday Pioneer*, December 20, 1890; cited in David Stannard, *American Holocaust: Columbus and the Conquest of the New World* (New York: Oxford University Press, 1992), 126.

21. Arnold J. Toynbee, *A Study of History*, 12 vols. (London: Oxford University Press, 1935-1962), 3:4-7.

22. See Kirk Bryan, "PreColumbian Agriculture in the Southwest, as Conditioned by Periods of Alluviation," *Annals of the Association of American Geographers* 31, no. 4 (1941): 219-42. See also R. Gwinn Vivian, "An Inquiry into Prehistoric Social Organization in Chaco Canyon, New Mexico," in *Reconstructing Prehistoric Pueblo Societies*, ed. William Longacre (Albuquerque: University of New Mexico Press, 1970), 75-76.

23. See Philip Drucker, *Cultures of the North Pacific Coast* (New York: Chandler Publishing Company, 1902), 136.

24. A. I. Hallowell, "Some Empirical Aspects of Northern Saulteaux Religion," *American Anthropologist* 36 (1934): 391.

25. Dorothy Lee, "Linguistic Reflection of Wintu Thought," in *Freedom and Culture* (Prospect Heights, Ill.: Waveland Press, 1987), 124.

26. Victor Barnouw, *Wisconsin Chippewa Myths and Tales and Their Relation to Chippewa Life* (Madison: University of Wisconsin Press, 1977), 25.

27. A. I. Hallowell, "Ojibwa Metaphysics of Being and the Perception of Persons," in *Person Perception and Interpersonal Behavior*, eds. Renato Taquiri and Luigi Petrullo (Palo Alto, Calif.: Stanford University Press, 1958), 65-55.

28. Hallowell, *"Aspects of Northern Saulteaux Religion,"* 65-66.

29. Gladys A. Reichard, *Navajo Religion: A Study of Symbolism*, 2d. ed. (Princeton, N.J.: Princeton University Press, 1950), 556.

30. Milfort, *Memoirs*, 133-34.

31. Vine Deloria, Jr., *God Is Red* (New York: Dell Publishing Company, 1973), 73-74.

32. Ibid., 73.

33. Merchant, *Major Problems in American Environmental History*, 543.

34. The term is David Stannard's, in *American Holocaust*.

35. Bruce Trigger, Review of Axtell's *After 1492, Ethnohistory* 40, no. 3 (Summer 1993): 467.

36. Ibid.

37. Ibid., 468.

Duwamish leader Chief Seal'th or Seattle. 1865 photograph by E. M. Sammis. Courtesy of Museum of New Mexico. Neg. No. 88464.

Chapter One

Native Americans: America's First Ecologists?

In the late twentieth century, increased pollution of air, water, and soil has spurred a mushrooming environmental movement. Increased attention to environmental problems has also fostered examination of the history of ecological thought, including the attitudes of Native Americans toward the natural world. Environmental philosophy has called the native example into service to question the basic assumptions of a technologically driven, resource-extracting economy. Study of many native cultures reveals a reverence for nature that was intertwined with daily life, solidified by rituals. In our time, many native peoples who practiced such a "natural theology" now face deadly pollution in their homelands, following the growth of industry. In fact, today some native reservations contain some of the worst toxic dumps in North America.

Native American Perspectives on the Environment

Environmental conservation was not a subject of general debate and controversy in the mid-nineteenth century, as Euro-American settlement spread across the land mass of the United States. Yet, from time to time, the records of the settlers contain warnings by native leaders whose peoples they were displacing describing how European attitudes toward nature would ruin the land, air, and water. Perhaps the most famous warning of this type came from Chief Seal'th, a leader of the Duwamish, who in 1854 prepared to move his people across Puget Sound, away from the growing city of Seattle.[1] He expresses the reverence his people have for the land:

*Our dead never forget the beautiful world that gave
them being. They still love its verdant valleys, its mur-
muring rivers, its magnificent mountains, sequestered
vales and verdant-lined lakes and bays. . . . Every part
of this soil is sacred in the estimation of my people.
Every hillside, every valley, every plain and grove has
been hallowed by some sad or happy event in days long
vanished. Even the rocks, which seem to be dumb and
dead as they swelter in the sun along the silent shore,
thrill with memories of stirring events connected with the
lives of my people. . . .*[2]

In the development of an environmental philosophy,
Chief Seal'th's words are often cited in the late twentieth century as evidence that many Native Americans practiced a
stewardship ethic toward the earth long before such attitudes
became popular in non-Indian society. The debate ranges
from acceptance of several versions of Chief Seal'th's speech
(some of them embellished) to a belief that the original trans-
lator, Dr. Henry Smith, as well as many people who followed
him, put the ecological concepts into the chief's mouth.

However, it is difficult to believe that Smith, in 1854,
would have fabricated an environmental message for an
English-speaking audience for whom conservation was not an
issue, and no one has provided any motive for such a fabrica-
tion. Regardless of the exact wording of Seal'th's speech, it
did contain environmental themes. Chief Seal'th was not
telling the immigrants what they wanted to hear because they
displayed no such ideological bent. If there was an environmental movement among whites in 1850s Seattle, local historians have yet to find any evidence of it.

Embellishment of the speech *did* occur, however, for a
willing audience in 1972 after the modern advent of Earth
Day. Ted Perry, a scriptwriter, put several phrases in the
chief's mouth in his 1972 film *Home.* Two examples: Seal'th
never said, "The earth is our mother" in those words. Nor did
he discourse on the whites' slaughter of buffalo—his people's
culture was based on salmon and other fish. It should be
noted, however, that references to the earth as "mother" were

not uncommon across North America in the early years of Euro-American settlement. Despite its lack of authenticity, Perry's paraphrased version of Seal'th's speech enjoyed wide coverage in the 1970s through the 1990s. On Earth Day 1992, organizers asked religious leaders to read the revised version of Seal'th's speech from a children's book, *Brother Eagle, Sister Sky: A Message from Chief Seattle.* The book was released in September 1991 and sold 280,000 copies by May 1992. Two decades after his film paraphrased Chief Seal'th, Perry, a professor at Middlebury College in Vermont, said he has been trying to set the record straight: "Why are we so willing to accept a text like this if it's attributed to a Native American?" he asked. "It's another case of placing Native Americans up on a pedestal and not taking responsibility for our own actions."[3]

Other environmentalists see attribution of their ideas to Native Americans as simple historical accuracy. On Earth Day 1992, several thousand participants in Kansas City decided to unify historical and ecological themes in looking at the consequences of five hundred years since the discovery of America by Columbus. Among other activities, in a Kansas City park they assembled from recyclable materials a turtle that was larger than two football fields end to end. The turtle was meant to observe the Iroquois creation myth in which North America (Turtle Island) is said to have come into being on the back of a turtle.

Unlike the quotations from Chief Seal'th, there has been no controversy regarding the authenticity of material from Luther Standing Bear, who watched the last years of settlement on the Great Plains. He contrasts the Euro-American and Native American conceptions of the natural world of North America:

We did not think of the great open plains, the beautiful rolling hills, and winding streams with tangled brush, as "wild." Only to the white man was nature "a wilderness" and only to him was the land "infested" with "wild" animals and "savage" people. To us it was tame. Earth was bountiful, and we are surrounded with the blessings of the Great Mystery.[4]

In the late twentieth century, similar sentiments were expressed by Jewell Praying Wolf James, a Lummi native who is a lineal descendant of Chief Seal'th:

At one time our plains, plateaus, and ancient forests were respected and not considered a wilderness. The skies were darkened by migrating fowl; the plains were blanketed with massive herds of buffalo. Our mountains teemed with elk, deer, bear, beaver, and other fur-bearing animals. All the rivers were full of salmon and [other] fish—so much that you could walk across their backs to get to the other side. The plants and trees were medicines and food for us. . . . In 1492 . . . our holocaust began. . . .[5]

Vine Deloria, Jr., suggests that scholars who contend that Euro-Americans have "invented" the image of the Indian as ecologist may be showing their own ignorance of history. Deloria cites Sam Gill's *Mother Earth* (1987) in which the author says he can find only two native references to earth as "mother":

As a by-product of researching Indian treaties, I have come up with numerous references to Mother Earth. Of course I did not find these references in ethnographic materials—I found them in minutes of councils and treaty negotiations. . . . Indians were not sitting around in seminar rooms articulating a nature philosophy for the benefit of non-Indian students, after all. They were trying to save their lands from exploitation and expropriation.[6]

Deloria documents the metaphor of earth as mother as far back as 1776. On June 21, at a conference in Pittsburgh during the Revolutionary War, Cornstalk, who was trying to convince the Mingos (Iroquois) to ally with the Americans, said:

You have heard the good Talks which our Brother [George Morgan] Weepemachukthe [The White Deer]

On Earth Day 1992, residents of Kansas City, Missouri, constructed a giant turtle out of materials to be recycled as a tribute to the Iroquois concept of Turtle Island. Photograph by Marty Kraft/Heartland All Species Project.

has delivered to us from the Great Council at Phil-
adelphia representing all our white brethren who have
grown out of this same ground with ourselves[,] for this
Big [Turtle] Island being our common Mother, we and
they are like one Flesh and Blood.[7]

Native Ecology's Opponents

Euro-American observers have sometimes scoffed at assertions that Native American culture displayed any sort of ecological ethos, occasionally charging that the natives had
engaged in massive "buffalo kills," driving the animals off
cliffs to their deaths. This practice came into use after Plains
Indians adapted to use of the horse, a European contribution
to North America's modern ecology. Even apart from buffalo
killed during drives that the horse made possible, the Great
Plains still were home to millions of buffalo during the
mid-nineteenth century, as Euro-American settlement spread
across the region. Actually, it was Europeans and immigrant
Americans who obliterated the buffalo herds. The U.S. government at times subsidized hunters who slaughtered vast
numbers of buffalo for their hides, or even only for their
tongues. The government also subsidized the railroads which
brought the non-Indian hunters to the buffalo. Carcasses of
animals stripped of their skins were left on the Plains to rot
in mountainous piles. The near-extermination of the buffalo
by invading Euro-Americans was no accident. It was partly
due to the profit motive and partly due to intentional government policy designed to deprive native peoples of their economic base as well as to (as one popular phrase of the day
put it) "kill the Indian and save the man." Since the Plains
tribes typically used every part of the buffalo—meat, hides,
horns, and teeth, without the buffalo, native life as it had
been became impossible.

Those who believe that Native Americans had no general
ecological ethic also sometimes point to native complicity in
the slaughter of the beaver and other fur-bearing animals for
trade. European or Euro-American traders contracted with

Indians for so many pelts that the animals almost disappeared. Calvin Martin has speculated that some native peoples held the beaver responsible for the incursions of immigrants and so took "revenge" on the animals. In *Keepers of the Game: Indian-Animal Relationships and the Fur Trade,* Martin contends that the image of Native Americans as conservationists is just another stereotype of Native Americans by non-Indians:

> *Late in the 1960s, the North American Indian acquired yet another stereotypic image in the popular mind: the erstwhile "savage," the "drunken" Indian, the "vanishing" Indian was conferred the title of "ecological" (i.e., conservationist-minded) Indian. Propped up for everything that was environmentally sound, the Indian was introduced to the American public as the great high priest of the Ecology Cult.*[8]

In Martin's view, millions of dead beaver effectively destroy the veracity of any argument that native peoples generally held nature to be sacred and that most native peoples took from nature only what they needed. For as long as harvestable numbers of beaver remained, native hunters teamed with Europeans and Euro-Americans to take as many as possible in the shortest time, using the motivations of a market economy rather than a conservation ethic.

However, the native peoples did not initiate the commercial fur trade. They had lived in natural symbiosis with the beaver and other fur-bearing animals for thousands of years before Europeans, so intent on remaking others in their own image, imposed mercantile capitalism on them. European immigrants employed the native peoples in this endeavor not vice versa. Further, by the time of the fur trade, the market economy was destroying more than the beaver populations. The native societies themselves were being destroyed through the spread of trade goods, liquor, and disease, as well as because of the loss of game animals and land base. Simply put, during early contact native peoples were trying to survive under rules imposed upon them. Native peoples who took part in the fur trade often did so to acquire trade goods that created other dependencies and caused them to abandon traditional beliefs and modes of economy. Beginning as early as 1700, native peoples realized what was happening to them and debated in their councils whether European trade goods should be accepted at all. It is clear that the fur trade was a post-contact phenomenon and that if a trading industry had not existed, the beaver would not have been hunted to near extinction.

Some ethnohistorians maintain that Native Americans possessed little or no environmental philosophy, and that any attempt to assemble evidence to sustain a Native American ecological paradigm is doomed to failure because the entire argument is an exercise in wishful thinking by environmental activists seeking support for their own views. William A. Starna, professor of anthropology at the State University of New York at Oneonta, has called the argument that Native Americans had an environmental ethic "pan-Indian mythology."[9] As he does in the face of evidence that the Iroquois helped inspire democracy, Starna asserts that modern Indian "activists" made up the idea of native environmentalism.

To the contrary, anyone who believes that American Indians only recently began using the metaphor of earth as mother knows precious little history. It has been documented that European colonists began hearing such references shortly after the first Pilgrims arrived. In *Brave Are My People: Indian Heroes Not Forgotten*, Frank Waters describes a "purchase" by Miles Standish and two companions of a tract of land fourteen miles square near Bridgewater, for seven coats, eight hoes, nine hatchets, ten yards of cotton cloth, twenty knives, and four moose skins. When native people continued to hunt on the land after it was "purchased" and were arrested by the Pilgrims, the Wampanoag sachem Massasoit protested:

What is this you call property? It cannot be the earth. For the land is our mother, nourishing all her children, beasts, birds, fish, and all men. The woods, the streams, everything on it belongs to everybody and is for the use of all. How can one man say it belongs to him only?[10]

While Standish and his companions thought they had an English-style deed, Massasoit argued that their goods had paid only for use of the land in common with everyone.[11]

The metaphor of earth as mother recurs time and again in the statements of Native American leaders recorded by Euro-American observers, in many areas of North America and long before Chief Seal'th's well-known speech. Tecumseh, rallying native allies with an appeal for alliance about 1805, said, "Let us unite as brothers, as sons of one Mother Earth. . . . Sell our land? Why not sell the air. . . . Land cannot be sold."[12] Black Hawk, exiled to a reservation near Fort Madison, Iowa, after the three-month war that bears his name, opened a Fourth of July address to a mainly non-Indian audience in the late 1830s by observing, "The Earth is our mother; we are on it, with the Great Spirit above us."[13]

In 1877, the Nez Perce Chief Joseph, who likely knew nothing of Massasoit, replied to an Indian agent's proposal that he and his people move to a reservation and become farmers. This statement was made a few months before Joseph and his band fled 1,700 miles across some of the most rugged land in North America to avoid subjugation. Chief Joseph said: "The land is our mother. . . . She should not be disturbed by hoe or plow. We want only to subsist on what she freely gives us."[14] Smohalla, a religious leader of the Nez Perce, said at the same meeting:

> *You ask me to plow the ground? I should take a knife and tear my mother's bosom? Then when I die, she will not take me to her bosom to rest. . . . You ask me to dig for stone! Shall I dig under her skin for her bones? Then when I die I cannot enter her body to be born again. You ask me to cut grass and make hay and sell it, to be rich like white men! But how dare I cut off my mother's hair?*[15]

A third Nez Perce chief, Tuhulkutsut, joined in: "The earth is part of my body. I belong to the land out of which I came. The earth is my mother." In response to these statements, it is recorded that U.S. negotiator General Oliver O. Howard protested, "Twenty times over [you] repeat that the earth is your mother. . . . Let us hear it no more, but come to business."[16]

In addition to the numerous references to the earth as mother, the ecological metaphors of Lakota holy man Black Elk, as told to John Niehardt, emphasize the utmost reverence for the natural world. In the late nineteenth century, long before "pan-Indian mythology" and long before environmental contamination became a widespread problem, Black Elk said: "Every step that we take upon You [the earth] should be done in a sacred manner; every step should be taken as a prayer."[17]

Ecological metaphors also were woven into the languages of many Native American cultures. For example, the Maya word for "tree sap" is the same as the word for "blood."[18] "Who cuts the trees as he pleases cuts short his own life," said the Mayas, long before pan-Indianism.

Indeed, it is remarkable that, at the time of the first sustained contact with Europeans, so many diverse native cultures—2,000 distinct societies speaking several hundred different languages—all shared ways of life which involved symbiosis with the natural world. Some evidence indicates that population densities were generally lower than those of twentieth-century North America, not because resources were scarce or because native technology was limited but because they were *kept* low. The Cherokees' oral history, for example, contains stories in which animals worry about the land becoming too crowded with human beings.[19] Very possibly, these stories were an example of the Cherokee "Harmony Ethic," which pervaded not only the relationships between people but also people's regard for the earth. Many native peoples consciously spaced the birth of children, and certain plants were used as contraceptives. Indeed, Thomas Jefferson comments: "[T]hey have fewer children than we do . . . [and] have learned the practice of procuring abortion by the use of some vegetable."[20] Jefferson also noted that such herbal birth control practices prevented "conception for a considerable time after."[21]

While many Native American customs and rituals also

indicate a reverence for the earth as provider, or "mother," the tidal wave of settlers who swept across North America in the nineteenth century typically thought of the earth in terms of a "mother lode" to be exploited for profit. Most Euro-Americans did not quote the words of Seal'th and Standing Bear with frequency until long after they were spoken.

Christopher Vecsey and Robert W. Venables, in *American Indian Environments: Ecological Issues in Native American History*, make a case that concepts of the earth as sustainer (or "mother") and the sky as "father," realm of the Creator, or "Great Mystery," are shared by many native cultures across the continent and that the "sacred circle" (or "hoop") is symbolic of encompassing creation or the sacred interdependence of all things in contrast to Euro-American notions of exploitation:

> *The American Indians' concept of a sacred circle expresses a physical and spiritual unity. This circle of life is interpreted according to the particular beliefs of each Indian nation, but is broadly symbolic of an encompassing creation. . . . While non-Indians quite willingly admit to the complexity of the circle of "things" around them, what has been left behind by the scientific, post-Renaissance non-Indian world is the universal sacredness—the living mystery—of creation's circle. One of the themes of this book is the consequences of a conflict during which indigenous Indian nations, who saw their environments as the sacred interdependence of the creator's will, confronted waves of post-Renaissance Europeans who saw in the environment a natural resource ordained by God for their sole benefit.*[22]

The circle often becomes the primary native symbol for the world of nature. J. R. Walker's *The Sun Dance and Other Ceremonies of the Oglala Division of the Teton Sioux* attributes the following to an Oglala Lakota informant named Tyon:

> *The Oglala believe the circle to be sacred because the Great Spirit caused everything in nature to be round*

*except stone. Stone is an implement of destruction. . . .
Everything that breathes is round, like the body of man.
Everything that grows from the ground is round, like the
stem of a tree. Since the Great Spirit has caused everything to be round, mankind should look upon the circle
as sacred for it is the symbol of all things in nature
except stone. It is also the symbol of the circle that marks
the edge of the world and therefore the four winds that
travel there. Consequently, it is also the symbol for a
year. The day, the night, and the moon go in a circle
above the sky. Therefore, the circle is a symbol of these
divisions of time and hence the symbol of all time.*[23]

A similar attitude of reverence toward the earth as mother may be found among the Pueblos of the Southwest:

*We might consider the Pueblo view that in the spring-
time Mother Earth is pregnant, and one does not mistreat her any more than one might mistreat a pregnant
woman. When our technologists go and try to get
Pueblo farmers to use steel plows in the spring, they are
usually rebuffed. For us it is a technical idea—"Why
don't you just use the plows? You plow, and you get 'X'
results from doing so." For the Pueblos, this is meddling
with the formal religious idea. . . . It is against the way
in which the world operates. It is against the way things
really go. Some Pueblo folks still take the heels off their
shoes, and sometimes the shoes off their horses, during
the spring. I once asked a Hopi whom I met in the country, "Do you mean to say, then, that if I kick the ground
with my foot, it will botch everything up, so nothing will
grow?" He said, "Well, I don't know whether that would
happen or not, but it would just really show what kind
of person you are."*[24]

The Mohawks of Akwesasne expressed a similar reverence
for nature as a living entity for hundreds of years before their
homeland was degraded by pollution. More recently in 1990
Mohawk Nation Council subchief Tom Porter offered a tradi-

tional thanksgiving prayer to open the New York Assembly hearings into the crisis at Akwesasne in which he asked how humans could have forgotten our place in the order of nature. This thanksgiving prayer illustrates how intricately love and respect for the earth are woven into Mohawk culture, and how deeply pollution has wounded the traditional way of life:

> *[Before] our great-great grandfathers were first born and given the breath of life, our Creator at that time said the earth will be your mother. And the Creator said to the deer, and the animals and the birds, the earth will be your mother, too. And I have instructed the earth to give food and nourishment and medicine and quenching of thirst to all life. . . . We, the people, humbly thank you today, mother earth.*
>
> *Our Creator spoke to the rivers and our creator made the rivers not just as water, but he made the rivers a living entity. . . . You must have a reverence and great respect for your mother the earth. . . . You must each day say "thank you" [for] every gift that contributes to your life. If you follow this pattern, it will be like a circle with no end. Your life will be as everlasting as your children will carry on your flesh, your blood, and your heartbeat.*[25]

A tribute to the Creator and a reverence for the natural world is reflected in many native greetings over the entire North American continent. More than 2,500 miles from the homeland of the Mohawks, the Lummis of the Pacific Northwest coast might begin a public meeting this way:

> *To the Creator, Great Spirit, Holy Father: may the words that we share here today give the people and [generations] to come the understanding of the sacredness of all life and creation.*[26]

The natural world presented icons to the Iroquois. The eastern white pine has had a deep spiritual and political meaning as well as many practical uses for the Iroquois.

British naval officers, on the other hand, found a different practical use for the tallest trees in eastern North America: they provided British ships with taller, stronger masts than their French counterparts and thus gave the British a military advantage.

The origin story of the Iroquois Confederacy holds that a Peacemaker planted a Great Tree of Peace at the Onondaga Nation (near present-day Syracuse, New York) to solve the internecine blood feuds that had been dividing the Haudenosaunee people. Through the symbolic tree planting, Deganawidah, the Peacemaker, stopped blood feuds as he and his spokesman, Hiawatha (or Aionwantha), instituted peace, unity, and clear thinking among the Haudenosaunee. Today's environmental devastation of the pine forests of the Northeast caused by acid rain is, to the traditional Iroquois, a deeply troubling tragedy. The eastern white pine is not only a symbol of peace and unity but also of practical use as a forest product to them. Such an ecological change is perceived clearly as a threat not only to the physical environment but also to the spiritual and political well-being of the traditional Haudenosaunee.

Native perspectives on the environment often were virtually the opposite of the views of many early settlers, who sought to "tame" the "wilderness." Many native peoples endowed all living things with spirit, even objects that Europeans regarded as nonliving, such as rocks. Most Native Americans saw themselves as enmeshed in a web of interdependent and mutually complementary life. As Black Elk said: "With all beings and all things, we shall be as relatives."[27]

If Native American ecological philosophy has suffered from oversimplification, so have interpretations of native attitudes toward land tenure. Often the vastly oversimplified notion that Indians had no concept of land ownership has served two contrary purposes to Europeans—to bolster the stereotype of the "noble savage" and to salve the conscience of those who were actively expropriating the land for their own uses. Some early New England colonists assumed that native people had no land tenure ethic because they did not fence land or raise domestic animals on it. But although

Native Americans did not have land deeds or trade in real estate, they did *use* the land. William Cronon reminds us to consider the differences between individual ownership of land, which most Native Americans did not practice, and collective sovereignty:

> *European property systems were much like Indian ones in expressing the ecological purposes to which a people intended to put their land; it is crucial that they not be oversimplified if their contributions to ecological history are to be understood. The popular idea that Europeans had private property, while the Indians did not, distorts European notions of property as much as it does Indian ones.*[28]

According to Cronon, both European and Native American property systems involved distinctions between individual ownership and community property; and both "dealt in bundles of culturally defined rights that determined what could and could not be done with land and personal property."[29] Customs of land tenure varied greatly in detail across New England (and the rest of North America); generally, however, Native Americans owned the implements of their work, their clothing, and other items used in their daily lives. An extended family which occupied the same lodge usually exercised a sense of ownership. Land, however, was usually held collectively. America was not a "virgin land" (in the words of George Bancroft) when Europeans arrived. Large tracts were under intensive management for hunting and agriculture by Native Americans. Because Indians often did not farm or raise domestic animals in a European manner, non-native observers often misunderstood this.

Because attitudes toward land tenure varied, negotiations which Europeans took to involve acquisition of land from native people often involved a high degree of intercultural misunderstanding. When the English colonists of New England thought they were *buying* land, Native Americans often took the same agreements to mean that they were agreeing to *share* it.[30]

A Critique of Technology through Native Eyes

The use of sometimes-embellished Native American points of view to critique "modern" society is at least as old as the time of Benjamin Franklin, who used fictionalized natives to twit pompous British lawyers. Whether Chief Seal'th said everything that has been attributed to him may be largely beside the point. Native thought contains a reverence for the earth as provider that has become apparent on a mass scale in non-Indian society in our own time. In recent years, there has been a concerted effort to fuse native points of view with environmental philosophy. One example of this fusion is Jerry Mander's *In the Absence of the Sacred*. Mander, a former advertising executive turned critic of technology, introduces native points of view on the environment as a counterpoint to what he regards as a society overly driven by technology. Mander introduces Native Americans as "guardians of an earth-centered way of life, an outlook which may, even on the periphery of modern civilization, serve to call our collective spirit home."[31]

Utilization of a Native American example to sharpen a critique of corporate capitalism also is not new. The patriots who dumped East India Company tea into Boston Harbor dressed as Mohawks. Today, such critiques seek to overturn an entire ingrained way of thinking about the earth that has supported expropriation, development, and "progress" for centuries. After more than five centuries of aggressive expansion, these ingrained modes of thinking are only slowly receding as their environmental consequences become more evident to non-native people.

Ironically, just as corporate activity invades the last parcels of indigenous land in places such as the Brazilian and Central American rainforests, the assumptions which underlie "technotopia" seem to be unraveling. In Peter MacDonald's article in *Akwe:kon Journal*, he writes that Mander

has written a book which poignantly tells a story . . . which suggests that the great legacy of indigenous knowledge and culture may be all that stands between

*the natural world of redemption and the creeping
Disney makeover of our environment which glosses over
the shaved forests and our fetid rivers of toxins.*[32]

Mander's critique reflects a growing knowledge of native
lifeways among non-Indians who are sensitive to environmental problems created by modern technology. His point of view
echoes that of native people around the United States, and
the world, encapsulated here by the Lummi Jewell Praying
Wolf James:

*The quest for the "higher standard of living" as defined
by most Americans in the United States is the nightmare
of the rest of the world. This standard has placed
America at the top of the list as users of natural resources and producers of toxic contamination.
Technology and science have "objectively" separated
care and consideration of the cumulative impacts of
humankind's collective behavior away from social
responsibility. The global community must discover an
orientation that teaches the world to do with the minimal and not the maximum. We have to address our levels of consumption before the whole global community
dies of ecocide.*[33]

James calls for creation of a "world court of the environment" which would publicize the behavior of "environmentally criminal activity" around the world. That proposal was
originally contained in a declaration by a group of native
and non-native writers, scientists, and environmentalists who
met during 1991 in Morelia, Mexico, sometimes called the
"Group of 100," of which James was a member. The "Group
of 100" seeks to reshape the assumptions of political economy, and, by doing so, to change modern life. (See "The
Morelia Declaration," page 255). To do so would require radical surgery on dominant assumptions of a way of life that
Mander calls "technoutopic." Believing that the incentive of
profit must be mitigated by concern for people and the earth,
Mander states: "No notion more completely confirms our

technological somnambulism than the idea that technology contains no inherent political bias."[34] Mander argues that technology *is itself* an ideology, compelling the ruin of the earth's ecology for innovation and monetary profit.

Native Ecological Rituals

Most native peoples incorporated nature into their rituals and customs because their lives depended on the bounty of the land around them. Where a single animal comprised the basis of a native economy (such as the salmon of the Pacific Northwest or the buffalo of the Great Plains), strict cultural sanctions came into play against the killing of these animals in numbers which would exceed their natural replacement rate.

On the Great Plains, the military societies of the Cheyennes, Lakotas, and other peoples enforced rules against hunting buffalo out of season and against taking more animals than could be used. Similarly, Northwest coast peoples treated the salmon with great respect. The fishing economy formed a base of their subsistence, filling a role similar to that of the buffalo on the Great Plains. Many native peoples who subsisted mainly on salmon runs intentionally let the fish pass after they had taken enough to see them through the year. They were acting through conscious knowledge that the salmon runs would vanish if too few fish escaped their nets to reach spawning grounds at the headwaters of rivers and streams. In addition, respect for these fish was shown through the custom of thanking them for offering themselves to sustain human beings.

The salmon were also part of the spirit world of Northwest peoples. They were believed to be spirit beings who had their village under the western ocean. Indians who visited them in visions saw them living in great houses like human beings. Their annual pilgrimages to the rivers and bays were seen as acts of voluntary sacrifice for the benefit of their human friends. Though they seemed to die, the spirits had simply removed their outer "salmon robes" and journeyed back to their undersea homes. But they would return again only if their gifts of flesh were treated with respect.[35]

All along the Northwest coast, the first catch of salmon in the late summer or early fall was laid along a riverbank, often with their heads pointed upstream, sometimes on a woven mat or cedar board. Sometimes a special shelter was constructed to catch the first salmon. This first catch might be sprinkled with birds' down as a formal speech of welcome, such as the following, was given:

> *Oh friends! Thank you that we meet alive. We have lived until this time when you came this year. Now we pray you, Supernatural Ones, to protect us from danger, that nothing evil may happen to us when we eat you, Supernatural Ones! For that is the reason why you come here, that we may catch you for food. We know that only your bodies are dead here, but your souls come to watch over us when we are going to eat what you have given us . . .*[36]

The people assembled around the fish would respond with affirmations as the bodies were cooked and divided among them. Such ceremonies might last for several days of feasting and gift-giving, as large numbers of migrating salmon were allowed past the Indians' nets to ensure the continuation of the salmon runs; then fishing resumed.

Peoples across the continent customarily feted their main food source with events such as the First Salmon Ceremony of the Pacific Northwest Indians. On the Great Plains, the buffalo was held in similarly high regard; among agricultural peoples of the Northeast, the Iroquois for example, festivals celebrated the vital role of the "three sisters"—corn, squash, and beans.

The Sun Dance ceremonies of the Plains Indians also reflect celebrations of the cycle of life. Like the Christian Easter, the Sun Dance (which the Cheyennes call the "New Life Lodge") is associated with the return of green vegetation in the spring and early summer, as well as the increase in animal populations, especially the buffalo. The ritual is communal and expresses a tribe or nation's unity with the earth and dependence on it for sustenance. The Sun Dance pole is said to unite sky and earth, and the four sacred directions are incorporated into the ceremonial design. The parts of the dance in which the skin is pierced are not required of anyone not wishing to participate in them. Some native peoples do not even practice skin piercing during the Sun Dance. In some ways, the aim of the Sun Dance is similar to that of the First Salmon Ceremony: each is part of a cycle of life and sustenance, and each demonstrates respect for a people's main food source.

Many native peoples honor and celebrate the plants as well as the animals that they consume, out of a belief that the essence of life that animates human beings is also present in the entire web of animate and inanimate life. Long before a science of "sustained yield" forestry evolved natives along the Northwest coast harvested plants in a way that would assure their continued growth, as part of a belief that the trees were sentient beings.[37]

Corn, the major food source for several agricultural peoples across the continent, had a special spiritual significance. Often corn and beans (which grow well together because the beans, a legume, fix nitrogen in their roots) were said to maintain a spiritual union. Some peoples, such as the Omahas of the eastern Great Plains, "sang up" their corn through special rituals. In addition to "singing up the corn," the Pueblos cleaned their storage bins before the harvest, "so the corn [would] be happy when we [brought] it in."[38] The Pawnees grew ten varieties of corn, including one that was used only for religious purposes (called "holy," or "wonderful," corn), and was never eaten.[39] The Mandans had a corn priest who officiated at rites during the growing season.[40] Each stage of the corn's growth was associated with particular songs and rituals, and spiritual attention was said to be as important to the corn as proper water, sun, and fertilizer. Among the Zuñis, a newborn child was given an ear of corn at birth and endowed with a "corn name." An ear of maize was put in the place of death as the "heart of the deceased" and was later used as seed corn to begin the cycle of life anew. To Navajos, corn was as sacred as human life.[41]

Some native peoples also used fire to raze fields for farm-ing, to drive game while hunting, and to aid regeneration of vegetation. These were not fires left to blaze out of control; instead, Navajos who, for example, used range fires custom-arily detailed half of their hunting party to control the fire and to keep it on the surface, where the flames would clear old brush so that new plant life could generate, instead of destroying the forest canopy. Donald J. Hughes, in *American Indian Ecology*, points out that when Europeans first laid eyes on North America, it was much more densely forested than today: "Eastern America was a land of vigorous forests, not a fire-scarred wasteland."[42] The park-like appearance of many eastern forests was a result of native peoples' efforts to manage plant and animal life, not a natural occurrence.[43]

Although a majority of native peoples did not possess a concept of individual land ownership per se, their rituals and rites, as well as their daily lives, displayed a reverence for the land with which their lives were so closely intertwined. Land was typically (but not always) held in common by a particu-lar group—clan, tribe, or native nation. In the Cherokee lan-guage, the word that means "land" *(eloheh)* also denotes cul-ture, history, and religion.[44]

The interweaving of ecological and religious themes is a constant among most native peoples across North America. The application of Western environmental and religious ter-minology to native worldviews sometimes does not fit:

> *[Among many native peoples] religion is viewed as embodying the reciprocal relationships between people and the sacred processes going on in the world. It may not involve a "god." It may not be signified by praying or asking for favors, or doing what may "look" religious to people in our culture. For the Navajo, for example, almost everything is related to health, [while] for us health is a medical issue.*[45]

Native modes of perception differ markedly in this regard from Western "knowledge" and ways of knowing. Sometimes ways of seeing are not directly translatable across cultures.

The term "sacred," used by native peoples to describe certain places, does not carry the same meaning to a devout Catholic, although it is the closest term English-speaking people have to express the Indian concept. Few native peoples thought of their attitude toward the land as simply a "conservation ethic." For example, when a Nootka thanked a salmon for offering itself to him, he also was engaging in a religious ritual.

Native Population Estimates

As we gain a more complete understanding of the native societies that flourished in North America before the voyages of Columbus, evidence accumulates that many were ecologically successful—that is, native societies provided a larger than previously thought number of people with the human relationships and technology with which to wrest a satisfactory material and spiritual life from the environment without destroying it. Of course, America was no stereotypical Garden of Eden. People sometimes went hungry (usually due to natural rather than societal circumstances); wars were fought, and people died in them. Occasionally, a native civilization overtaxed its environment and collapsed. Generally, however, native peoples lived well, especially compared to conditions prevailing after the invasion of the Europeans.

The question of the variety and numbers of peoples who lived in the Americas prior to permanent contact with Europeans has opened a lively debate during the last third of the twentieth century. This debate involves two very different ways of looking at historical and archaeological evidence. One side in the population debate restricts itself to strict interpretation of the evidence at hand. Another point of view accepts the probability that observers (usually of European ancestry) recorded only a fraction of phenomena that actually occurred in the Americas.

The fact that disease was a major cause of native depopulation is not at issue here—both sides agree on the importance of disease in the depopulation of the Americas to the point where many settlers thought they had come to an empty land that was theirs for the taking. The debate is over the *number* of native people who died. There also seems to be little disagreement about the fact that the plagues loosed on the Americas by contact with the Old World have not ended, even today. For example, between 1988 and 1990, 15 percent of the Yanomamis of Brazil, who had only limited contact with people of European descent until this time, died of malaria, influenza, and even the common cold.[46]

Henry F. Dobyns, of the Newberry Library, estimates that at the time of Columbus's first voyage about 16 million Native Americans lived in North America north of Mesoamerica, the area populated by the Aztecs and other Central American native nations.[47] Since population densities were much greater in Central America and along the Andes, an estimate of 16 million north of Mesoamerica indicates to Dobyns that 90 to 112 million native people lived in the Americas before A.D. 1500, making some parts of the New World as densely populated at the time as civilized areas of Europe and Asia.[48]

Dobyns's estimates of indigenous population at contact represent a radical departure from earlier tallies, which depended for the most part on actual historical and archaeological evidence of the dead, assuming that Euro-American scholars were capable of counting native people who had, in some cases, been dead for several centuries. Although anthropologists usually date the first attempt at measuring native populations to Henry Schoolcraft in the 1850s, Thomas Jefferson's *Notes on the State of Virginia* (published in several editions during the 1780s) contained an extensive (if fragmentary) Indian "census." Jefferson did not attempt to count the number of native people inhabiting North America during his time—no one then even knew how large the continent might be, not to mention the number of people inhabiting it. Instead, he prudently settled for estimates of the population of Indian nations bordering the early United States.

The first systematic count of Indian populations was compiled during the early twentieth century by James Mooney, who maintained that at contact 1,153,000 people lived in the land area which is now the United States. Mooney calculated the 1907 native population in the same area at 406,000. Dividing the country into regions, he then calculated the percentage loss to be from 61 percent in the North Atlantic states to 93 percent in California.[49]

Following Mooney's "census," the most widely accepted population estimates were provided beginning in 1939 by A. L. Kroeber in his *Cultural and Natural Areas of Native North America*.[50] By Kroeber's determination, only about 900,000 native people occupied North America north of Mexico at contact. According to Ann F. Ramenofsky, Kroeber did not consider disease as a factor in depopulation because he feared that such an emphasis would lead to an overestimation of precontact population.[51] One may speculate whether this was a case of deliberate scientific oversight or simple prudence, but the fact was that for nearly a half-century his conservative figures were accepted as authoritative (it was a time when one could appear radical by arguing that in 1492 perhaps 2 million natives occupied the area now known as the United States). Sooner or later a challenge was likely to arise. Dobyns, who *did* consider disease (some say he overemphasized it), challenged Kroeber's figures along with others, to initiate the present debate.

Defending his own precontact population estimates, Dobyns argues that "absence of evidence does not mean absence of phenomenon," especially where written records are scanty, as in America before or just after European contact.[52] Dobyns's position is that European epidemic diseases invaded a relatively disease-free environment in the Americas with amazing rapidity, first in Mesoamerica (via the Spanish) and then in eastern North America along native trade routes long before English and French settlers arrived. The fact that Cartier observed the deaths of fifty natives in the village of Stadacona in 1535 indicates to Dobyns, for instance, that many more may have died in other villages that Cartier never saw. Because of lack of evidence, conclusions must be drawn from what little remains, according to Dobyns, who extends his ideas to other continents as well. "Lack of Chinese records of influenza does not necessarily mean that the Chinese did not suffer from influenza; an epidemic could have gone unrecorded, or records of it may not have survived," Dobyns has written.[53]

Critics of Dobyns assert that "there is still little certain knowledge about pre-1500 population levels." On a historiographic level, Dobyns has been accused of misusing a few scraps of documentary evidence we have in an effort to sustain his argument for widespread 16th-century epidemics.[54] To Dobyns's critics, the fact that fifty natives were recorded as dying at Stadacona means just that: fifty natives died, no more, no less. To Dobyns, however, such arguments "align themselves with the Bandelier-Rosenblatt-Kroeber-Steward group," which minimizes Native American population magnitude and social structural complexity.[55]

While Snow and Lanphear, of the State University of New York at Albany, maintain that "there were often buffer zones between population concentrations or isolates that would have impeded the spread of diseases,"[56] Dobyns replies that the practice of trade, war, diplomacy, and other demographic movements obliterated such buffer zones and aided in the spread of disease.[57] Snow and Lanphear also assert that the sparseness of native populations in North America itself impeded the spread of disease, a point of view which does not account for the speed with which smallpox and other infections spread once they reached a particular area.

Dobyns not only denies that buffer zones existed but maintains that smallpox was only the most virulent of several diseases to devastate New World populations. The others, roughly in descending order of deadliness, included measles, influenza, bubonic plague, diphtheria, typhus, cholera, and scarlet fever.[58] According to Dobyns, the "frontier of European/Euroamerican settlement in North America was not a zone of interaction between people of European background and vacant land, nor was it a region where initial farm colonization achieved any 'higher' use of the land as measured in human population density. It was actually an interethnic frontier of biological, social, and economic interchange between Native Americans and Europeans and/or Euroamericans."[59] The most important point to Snow and Lanphear, however, is "where one puts the burden of proof in this argument . . . in any argument of this kind." They maintain that we "cannot allow ourselves to be tricked into assuming the burden of disproving assertions for which there is no evidence."[60]

Given the evidence they have in hand, however, even Snow and Lanphear acknowledge that between two-thirds and 98 percent of the native peoples inhabiting areas of the northeastern United States died in epidemics between roughly 1600 and 1650. The population of the Western Abenakis, for example, declined from 12,000 to 250 (98 percent), the Massachusetts (including the Narragansetts) from 44,000 to 6,400 (86 percent), the Mohawks from 8,100 to 2,000 (75 percent), and the Eastern Abenakis from 13,800 to 3,000 (78 percent).[61]

David Henige, of the University of Wisconsin at Madison, also criticizes Dobyns for a "remorseless attention to disease to the exclusion of all else," as the major cause of depopulation among native peoples and asks "why he [Dobyns] does not consider the possible role of such factors as warfare, land exhaustion, climatic pressure, or cultural changes."[62]

It is clear from the preceding debate that the range of population estimates at contact reflects diverse viewpoints on the role of disease and other factors. William M. Denevan, who edited a collection of articles surveying population estimates for 1492 across North and South America,[63] arrived at a consensus figure of 53.9 million native people for the entire hemisphere, including 3.8 million north of Mesoamerica. These figures represent a small decline from his first set of estimates, made in 1976.

Given the number of people killed and the lengthy period during which they have died, the world has probably not again seen such continuous human misery over such a large area. One good example is the fate of the Aztec capital city Tenochtitlán, which occupied the site of present-day Mexico City. Tenochtitlán impressed Hernán Cortés as a world-class metropolis when he first saw it shortly after the year 1500. It is estimated that the Aztec capital had a population of 250,000 people at a time when Rome, Seville, and Paris had a population of only about 150,000 each. Before he destroyed it, Cortés viewed the splendor of the Aztec capital and called Tenochtitlán the most beautiful city in the world.

Spanish chronicler Bernal Diaz del Castillo stood atop a great temple in the Aztec capital and described causeways eight paces wide, teeming with thousands of Aztecs, crossing lakes and channels dotted by convoys of canoes. He said that Spanish soldiers who had been to Rome or Constantinople told Diaz that for "convenience, regularity and population, they have never seen the like."[64] The comparisons of life among the Aztecs with what the Spanish knew of Europe acquire some substance as one realizes that, in 1492, the British Isles held only about 5 million people, while Spain's population has been estimated at 8 million.[65] Even nearly three centuries later, at the time of the American Revolution, the largest cities along the eastern seaboard of the new United States—Boston, New York, and Philadelphia—had a population of no more than 50,000 people each.

Within a decade of Cortés's first visit, Tenochtitlán was a ruin. Ten years after the Aztec ruler Montezuma had hailed Cortés with gifts of flowers and gold (and had paid for such hospitality with his life), epidemics of smallpox and other diseases carried by the conquistadors had killed at least half the Aztecs. One of the Aztec chroniclers who survived wrote: "Almost the whole population suffered from racking coughs and painful, burning sores."[66]

The plague followed the Spanish conquest as it spread in roughly concentric circles from the islands of Hispaniola and Cuba to the mainland of present-day Mexico. Bartolomé de las Casas, the Roman Catholic priest who questioned Spanish treatment of the natives for decades, said that when the first visitors found it, Hispaniola was a beehive of people. Within one lifetime, the forests were silent. Within thirty years of Cortés's arrival in Mexico, the native population decreased from about 25 million to roughly 6 million. After Spanish authorities set limits on money wagers in the New World, soldiers in Panama were said to have made bets with Indian lives instead. When natives were not killed outright by disease, conquerors killed them slowly through slavery. Las Casas, who arrived in the New World ten years after Columbus, described one form of human servitude, pearl diving: "It is impossible to continue for long diving into the cold water and holding the breath for minutes at a time . . . sun rise to sun set, day after day. They die spitting blood . . . looking like sea wolves or monsters of another species."[67] Other conquistadors disemboweled native children. According to Las Casas, "they cut them to pieces as if dealing with sheep in a slaughterhouse. They laid bets as to who, with one stroke of a sword, could cut off his head or spill his entrails with a single stroke of the pike."[68]

A century later, entering North America the Puritans often wondered why the lands on which they settled, which appeared so bountiful otherwise, appeared to have been wiped clean of their original inhabitants. Four years before the *Mayflower* landed, a plague of smallpox had swept through Indian villages along the coast of the area the settlers would rename New England. John Winthrop admired abandoned native cornfields and declared that God had provided the epidemic that killed the people who had tended them as an act of divine providence: "God," he said, "hath hereby cleared our title to this place."[69] As settlement spread westward, native people learned to fear the sight of the honeybee. These "English flies" usually colonized areas about a hundred miles in advance of the frontier, and the first sight of them came to be regarded as a harbinger of death. The virulence of the plagues from Europe may be difficult to comprehend in our time. Even in Europe, where immunities had developed to many of the most serious diseases, one in seven people died in typical smallpox epidemics. Half the children born in Europe at the time of contact never reached the age of fifteen; and life expectancy on both sides of the Atlantic averaged thirty-five years.

Before contact, outside of a few specific areas (such as Mayan cities and Cahokia), population density was not great enough to devastate the environment generally. Instead, early European observers marveled at the natural bounty of America—of Virginia sturgeon six to nine feet long, of Mississippi catfish that weighed more than one hundred pounds, of Massachusetts oysters that grew to nine inches across, as well as lobsters that weighed twenty pounds each. The immigrants gawked at flights of passenger pigeons that sometimes nearly darkened the sky and speculated that a squirrel could travel from Maine to New Orleans without touching the ground. Bison ranged as far east as Virginia. George Washington observed a few of them and wondered if they could be cross-bred with European cattle.

Despite the dispute over population size and density before the devastation of European diseases, it is rather widely agreed that native populations in North America bottomed at about half a million in the early twentieth century (using Mooney's contemporary figures) and that they have been increasing again since then. The latest figures for the United States, contained in the 1990 census, indicate that roughly 2 million people list themselves as Native American. Such a measure may not be as precise as it sounds, however, because the census allows people to categorize themselves racially.

Scholars who assert that Native Americans possessed no more of an environmental ethic than invading Europeans fail to look at land-use patterns in North America before and after contact with Europe. The advent of widespread pollution, and a social and political movement to restrain it, is a European import to the Americas. Despite populations that were as dense in some areas as habitation today, Native Americans as a whole lacked a philosophy that stressed "development" of the earth for profit, although they did develop resources to sustain their lives and societies. Native societies also lacked the technological drive to transform the environment in the name of profit, although native people did adapt technology to suit their needs.

A supreme irony of our time is that peoples who have tried to live within the bounds of a natural ethic today face some of the worst pollution in North America. Almost without exception, these conditions have been imposed on native peoples by the dominant society. A sense that "this is the time at the end of time" conveys a sense of urgency in contemporary native appeals to save unspoiled areas of North America from logging, ranching, and mineral extraction. Even as Western technology and resource exploitation spread to the final frontiers of the continent, a rising environmental movement is paying more attention to the ways in which native peoples in the Americas managed their relationships with the environment before industrialization—in a search for answers to contemporary ecological problems.

While some scholars may argue that the idea of Indian as ecologist is simply stereotyping and wishful thinking among present-day environmental advocates, the written and oral histories of many Native American peoples indicate that their cultures evolved over thousands of years largely in symbiosis with the earth that sustained them. Often these customs were incorporated into religious rituals that held the earth to be the sustainer of all things and linked the welfare of the earth to the survival of people who lived upon it.

Notes

1. "Seattle" is an anglicized version of the chief's name. Pronounced in the original Duwamish, the name ends with an intricate twist of the tongue that is unknown in English and is most accurately transcribed as "Seal'th," or "Seath'l." The name of the city was adapted from the name of the chief to suit people who spoke English.

2. W. C. Vanderwerth, ed., *Indian Oratory: Famous Speeches by Noted Indian Chieftains* (Norman: University of Oklahoma Press, 1971), 120-21.

3. Malcom Jones, "Just Too Good to Be True: Another Reason to Beware of False Eco-Prophets," *Newsweek*, May 4, 1992, 68.

4. Luther Standing Bear, *Land of the Spotted Eagle* (Lincoln: University of Nebraska Press, 1978), 98.

5. Jewell Praying Wolf James, in *Our People, Our Land: Perspectives on the Columbus Quincentenary*, ed. Kurt Russo (Bellingham, Wash.: Lummi Tribe and Kluckhohn Center, 1992), 33.

6. Vine Deloria, Jr., "Comfortable Fictions and the Struggle for Turf: An Essay Review of James Clifton, *The Invented Indian* . . ." *American Indian Quarterly* 16, no. 3: 406.

7. Cornstalk, Shawnee chief, in speech to the Mingos at the Kiskapoo village, June 21, 1776, *Morgan's Journal*, 31-32; cited in Deloria, "Comfortable Fictions," 406.

8. Calvin Martin, *Keepers of the Game: Indian-Animal Relationships and the Fur Trade* (Los Angeles: University of California Press, 1978), 157.

9. William A. Starna, review of Vecsey and Venables, *American Indian Environments*, in *American Anthropologist* 84 (1982): 468.

10. Frank Waters, *Brave Are My People: Indian Heroes Not Forgotten* (Santa Fe, N.M.: Clear Light Publishers, 1993), 28.

11. Such conflicts over the notion of land use bred the term "Indian giver" among colonists since they were unable or unwilling to accept American Indian concepts of shared land use. The exclusive use of land through private property, of course, was imposed through the use of colonial military force and the proliferation of white settlers.

12. Waters, *Brave Are My People*, 62–63.

13. Ibid., 76.

14. Ibid., 172.

15. Ibid., 172–73.

16. Ibid., 173.

17. Black Elk, *The Sacred Pipe*, ed. Joseph Epes Brown (New York: Penguin Books, 1973), 13–14.

18. George E. Stuart, "Maya Heartland under Siege," *National Geographic*, November 1992, 95.

19. Charles Hudson, "Cherokee Concept of Natural Balance," *Indian Historian* 3:54.

20. See Paul L. Ford, ed., *The Writings of Thomas Jefferson*, vol. 3 (New York: G. P. Putnam Sons, 1892–1899), 441.

21. Ibid.

22. Christopher Vecsey and Robert W. Venables, *American Indian Environments: Ecological Issues in Native American History* (Syracuse, N.Y.: Syracuse University Press, 1980), x; cited in George Cornell, "Native American Perceptions of the Environment," *Northeast Indian Quarterly* 7, no. 2 (Summer 1990): 4.

23. J. R. Walker, *The Sun Dance and Other Ceremonials of the Oglala Division of the Teton Sioux* (New York: AMS Press, 1971), 160; cited in Cornell, "Native American Perceptions," 6.

24. Barre Toelken, "Seeing with a Native Eye: How Many Sheep Will It Hold?" in *Seeing with a Native Eye: Essays on Native American Religion*, ed. Walter Holden Capps (New York: Harper Forum Books, 1976), 14.

25. Tom Porter, New York State Assembly Hearings, "Crisis at Akwesasne" (Ft. Covington, N.Y.), July 24, 1990, transcript, 24–28.

26. Kurt Russo, ed., *Our People, Our Land: Perspectives on the Columbus Quincentenary* (Bellingham, Wash.: Lummi Tribe and Kluckhohn Center, 1992), frontispiece.

27. Black Elk, *The Sacred Pipe*, 105.

28. William Cronon, *Changes in the Land: Indians, Colonists and the Ecology of New England* (New York: Hill & Wang, 1983), 68–69.

29. Ibid., 69.

30. Ibid., 70.

31. Quoted in Peter MacDonald, "Technology and Indigenous Thought," *Akwe:kon Journal* (Spring 1992): 35.

32. Ibid., 46.

33. James, in *Our People, Our Land*, 33.

34. Ibid.

35. J. Donald Hughes, *American Indian Ecology* (El Paso: Texas Western Press, 1983), 45.

36. Franz Boaz, *Contributions to the Ethnology of the Kwakiutl*, vol. 3 of *Columbia University Contributions to Anthropology* (New York: Columbia University Press, 1925), 611–12.

37. Hughes, *American Indian Ecology*, 54.

38. William Brandon, *American Heritage Book of Indians* (New York: Dell, 1961), 116.

39. Peter Iverson, "Taking Care of the Earth and Sky," in *America in 1492: The World of the Indian Peoples Before the Arrival of Columbus*, ed. Alvin Josephy (New York: Alfred A. Knopf, 1992), 98.

40. Ibid., 67–68.

41. Ibid., 74.

42. Ibid., 54.

43. Peter Nabokov and Dean Snow, "Farmers of the Woodlands," in *America in 1492*, ed. Alvin Josephy, 124.

44. Ruth Underhill, *Red Man's Religion: Beliefs and Practices of the Indians North of Mexico* (Chicago: University of Chicago Press, 1965), 206.

45. Toelken, "Seeing with a Native Eye," 14.

46. Ronald Wright, *Stolen Continents: The Americas through Indian Eyes Since 1492* (Boston: Houghton-Mifflin, 1992), 14.

47. Henry F. Dobyns. *Their Numbers Became Thinned* (Knoxville: University of Tennessee Press, 1983), 42.

48. Dobyns's population estimates have risen over time. His initial estimate of 12.5 million in North America north of the Rio Grande is analyzed in "Estimating Aboriginal American Population," *Current Anthropology* (October 1966): 395–412. His estimate of 16 million appears in *Their Numbers Became Thinned*, published in 1983. Scholars other than Dobyns, including Borah, Simpson, and Cook, agree with his hemispheric estimate of about 100 million. See Woodrow Borah, "The Historical Demography of Aboriginal and Colonial America: An Attempt at Perspective" in *The Native Population of the Americas in 1492*, ed. William M. Denevan (Madison: University of Wisconsin Press, 1976) and Sherburne F. Cook and Leslie B. Simpson, "The Population of Central Mexico in the Sixteenth Century," *Ibero-Americana*, vol. 31 (Berkeley and Los Angeles: University of California Press, 1948). In the meantime, the Smithsonian Institution, under pressure from rising population estimates, raised its own estimate of aboriginal population, doubling its estimate of population north of the Rio Grande to 2 million, from half that number. See: Douglas Ubelaker, "The Sources and Methodology for Mooney's Estimates of North American Indian Populations," in *Native Population of the Americas in 1492*, ed. William M. Denevan (Madison: University of Wisconsin Press, 1972).

49. See James Mooney, "Population," in *Handbook of American Indians North of Mexico*, ed. F. W. Hodge, Bureau of American

Ethnology Bulletin 30, no. 2 (Washington, D.C.: Government Printing Office, 1910), 28–87; and James Mooney, *The Aboriginal Population of North America North of Mexico*, in *Smithsonian Miscellaneous Collections* 80, no. 7, ed. J. R. Swanton (Washington, D.C.: Smithsonian Institution, 1928).

50. A. L. Kroeber. *Cultural and Natural Areas of Native North America*, vol. 38 of University of California Publications in American Archaeology and Ethnology (Berkeley: University of California Press, 1939).

51. Ann F. Ramenofsky, *Vectors of Death: The Archaeology of European Contact* (Albuquerque: University of New Mexico Press, 1987), 9.

52. Henry F. Dobyns, "More Methodological Perspectives on Historical Demography," *Ethnohistory* 36, no. 3 (Summer 1989): 286.

53. Ibid., 296.

54. Dean R. Snow and Kim M. Lanphear, "European Contact and Indian Depopulation in the Northeast: The Timing of the First Epidemics," *Ethnohistory* 35, no. 1 (Winter 1988): 16.

55. Dobyns, "More Methodological Perspectives," 289.

56. Snow and Lanphear, "European Contact," 16.

57. Dobyns, "More Methodological Perspectives," 291.

58. Dobyns, *Their Numbers Became Thinned*, 11–24.

59. Ibid., 43.

60. Dean R. Snow and Kim M. Lanphear, "'More Methodological Perspectives:' A Rejoinder to Dobyns," *Ethnohistory* 36, no. 3 (Summer 1989): 299, 300.

61. Snow and Lanphear, "European Contact," 24.

62. David Henige, "On the Current Devaluation of the Notion of Evidence: A Rejoinder to Dobyns," *Ethnohistory* 36, no. 3 (Summer 1989): 306; see also William Engelbrecht, "Factors Maintaining Low Population Density among the Prehistoric New York Iroquois," *American Antiquity* 52 (January 1987): 13–27.

63. William M. Denevan, ed. *The Native Populations of the Americas in 1492* (Madison: University of Wisconsin Press, 1976).

64. Bart McDowell, "The Aztecs," *National Geographic*, December 1980, 753.

65. Wright, *Stolen Continents*, 11.

66. Miguel Leon Portilla, *The Broken Spears: The Aztec Account of the Conquest of Mexico* (Boston: Beacon Press, 1962), 132.

67. Bartolomé de las Casas, *The Devastation of the Indies* [1542] (New York: Seabury Press, 1974), 15.

68. Ibid., 43.

69. Lewis Lord and Sarah Burke, "America Before Columbus," *U.S. News & World Report*, July 8, 1991, 36.

Section of an old map of America, from Abraham Ortelius's Epitome Theatri Orbis Terrarum, *printed by Joa Keerberg. Notice that the Rio Grande runs into the Pacific Ocean!*

Chapter Two

Ecological and Spiritual Dimensions of the 1680 Pueblo Revolt in Colonial New Mexico

Water for irrigation of land produced conflict in colonial New Mexico. Spanish economic exploitation of the land and labor of the Pueblo Indians from 1598 to 1680 caused the Pueblos to revolt. Ironically, the Pueblos would use various environmental factors, including the waters of the Rio Grande to defeat the Spanish and oust the Spanish government. The struggle to overthrow Spanish oppression utilized political, economic, spiritual, and ecological factors to reinstitute Indian autonomy and traditional Indian ways. In essence, Spanish colonization in New Mexico was for profit, and the Pueblos suffered under a land-use system that became unbearable during drought and hard times. The Pueblo response to this exploitation was passive at first, then active.

During the early years of Spanish settlement in New Mexico, colonial governors tried to retrieve their investments in the colony, surveying a landscape that was utterly bereft of easily accessible gold and silver. Unable to wrest wealth from minerals in the land, the colonists squeezed more harshly on the Pueblos for produce and labor. The priests railed against their "devil worship," and from time to time whipped some of the Pueblos' most respected elders (sometimes to death) in public displays. All these acts fired resentment among the native people. Over fifty years after the first colonization, in 1650, the Pueblos joined with their ancient enemies the Apaches in an abortive effort to drive the Spanish out. Thirty years later, however, in 1680, a coalition of Pueblos united by the war captain Popé (po-pé), raised a furious revolt that killed a quarter of the settlers, destroyed the hated Catholic churches, and drove the Spanish to El Paso del Norte, leaving behind almost everything they owned. The governor summed up the situation: "Today they [the Pueblos] are very happy without religion, or Spaniards."[1]

Tension between the Spanish and the Pueblos was influenced by the changing nature of land use in northern New Mexico. Lying at the southern end of the Rocky Mountains, three major rivers originate in Pueblo country and are of great economic importance to northern New Mexico: the Rio Grande, the Canadian River, and the Pecos River. When the water level is lowered at the source of these rivers, either by human activity or nature, distant areas are directly influenced. The Pueblos and later settlers from New Spain inhabited the upper Rio Grande Valley in northern New Mexico, a three-hundred-mile swath of land, from Socorro in the south northward through Albuquerque to the Colorado state line. The area includes nearly a half-million acres of land that can be irrigated and 12 million acres of grazing land of varying quality. The lower Rio Grande Valley, south of Santa Fe, receives less rainfall and snow than the upper Rio Grande Valley to the north. Historically, the Spanish used the lower area primarily for grazing, while the upper area was characterized by intensive Pueblo agriculture based on an extensive irrigation system. The settlers from New Spain imposed a harsh and exploitative system which oppressed the Pueblos and produced resentment, then revolt.[2]

Historical Context of the Pueblo Revolt

The Pueblos of the Rio Grande are cultural and economic descendants of the Mogollon, Anasazi, and Hohokam communities to the west and southwest of the upper Rio Grande Valley. Cultivation of corn was introduced into the area about 3000 B.C. About 2000 B.C. beans and squash were added, and cotton later became a fourth staple crop. About two thousand years ago, irrigation was introduced to supplement the dry farming in the area. The Pueblos used brief, heavy precipitation to advantage by constructing some of

The oldest printed picture of an ear of maize, *from* Oviedo's Historia Natural, *Seville, 1535.*

their irrigation works at the bases of steep cliffs that collected runoff. The vital role of water and irrigation in Pueblo country is illustrated by the fact that the great classic Pueblo civilizations were destroyed by a drought so severe that not even ingenious water management could cope with it. By A.D. 1200, most Pueblo settlements outside of the Rio Grande Valley had been abandoned after fifty years of severe drought.[3]

Irrigation is the key factor in Pueblo land use. In order to plan, construct, and maintain elaborate land systems, cooperation between several villages was crucial. Irrigation systems needed routine maintenance which rendered clans inefficient, so nonkinship associations were created to cope with such work. This organizational framework had other community functions, and it revolved primarily around the spiritual life of the Pueblos. The basic rationale for the nonkinship associations was irrigation, however.[4]

Pueblos regulated water by ritual. Since no group within a pueblo could control resources other than its own, family and religious feasts redistributed much of the material wealth of the people to minimize human misery. Because no single authority controlled the food supply, food redistribution through agricultural rites and other rites attending marriage, birth, death, and illness alleviated class tensions, particularly in times of drought and lean harvests. Climate and ritual are key factors in a system designed to manipulate an arid environment, which is regulated by ritual rather than laws.[5]

The Spanish colonization of New Mexico was undertaken to manipulate the Pueblos' environment for economic gain within a system of mercantile capitalism. The Spanish Crown accepted bids for the colonization of an area. Money, men, and material goods all were needed for a successful colonizing venture. Don Juan de Oñate, who was related to several conquistadors by blood and marriage, obtained the colonization contract for New Mexico not only because of his wealth but through family influence. After Spanish approval, the colonization of New Mexico began in earnest in 1598.

Social structure and economic gain were tied together in such a venture. Oñate asked the Spanish authorities to confer the title *hidalgo* to his soldiers. A few years after the conquering of New Mexico, this title and the privilege of inheritance was given to the soldier-settlers of New Mexico. *Hidalgos* were forbidden to leave New Mexico, and if they did, were considered military deserters.[6]

Just a few months after initial settlement a small minority of Spanish and Mexican servants gained control over Ácoma Pueblo through acts of violence and a divide-and-conquer strategy, but they were pushed out by the people of Ácoma. The massacre that followed illustrates the colonizers' willingness to use extreme violence to establish their rule. A force of seventy soldiers was sent to Ácoma in the winter of 1598 to 1599 to avenge the death of several Spanish soldiers. Oñate proclaimed a "war by fire and blood" against Ácoma.

After three days of fierce fighting, the Spanish reached the top of the mesa where Ácoma was built. They loaded cannons with two hundred balls apiece and fired into the Pueblos' ranks, piling up masses of dead and wounded Indians. About a thousand Indians were killed. Ácoma Pueblo was set on fire, and prisoners were captured. The prisoners were taken to San Juan Pueblo, given a mock trial, and found guilty; adult males had a foot cut off, and the

women were sentenced to "personal service," a euphemism
for slavery and concubinage. Shortly after this bloody massacre, two other pueblos were sacked and well over a thousand more Indians were killed while other captives were tor-
tured. These violent acts enforced an uneasy peace over the
Rio Grande Valley.[7]

Once Spanish military rule was established, Oñate relo-
cated many Pueblos and employed some Pueblo warriors to
deal with other recalcitrant Pueblos. Animosities also developed between the Navajos, the Apaches, and the Pueblos.
This forced the Pueblos to depend upon the Spanish for
defense against their Athabascan (Navajo and Apache)-
speaking neighbors. Pueblo warriors, directed and encouraged by the Spanish, began to engage in slave raids on the
Apaches and Navajos. By 1650, slave raiding was a significant part of New Mexico economy, although land was still the
most important factor.[8]

Land was the most significant form of wealth in the New
Mexico economy, and land tenure greatly influenced Spanish
colonial administration. Consequently, exploitative forms of
land tenure and land labor were introduced. The Spanish
Crown awarded a *capitalacion* to the head of a colonizing
expedition. A *capitalacion* was the fundamental code of law
for a given territory, one that had authority over the personal
interests of the settlers. Much of a *capitalacion* dealt with the
Crown's ability to tax and regulate trade, and the Crown
profited a great deal in taxes from such self-interest. Under
authority of the *capitalacion*, an *encomienda* was granted to
an individual. The *encomienda* gave a person control over an
area in order to extract tribute which was then shared with
the Crown. The theology of *repartimiento* empowered the
encomendero to extract forced labor from natives.

Since the majority of tribal land was allotted as feudal
encomiendas which the governors of New Mexico used as
patronage, under Spanish law Indian lands and the labor of
the Indians who lived on it became the property of the
Spanish because they were Christians. Thus through *repartimiento* Indians were forced to work for European masters
in fields that were formerly theirs and had to pay heavy

taxes to their new lords. Their taxes were usually in the form of woven cloth or corn from what little land they were allowed to keep.[9]

Missions comprised another type of Spanish economic activity; as native people were compelled to convert to Christianity, their labor belonged to the missions and provided revenue for the Church. This process of land tenure was exploitative and fraught with corruption and abuses. Governors often created illegal workshops where Indians were forced to work long hours to produce goods that the governor sold for personal gain. The only major source of internal criticism of this system was the Church, which periodically resented manipulation by the governor and wished for a larger share of revenues.

Spanish colonization in New Mexico utilized violence, divisiveness, control of land, and forced labor in an economy in which Indians were grossly exploited. For more than eighty years, the Spanish profited from this system before the Pueblos' major revolt in 1680 drove them from the region for a dozen years.[10]

The Pueblos revolted in 1680 for political, economic, ecological, and religious reasons. The Pueblo uprising was more than just a revolt against Spanish oppression in order to reinstitute political autonomy and traditional Indian ways. The shaman Popé, the Indian who united the Pueblos in their revolt, fashioned a vision that directed Pueblo discontent into a unified cosmological solution to Spanish oppression. The essence of Popé's vision involved ousting the Spanish and returning to traditional ways, but the nature of the vision he used was innovative and represented a synthesis of the various Pueblo experiences with the Spanish colonials.

Popé's Spiritual and Ecological Design

Popé's shamanic vision stimulated the Pueblo Revolt and unified the mythic experience of the Pueblos vis à vis the Spanish. The primary axes of this mythic and totemic system are the four directions of the earth and a world axis that passes through the center of the intersecting axes. The world pole, or axis, connects the three worlds of sky, earth, and underworld. Thus, a mandala is formed whose center encourages a break in space and time. Through this break, the spiritual worlds of above and below are generated. These worlds exist in a dimension of inner experience. Thus, the shamanic vision is not a flight into the supernatural but an inner symbolic journey. The shaman does not fly up or down but into the meaning of things. This vision unifies the inner, hidden, and experiential dimensions that eliminate space, time, and distance as well as the differentiation of subject and object. The shamanic vision is a universal human experience, but it tends to be an overall unifying force only in tribal societies.[11] The geometrical axes of the shamanic cosmos are used as the basis of infinite structural oppositions, meditations, and syntheses. Briefly, this is the inner world that Popé and his people kept alive in spite of Spanish religious fanaticism and intolerance.

After eighty-two years of peonage and forced conversion to Catholicism, the Pueblo Indians still passed down their way of life through an oral tradition. The spoken word cannot be burned or otherwise controlled as easily as the written word. Between 1598 and 1680, the Pueblos gradually learned to conform outwardly to the Roman Catholic religion while inwardly keeping their own faith alive. Few Spaniards realized until Popé's rebellion that conversion of the soul by the sword had been such a dismal failure in seventeenth-century New Mexico. One bitter European stated after the revolt that most Pueblos "have never forsaken idolatry, and they appear to be Christians more by force than to be Indians who are reduced to the Holy Faith."[12] An old Indian testified that because "the Spaniards punished sorcerers and idolaters, the [Pueblos] had been plotting to rebel and kill the Spaniards and the [priests]."[13]

The persistence of Pueblo culture in the face of Spanish intolerance provided fertile ground for spiritual leaders. As Spanish influence increased and Catholic priests sought to destroy the power of the medicine men, many Indians converted to Christianity but many others resisted the priests and clung tenaciously to their own beliefs. Popé, the political leader of San Juan Pueblo, also was one of the Pueblos' staunchest traditionalists. The Spanish denied Popé the right to conduct his rituals publicly and even enslaved his older brother. Gradually, Popé became a symbol of resistance. From 1660 onward, drought and overgrazing produced severe economic hardship in New Mexico, and Popé and others became certain that they had displeased the gods. The increasing Spanish population added to the harsh conditions; in the eighty-two years of Spanish domination, the Pueblo population had been cut in half while the Spanish population had increased as more settlers arrived.[14]

Given the religious intolerance spawned by the Spanish Inquisition, economic exploitation, and adverse natural phenomena such as drought, seventeenth-century New Mexico had all the necessary ingredients to foment rebellion. And Popé's vision became the catalyst for such a revolt.

The personal road of Popé to his shamanic vision was fraught with as much misery as that of the people to whom he sought to provide spiritual guidance. Popé was a trusted healer who began to struggle with his people's problems by asserting that "Indians must be Indian again." While Popé and his fellow shamans prayed and kept the ancient ways alive, the Spanish were not idle. Through a network of Christian Indian informants, the Spanish arrested forty-seven medicine men and accused them of witchcraft in 1675. While both Indians and Spaniards believed in witches, the Spanish in New Mexico most often sought evildoers outside their own community.[15]

Charged with sorcery, Popé was publicly whipped and thrown into jail. The people of San Juan Pueblo then demanded his release as well as the release of the other medicine men. Calmly, the Pueblos spoke to the Spanish governor in measured language. They informed the governor that one of two things would happen if he did not release the spiritual leaders. Either every Indian might move away, a situation which would leave the Spaniards without agricultural workers, or the Pueblos might stay in the valley and rise up against their Spanish oppressors. In the face of these alternatives, the governor of New Mexico released his captives.[16]

Weakened by flogging and imprisonment, Popé went to San Juan Pueblo to resume the very activities for which he had been jailed. For four years, the old man went into a kiva and made paintings, tracing designs with black and green and yellow lines as he had done before. He wanted counsel from Po-he-yemu, the "one who scatters mist," as to what he should do. Some accounts say that while in a Taos kiva, three spiritual messengers entered the ceremonial chamber from the lower world. Their names were Caudi, Tilimi, and Tleume. They said that they were sent by Po-he-yemu, who felt that the time was ripe for an uprising.[17] Thus, Popé had consulted the upper and lower worlds about the proper course of action in the world of the four directions.

The Pueblo medicine men and their subordinate war chiefs planned the revolt through the Society of Opi. For months, Popé and other leaders carried the message of revolt. Slowly, in virtually every pueblo, leaders emerged. The Spanish grew uneasy about Popé's activities at San Juan Pueblo. Although secrecy was of utmost importance and women and children were not told of the revolt, Popé's plans may have been leaked nevertheless through his daughter and her husband Nicolas Bua, governor of San Juan Pueblo. At any rate, Popé suspected that Bua was a traitor, so he was executed by Popé or one of his fellow conspirators.[18]

In spite of all these precautions, the Spanish learned conclusively of his plans through Christian Pueblo informants and ordered Popé to stop his agitation. Popé then decided he had to leave San Juan Pueblo and go to Taos Pueblo, where he would have no relatives advising him to be careful for their sakes and where he would be freer to speak and act.[19]

Planning the Revolt

Once Popé was clear about the message he had received from spirits in the upper and lower worlds, he earnestly worked to unify that shamanic vision with political reality. Popé had considerable political as well as spiritual knowledge. At Taos Popé took a radical step. He counseled the people there to seek the aid of their ancient enemies the Apaches. At first the people were astonished, but then they reasoned, as Popé had, that the Apaches hated the Spanish. Spanish soldiers and farmers had kidnapped Apache children and enslaved them. In fact, the Apaches often raided Spanish and Pueblo settlements not only for booty but also to recapture their children. When the Apaches raided, they took Spanish knives and guns to add to their arsenal. With Apache allies who had such weapons the Pueblos realized they would be stronger.[20]

To explain the nature of Spanish power, Popé thought of the Spanish influence along the Rio Grande as a long snake with its head in the north. Popé saw that by cutting off its head, Santa Fe, the Pueblos could kill the whole snake. He reasoned that by separating the capital from the outlying settlements, the Spanish would be weakened. His analogy of Spanish rule as a snake also helped to graphically communicate his ideas to the diverse Pueblos. Popé also planted rumors to further his revolt. Before the start of the revolt, Popé told his war chiefs to send word upriver that all territory downriver was under Indian control. These rumors would destroy Spanish morale and give incentive to his reluctant Indian allies. By guarding the trails and roads, the Indians could curtail Spanish intelligence and cause confusion.[21]

The fact that Popé found ready allies in most of the Pueblos meant that he was appealing to inner discontent; once this unrest was aroused, the vision that the spirits had given him added to the revolt's impetus.[22] The question then arose as to the timing of the revolt. All the Pueblo leaders agreed that they should rise up when the Spanish were the weakest. Popé knew that the Spanish were in the direst straits just before the arrival of their supply train from Mexico City. The supplies arrived every third year in the spring or summer. The year 1680 was when the supply train was due to bring such items as powder, shot, new swords, shields, armor, daggers, and horses—goods that were among the principal tools of Spanish oppression. Popé also knew that the supply train could be late.[23]

Popé and the Pueblos then focused on additional environmental factors to calculate the date of the revolt more

Rio Grande in New Mexico, circa 1935. Photo by T. Harmon Parkurst. Courtesy Museum of New Mexico. Neg. No. 88080.

specifically. They saw dramatic possibilities for revolution forming in the physical environment. They watched the weather, knowing that the activities of the rainmaker beings were of great importance. Popé and the Pueblos had noticed the heavy snowfall on the mountains above the Rio Grande in the winter of 1679 to 1680. A cool spring followed, which delayed the melting of the heavy snowpack. They knew that the hot days of July would turn the waters of the Rio Grande into a raging torrent. Usually, the Rio Grande was shallow enough for wagons to ford, but in a flood, with the river over its lower banks, the Rio Grande would be impossible to cross. When the gods provided appropriate weather, it would be a good time for the Pueblos to strike.[24]

Popé and the war chiefs watched the weather patiently. If the flood came early, the supply train would be held up. If the rainmaker gods looked upon them more favorably, the summer rains would come a little early and add further to the flood. As the level of the water rose, Popé and his cohorts knew that the supply train would be held up until the end of August. Obviously, the time to strike was early August, when the first corn was getting ripe and food was plentiful. So word went out that the total environment for revolt was right. Painted characters on deerskins were used by runners to explain the plan to the various pueblos. If the runners should be caught, they were to interpret the deerskins in some way without revealing the truth.[25]

Popé said that the most forceful attack must be on the environs of Santa Fe to isolate the Spanish Governor Don Antonio de Otermin. Once Otermin perceived that he was surrounded, Popé hoped that he would retreat peacefully. However, if he chose to stay, Otermin and the Spanish people were to die. In essence, force and bloodshed would be used to oust the Spanish, but once they were retreating Popé did not want to waste any more Pueblo lives.[26]

The war chiefs and Popé sent out runners as the corn began to ripen. With the runners, Popé sent out a knotted rope of palmilla leaf to signify the number of days until the attack would begin. The date was fixed as August 13, 1680. Although Popé had told leaders in the upriver pueblos near Santa Fe his general plans, only his closest advisors knew the details. Nevertheless, because Popé was concerned about informants and traitors, he changed the date to August 10. Consequently, if Otermin learned of the rebellion, he would think he had more time to prepare for it. So that Otermin would not be alerted Popé even prohibited pre-battle dances.[27]

During the night of August 9, 1680, preparations were made in the pueblos. War parties were organized: one to attack the Spanish farms farthest from the pueblo, another to strike the big estate, and yet another to surround the magistrate's house. Other warriors would attack the mission and the convent while parties would also be assigned to control the trails.[28]

The Fury Explodes

At dawn on August 10, the pent-up fury against Spanish oppression was unleashed. To show Otermin the ferocity of the rebellion, children were not spared. Very few Spaniards escaped from Taos to warn the governor, and over three dozen Spanish farmers and officials were killed.[29]

In the upriver Pueblos, the scene was much the same. Indians attacked the priests and killed them, leaving their bodies unburied. In revenge for the destruction of kachina masks, the Pueblos cut off the arms and legs of religious statues, and churches were set on fire. Farmhouses were looted for cattle, horses, and wagons. By the evening of August 10th, many Indians were armed with guns and swords, and many Spaniards and mestizos had been killed.

By nightfall, the upriver Pueblos were liberated according to Popé's plan. Only a few scattered Spanish settlers survived this onslaught. Initially, Santa Fe was not to be attacked until the surrounding countryside was secure. As the uprising gained momentum, news reached Santa Fe of the devastation. Downriver, the news was much the same as Pueblos rose up to throw off the yoke of Spanish domination. By the evening of August 10, a thousand refugees huddled into the government buildings in Santa Fe. Rumors were rampant about the revolt, and Indians had planted people inside the government buildings to exaggerate its success, including the rumor that Isleta Pueblo had fallen. This shocked Governor Otermin because Isleta was an important Spanish stronghold, and he had received no word from Lieutenant Governor Alonso Garcia at Isleta. Otermin believed that Isleta Pueblo had fallen when, in fact, Spanish messengers who would have told him it remained in Spanish hands in the initial stages of the uprising had been intercepted on the road by rebelling Indians.[30]

The truth was that although success of the Pueblo Revolt was nearly complete in the north by the evening of August 10, the downriver Pueblos were not all liberated. Spanish refugees crowded into Isleta and put a strain on precious Indian food supplies. The people of Isleta Pueblo had already given much of their food to the Spanish as taxes; now they would be required to give more. Although the Spanish refugees were uneasy with their circumstances at Isleta, Indian messengers reported that the upriver towns and Santa Fe had fallen and therefore the Spanish forces stayed at Isleta. Conversely, thinking Isleta was lost, Otermin, decided to forego any attempts to aid the pueblo. Popé's rumors had now isolated the two main contingents of Spanish power since each believed that the other was destroyed.[31]

Spanish inaction allowed the downriver Pueblos to consolidate their gains; their uprising had begun later in the day and was more sporadic. Between Isleta and Santa Fe, villages had begun to revolt on the afternoon of August 10. Churches were burned, and Indians in small villages took to the hills that were more defensible. Word of the revolt's beginning did not reach Jémez Pueblo until noon, where the people instantly moved against the missionaries.

At Ácoma, the attack was so well coordinated that not a single Spaniard survived. Runners from Ácoma went to Zuñi and announced the revolution. The Zuñis rose up and killed their priests and sent word to the Hopis, who did the same. At Pecos Pueblo, Christian and non-Christian Indians united to destroy the massive church they had built. The church showed no Indian influences in its architecture, and no Indian had been sent to Mexico City to become a priest. Such complaints probably were responsible for the uprising at Pecos Pueblo.³²

Now preparations were made for the siege of Santa Fe. The Spanish colonists spent an uneasy weekend huddled there. Then on Monday, August 12, 1680, sentries saw bands of Indians from downriver moving towards the city. By the next day, there were over five hundred Indians camped on the edge of Santa Fe. Otermin talked to an Indian leader named Juan, who gave the Spanish two choices: leave the country or die. On August 13, Otermin sallied forth from the garrison in Santa Fe and drove the Indians back into the foothills of the mountains to prove his resolve in staying. But at dusk, a thousand men arrived from the San Juan, Santa Clara, San Ildefonso, and Taos pueblos, and more Indians, including Popé, arrived during the night. Tension was mounting among the Spanish in the cramped quarters in Santa Fe.³³

On August 14, 1680, Lieutenant Governor Garcia at Isleta Pueblo ordered a southerly retreat to the Rio Grande at El Paso, thinking that he was alone. His reconnaissance efforts only reinforced the rumors of absolute destruction. On August 15, Garcia abandoned Isleta Pueblo. Otermin and his refugees in Santa Fe were now completely alone, and the Indian army at Santa Fe began to move toward the government stronghold in the center of town. Sometimes the fighting raged from house to house until Popé's army reached the main Spanish fortification, but the Pueblos were unable to penetrate the government headquarters on the plaza.³⁴ Meanwhile, Indians had dammed the ditch that brought water to the government buildings. Now there was no water for a thousand people and hundreds of animals in the stronghold. After two days, cattle started to bawl, sheep bleated, the children began to cry, and the people became sick in the August heat. Indians taunted the Spaniards, charging that their Christian god had failed them and that the Pueblo gods had never left them.³⁵

On August 20, the Spanish made one last attempt to break the siege, spurred by thirst and the threat of disease in close quarters. After attending mass, the Spanish burst out of the governor's palace and charged the Indians. Although the Indians ran, the Spaniards nevertheless killed three hundred Indians who were trapped in burning houses. The Spanish captured forty-seven prisoners and also repaired the water ditch, but it was a Pyrrhic victory. Santa Fe was laid waste, and the surrounding fields were now barren. There was no food. The Spanish had been miraculously victorious, but their future in Santa Fe was dim.[36]

Through interrogation of his forty-seven Indian prisoners, Governor Otermin learned that the Pueblo gods had decreed the death of every Spaniard in New Mexico. The prisoners claimed that the sentence had been carried out from Taos to Isleta—everywhere except in Santa Fe. With this knowledge, the governor executed his Indian prisoners. Since the situation seemed hopeless, Otermin decided to abandon Santa Fe and retreat towards Isleta and the south, where he hoped to find remnants of Lieutenant Governor Garcia's forces. On August 21, the exodus from Santa Fe began. The Spaniards feared for their lives as they filed into the plaza and then into the burnt rubble of Santa Fe. However, the Pueblos did not attack but merely watched as the bedraggled train of Spanish settlers made their way southward to safety. Popé and his people saw a vision coming true and did not want to risk another Indian life as long as the Spanish continued their retreat to the south.[37]

As the Indian army watched the Spanish retreat, Popé and his leaders knew that the supply train was still south of the ford at El Paso since mules, horses, and oxen could not ford the river. The Rio Grande was above the floodplain, and water was everywhere. Lieutenant Governor Garcia's group of fifteen hundred refugees was retreating southward from Isleta Pueblo while Otermin's band of one thousand from Santa Fe also was retreating. The supply train at El Paso was now powerless to change the course of events.[38]

Popé's focus on auspicious natural conditions had paid off. Heavy snows in the mountains at the headwaters of the Rio Grande, a late, cool spring, and early summer rains all created an environment conducive to the Pueblo Revolt. In the Pueblo worldview, the rainmaker gods had looked favorably upon them. For the Spaniards who sought to control man and nature, the defeat was followed by years of poverty near the present-day city of Juárez, Mexico.[39]

Twelve Years of Freedom

Once the Spanish left, old religious practices became public again. Popé urged his followers to wash in the Rio Grande with yucca roots to cleanse themselves of the taint of Christianity. The Spanish language was not to be spoken. Spanish names were to be forsaken for Indian names. Every vestige of Christianity was destroyed or mocked.[40]

Popé's policies sought to do more than reestablish Pueblo political and religious authority; however, he also forbade the use of Spanish manufactured goods and crops, in an attempt to restore the traditional ecology as well as traditional culture. But most of Popé's edicts regarding crops were ignored. Popé even ordered the execution of some of his reputed enemies, but the Pueblo confederacy that had expelled the Spanish became divided into two camps, one favoring Popé, the other opposing him. Popé was deposed but restored in 1688, shortly before he died. Four Spanish attempts at reconquest in eight years along with civil war and a plague of European diseases decreased the Pueblo population considerably after Popé's death. In 1692, the Spanish authorities returned to stay, until the United States ousted them in 1848.

During the Pueblos' twelve years of freedom, along with religious, economic, and ecological concerns, Popé focused on creating a new vision for his people. The rainmaker gods, the spiritual beings of the upper and lower worlds had been unified through his vision. Religious persecution had strengthened the resolve of spiritual men such as Popé. Before initiating the revolt Popé had prayed and waited for a sign from the gods. Finally, the physical environment and the Pueblo spiritual world had been unified to provide the power and conditions for a successful rebellion. Through excessive snow and early summer rains, the people were shown that their path back to the rainmaker gods was now open and that they would receive direction and help from the deities in the clouds. With the rout of the Spanish, the shamanic vision of the Pueblo people who lived in harmony with nature was complete.

A legendary joke about Popé's uprising illustrates the failure of the Spanish to understand the ecological and spiritual dimensions of the Pueblo Revolt. When Governor Otermin queried several Indians about the causes of the uprising, and who the leader of the revolt was, their replies seemed enigmatic to him. A Keresan-speaking captive alleged that the leader was Payastimo. When asked where he lived, the captive pointed to the mountains. A Tewa-speaking man answered the same question by asserting that the leader was Po-he-yemu, and he lived in the northern mountains, while another Tewa-speaking man said that the leader was Payatiabo, and he lived in the mountains. While the Spaniards actually thought that the Indians were referring to an actual leader of the revolt, in fact, all three words are the names of a deity whom the Pueblos address in their prayers to intercede for them with the one beyond the clouds. Generally, he is said to live in the north, on the highest mountain or in the clouds.[41]

In the Pueblo worldview, the "one who scatters mist," or Po-he-yemu, was the leader of the revolt but not in the way that the Spanish had imagined. Popé himself was merely Po-he-yemu's earthly vessel since the weather and environment necessary for the revolt could not be created by humankind. Once the natural forces converged, it was up to Popé and his people to be in contact with Po-he-yemu and act accordingly in the world of the four directions.

The Spanish documents of the period reflect the religious and racial bias of the times. Their charges of idolatry and devil worship among the Pueblos as a cause of the revolt give us little understanding as to the cultural dynamics of the conflict. However, it is clear that Popé's uprising was more than a religious conflict and struggle for freedom. It was a struggle between two worldviews—one in which man was in harmony with nature and another that sought dominion at all costs. Popé's vision of a people unified in harmony with the environment was indeed realized, for a time. The three realities were combined once again, and the physical, inner, and cultural aspects of Pueblo life were experientially and symbolically given meaning. In 1692, when the Spanish recolonized New Mexico, religious persecution was not as onerous as before. But although the Spanish may have learned a lesson in religious tolerance, they once again imposed their colonial land-use policies on the Pueblo people.

Notes

1. William Brandon, *American Heritage Book of Indians* (New York: Dell, 1969), 122.

2. See Roxanne D. Ortiz, "The Roots of Resistance: Pueblo Land Tenure and Spanish Colonization," *Journal of Ethnic Studies* 5 (Winter 1977): 4.

3. Edward P. Dozier, *The Pueblo Indians of North America* (New York: Holt, Rinehart and Winston, 1970), 1-10; and Joe S. Sando, *The Pueblo Indians* (San Francisco, Calif.: Indian Historian Press), 17-22.

4. Sando, *Pueblo Indians*, 28-30.

5. Ibid., 25-27.

6. Sando, *Pueblo Indians*, 52-53; and Alfonso Ortiz, ed. *New Perspectives on the Pueblos* (Albuquerque: University of New Mexico Press, 1972), 43.

7. Alvin Josephy, *The Patriot Chiefs* (New York: Viking Press, 1969), 82-83.

8. Ibid.

9. *Auto* of Antonio de Otermin, August 9, 1680, in *The Revolt of the Pueblo Indians of New Mexico and Otermin's Attempted Reconquest, 1680-1682*, vol. 2, ed. Charles Wilson Hackett (Albuquerque: University of New Mexico Press, 1970), 3; and Sando, *Pueblo Indians*, 52.

10. Sando, *Pueblo Indians*, 52-53; and Ortiz, "The Roots of Resistance," 8-9.

11. See Mircea Eliade, *The Sacred and the Profane* (New York: Harcourt, Brace and World, 1957), passim; and, more specifically, see Mircea Eliade, *Shamanism: Archaic Techniques of Ecstasy*, Bolingen Series, No. 76 (New York: Pantheon, 1964), Chapter 8. For such an application to the Pueblos, see Alfonso Ortiz, *The Tewa World* (Chicago: University of Chicago Press, 1969).

12. Declaration of Luis de Quintana, December 22, 1681, in *Revolt of the Pueblo Indians*, vol. 2, ed. Hackett, 291.

13. Declaration of one of the rebellious Christian Indians who was captured on the road, Place of El Alamillo, September 6, 1680, ibid., vol. 1, 61.

14. Declaration of Pedro Garcia, Pedro Namboa, and others, September 6, 1680, in *Revolt of the Pueblo Indians*, ed. Hackett, vol. 2, 62-62; and Edward H. Spicer, *Cycles of Conquest* (Tucson: University of Arizona Press, 1976), 169. See also Charles Wilson, ed. and trans., *Historical Documents Relating to New Mexico, Nueva Vizcaya, and Approaches Thereto, to 1773*, vol. 3 (Washington, D.C.: Carnegie Institute, 1923-1937), 17-18.

15. Ralph E. Twitchell, *The Leading Facts of New Mexico History* (Cedar Rapids, Ia.: Torch Press, 1912), i, 355-56; and Franklin Folsom, *Red Power on the Rio Grande* (Chicago,: Follett Publishing Co., 1973), 72.

16. Declaration of Diego Lopez, December 22, 1681, in *Revolt of the Pueblo Indians*, ed. Hackett, vol. 2, 301; and opinion of Fray Francisco de Ayeta, December 23, 1681, ibid., vol. 2, 310.

17. Declaration of Pedro Naranjo of the Queres Nation, December 19, 1681, ibid., vol. 2, 246.

18. Sando, *Pueblo Indians*, 52; and Declaration of the Indian Juan, December 18, 1681, in *Revolt of the Pueblo Indians*, ed. Hackett, vol. 2, 234.

19. Warren A. Beck, *New Mexico: A History of Four Centuries* (Norman: University of Oklahoma Press, 1969), 76; and Hackett, *Revolt of the Pueblo Indians*, vol. 1, xxii-xxiii.

20. *Auto* of Otermin, August 9, 1680, *Revolt of the Pueblo Indians*, ed. Hackett, vol. 1, 3-4; *Auto* and judicial process, August 13-20, 1680, ibid., vol. 1, 13.

21. *Auto* of Alfonso Garcia, August 23, 1680, ibid., vol. 1, 73-75; *Auto de junta de guerra*, October 1, 1680, ibid., vol. 1, 160; and Folsom, *Red Power*, 81-82.

22. Robert Silverburg, *The Pueblo Revolt* (New York: Weybright and Talley, 1970), 113-14; Folsom, *Red Power*, 83-84.

23. Ibid.

24. Silverburg, *Pueblo Revolt*, 127; and Folsom, *Red Power*, 84-85.

25. Twitchell, *New Mexico History*, 356; Silverburg, *Pueblo Revolt*, 114-15; Sol Stember, *Heroes of the American Indian* (New York: Fleet Press Corp., 1971), 33; and Folsom, *Red Power*, 86.

26. *Auto de junta de guerra*, October 1680, in *Revolt of the Pueblo Indians*, ed. Hackett, vol. 1, 160.

27. *Auto* of Otermin, August 9, 1680, ibid., vol. 1, 3-5; Declaration of the Indian Juan, December 18, 1680, ibid., vol. 2, 234-35; Declaration of Pedro Naranjo of the Queres Nation, December 19, 1681, ibid., vol. 2, 246.

28. *Auto* and Declaration of Maestre de Campo Francisco Gomez, August 12, 1680, ibid., vol. 1, 9-10; Declaration of Pedro Hidalgo, August 10, 1680, ibid., vol. 1, 6-7; and Twitchell, *New Mexico History*, 360.

29. *Auto* of Alfonso Garcia, August 24, 1680, in *Revolt of the Pueblo Indians*, ed. Hackett, vol. 1, 70–80; and *Auto* of Alfonso Garcia, August 14, 1680, ibid., vol. 1, 65–70.

30. *Auto* of Otermin, August 21, 1680, ibid., vol. 1, 17; Declaration of Pedro Hidalgo, ibid., vol. 1, 6–7; and Folsom, *Red Power*, 102.

31. Notification and arrest, September 6, 1680, in *Revolt of the Pueblo Indians*, ed. Hackett, vol. 1, 64; *Auto* for passing muster, reviewing arms and horses, and other things, September 29, 1680, ibid., vol. 1, 135.

32. *Auto* of Alfonso Garcia, August 14, 1680, ibid., vol. 1, 68; *Auto* of Alfonso Garcia, August 24, 1680, ibid., vol. 1, 70–80; *Auto* of Otermin, September 13, 1680, ibid., vol. 1, 113; *Auto* and judicial process, August 13–20, 1680, ibid., vol. 1, 177–83.

33. Judicial process and declaration, August 10, 1680, ibid., vol. 1, 8–9; Declaration of Diego Lopez, December 22, 1681, ibid., vol. 2, 292–303; ibid., vol. 1, xiii; and Folsom, *Red Power*, 110–12.

34. *Auto* and judicial process, August 13–20, 1680, in *Revolt of the Pueblo Indians*, ed. Hackett, vol. 1, 12–16; *Auto* of Alfonso Garcia, August 14, 1680, ibid., vol. 1, 67.

35. Declaration of Josephe, Spanish-speaking Indian, December 19, 1681, ibid., vol. 2, 239–40; *Auto* of Otermin, September 13, 1680, ibid., vol. 1, 113.

36. *Auto* of Otermin, September 13, 1680, ibid., vol. 1, 113–14.

37. *Auto*, August 21, 1680, ibid., vol. 1, 16–18.

38. *Auto* of Alfonso Garcia, August 14, 1680, ibid., vol. 1, 67; ibid., vol. 1, xxvi; see also another certified copy, *Auto* for holding a junta de guerra in El Paso. . . , August 25, 1680, ibid., vol. 1, 28.

39. Sando, *Pueblo Indians*, 53–54; and Folsom, *Red Power*, 121.

40. Folsom, *Red Power*, passim.

41. Ibid.; see also Henry Warner Bowden, "Spanish Missions, Cultural Conflict, and the Pueblo Revolt of 1680," *Church History* 44 (Summer 1975).

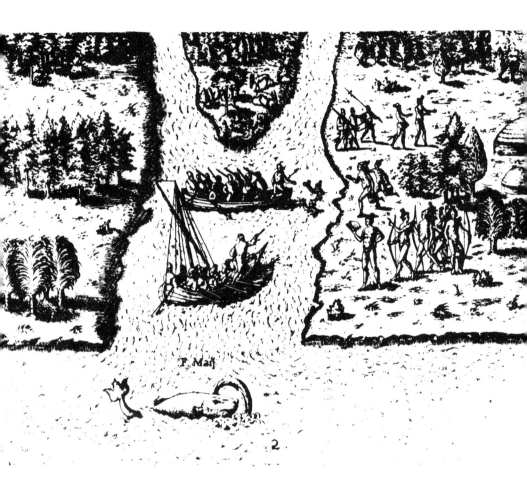

The French exploring the River May (St. John's River), from Jacques Le Moyne's Brevis Narratio eorum quae in Florida Americae, *engraved and published by Theodor de Bry, Frankfort/M., 1591. Note the "rotundas," or roundhouses.*

Chapter Three

Pre- and Post-Columbian Native Ecology: The Yamasees

To gain a more profound understanding of change over time for an important Native American tribe in Georgia and Florida, it is necessary to gather evidence from a variety of non-written sources concerning American Indian people subjected to colonialism and war in the American Southeast. The work of Michel Foucault and other deconstructionists is also important for this process. Foucault points out that in the eighteenth century, reformers postulated philosophic, political, and economic rationales to facilitate the transition from control over the physical body by such means as torture, dismemberment, and execution to a more subtle control that utilized "technologies of the body." These new intellectual developments were manifested in regulations, laws, administrative measures, prisons, scientific dogmas, philanthropy, morality, and other forms of social control. Thus, the body of the controlled (that is, colonized) people became the depository where power relationships were "contracted" rather than inflicted. It is this reality that creates a watershed in the treatment of Native Americans in the Caribbean that moves from genocide to a reality that attempts to preserve the physical body of the oppressed in order to exploit newly developing power relationships in the colonial system (slavery, peonage, and so forth).[1]

Such a deconstructionist awareness may be utilized along with archaeological, ethnological, historical, and ecological data on the Yamasee Indians to better understand Native American viewpoints and voices before and after the catastrophic consequences of the Yamasee War, a pivotal event not only for the Yamasees but also for power relationships in the American Southeast between Spain and England. This chapter will utilize a family ecology model to provide a convenient human dimension to structure information from Yamasee informants, ecological studies, archaeological data, and ethnohistorical accounts.

Yamasee family ecology in the precolonial Southeast was a threefold ecosystem. Obviously, the primary environed unit consisted of the family group, a bonded unit of interacting and interdependent persons who shared goals and resources. Secondly, the environment included nature and human beings, as well as air, water, space, food, and shelter, which were essential elements for subsistence. Being social in nature, humans also constituted a society, themselves the "human behavioral environment"; forming the third aspect of the ecosystem. . . family system nurtured the behavioral environment of roles, rules, and interactions that produced Yamasee society. The connection between the human-constructed aspects of the ecosystems (housing, equipment, clothing, and food) and the natural environment laid the basis for the physical maintenance of the ecosystem. This interaction between family and ecosystem was governed by two sets of rules: the unchangeable laws of nature and the human rules of the Yamasees.[2]

Energy in the forms of food and natural resources was the lifeblood of the system and was necessary for maintaining the individual and the group. The rules governing the relationship within and between systems were, however, human-defined and mutable. The human variables included allocation of resources, social customs, role expectations, and power distribution.[3]

Confusion over the term "Yamasee" and the scope of its application have caused considerable problems in understanding the people of coastal Georgia. This confusion has caused a proliferation of inaccurate literature and interpretive problems. Semantically, the term "Yamasee" is derived from a southeastern Indian village called Amacrisse. This village was one of the first Guale (pronounced "Wallie") towns that the Spanish used as an administrative center. Guale was a chief of coastal Georgia Indians at the time of initial Spanish contact in the early 1500s, so the Spanish began to refer to the area as Guale. In the early 1700s, the English began to refer to "Yamasees" as those Gualeans that were their trading partners and were nearest to Charleston. In reality, Cusabos, Guales, and Yamasees spoke a similar language, intermarried, and inhabited neighboring areas of the coast. The Spanish also used the term "Yamasee" to differentiate between the Appalachees of West Florida and Yamasees. Actually, Guales referred to themselves as "Tamathli" (tama-thlee), which means "people of the high ground." "Altamaha" is a common English spelling of this term. In essence, the term "Yamasee" was used by Spanish and English colonials to describe the people of the coastal zone of Georgia. Hence, Guale, Cusabo, and Yamasee are descriptive terms for the same people inhabiting different locales of the coastal zone of Georgia.[4]

The Yamasee Family Unit

The Yamasees usually divided labor among the sexes. The men specialized in political, religious, hunting, and military roles; they were ranked serially, with the mico (chief), shaman, heads of hunting societies, and war chiefs being the highest ranks. In kinship and in other ways, women held significant positions. Daughters of high-ranking micos assumed special status in the society. Evidence suggests that Yamasee kinship terminology was probably of the "Crow type," in which persons of the same sex in maternal lineages are designated by a single term. This ranking pattern was fairly prevalent among Muskogean peoples who had matrilineal clan structures within appropriate moieties.[5]

During the day women helped each other with household and garden chores. Younger women probably tended the gardens while the older ones engaged in child care and household duties. The warm season consisting of spring and summer meant hard work for Yamasee women. Gardens in the coastal sector were planted near lagoons and marshes, where "hills" of corn, beans, and squash were grown several feet apart. Soil exhaustion demanded that these cultivated areas be rotated periodically. Moving villages to adjacent bluffs and islands in the same locale every five to ten years seemed to have been a standard pattern.

Most Yamasees lived in small groups of a few families numbering 80 to 120 people. Several of these groups lived along a river, sound, or lagoon. Because of this subsistence structure, women's activities focused on gathering roots and nuts in the fall and winter.[6] While the activities of women were highly structured around agriculture in the warm months, they were less organized during the winter.

The men hunted and fished during the fall and winter. In the summer they garnered turtle eggs and shad (in season), but this was intermittent and akin to the women's seasonal gathering of nuts, acorns, firewood, and roots in the cold season.[7] Thus, the work was distributed between the sexes, with men working intensely in the cold season and women working less, and with the roles reversed in the warm season.

Clothing also distinguished genders. Most men wore a long breechcloth about five feet long and a half foot wide held up by a cord tied around the loin with the excess leather falling in front and behind. Sashes were often draped across the chest or over the shoulder, weather permitting. Moccasins made of deerskin were worn in cold weather.[8] Women wore deerskin skirts from the waist to the knees in the warm months, accompanied by a netlike material made of Spanish moss.[9]

Dwellings and Public Buildings

Materials used in the construction of dwellings and public buildings were fairly uniform in the coastal region from St. Augustine, Florida, to Charleston, South Carolina. "Rotundas" were the major village structures. These winter communal houses varied in size from 50 to 120 feet in diameter. They contained inner mat walls which formed sleeping compartments and a central court which was open to the sky. The walls were constructed of interlaced vines plastered with clay and tempered on the inside with Spanish moss. The interiors were covered with palmetto matting. Rotundas usually

Alligator hunt, from Jacques Le Moyne de Morgues's Brevis Narratio eorum quae in Florida Americae, *engraved and published by Theoror de Bry, Frankfort/M., 1591. Unlike agriculture, hunting is primarily a man's pursuit.*

housed around a hundred people, and some had palisades surrounding them that served as protection. The palisades do not appear to have been fortifications but served as barriers to keep out animals.

Yamasee behavior was governed by the ebb and flow of the natural environment, and guided by philosophical and religious doctrines based on the meanings of existence. Fertility and prosperity were goals of Yamasee society.[10] The Yamasees also professed a concept of immortality based on beliefs in an after-death place of punishment (cold) and a paradise (warm).[11] Various dietary and behavioral taboos were observed, while fertility management was practiced through abstinence and abortion. Herbs used for abortion were common, especially among unwed girls and women. In 1682, Robert Ferguson wrote of Indians in the low country of South Carolina:

> *the women destroy their bellies with the decoction of a certain bituminous root, that . . . root occasions stirility [sic]. This ancient custom is so invited into their females . . . till arriving at the age of twenty-seven . . . then they fancy to themselves that their children will grow most active, vigorous and valiant. . . .*[12]

In 1763, George Milliken-Johnson, a physician, witnessed Indian women in South Carolina using herbs to facilitate abortion. He stated that it "contributes to depopulate them."[13] Another observer, J. F. D. Smyth, stated there were "frequent abortions of young unmarried women . . . by medicinal simples that promote abortion . . ." Smyth also noted that such practices in their early youth subjected them to miscarriage even afterwards, ". . . and when it happens otherwise, they commonly have not more than two children, very seldom three during the whole course of their lives."[14]

Marriage was usually monogamous among the Yamasees. The micos were the only men allowed to have several wives. Premarital sex was accepted, but adultery was punished severely. Divorce and remarriage were allowed, but a waiting period was required until the community again accepted the person as a single individual. The dead were buried in several ways, depending on the age and station of the person. A Spanish observer wrote in 1526:

> *And on some small islands of the coast, there are certain mosques or temples of that idolatrous people, and many bones of dead men, those of the children and babies were separated from the adults; they are like ossuaries of charnel houses of the common people. The bones of principal men were by themselves in a chapel or temple separate from the rest of the community, and also on small islands.*[15]

Yamasee Subsistence

The Yamasees lived in the coastal zone and limited areas of the pine-barren sections of the Georgia, Florida, and South Carolina. This coastal zone had three sections: the strand, or beach; the marsh, or lagoon; and the delta. The beach was the most inhospitable area of the coastal zone. It was an undesirable place for settlement because of its exposure to storms and winds, including occasional hurricanes.[16] In addition, vegetation was sparse among the sand dunes, and flora important to aboriginal subsistence such as China brier, Spanish bayonet, yaupon, live oak, cabbage palm, saw palmetto, and prickly pear did not grow at the beach.[17] Animals indigenous to the beach were generally small and had adapted to the near-desert environment of the dunes. Although food was abundant further inland in the beach area, the sea turtle was the principal animal that the Yamasees depended on for food. Prized for its flesh and numerous eggs, its seasonal appearance was unfailing. The Yamasees also valued the coquina shell. This small bivalve still lives in large quantities on most Atlantic beaches.[18]

Aboriginal life centered on the lagoon-marsh area, a few hundred feet from the beach, because it was rich in resources. The islands, creeks, marshes, and lagoons that make up this environment were, and continue to be, extensive along the south Atlantic Coast. Due to the tide, the drainage of the salt marshes caused heavy silting. It was impossible to traverse the marsh on foot at low or high tide, so the Yamasees traveled in dugout canoes.[19] On the Georgia and Carolina coasts, high ground in the lagoon and marshy sections created large freshwater or brackish swamps. The diverse flora consisted of palmetto scrub oak and varieties of yucca. But none of these plants were a part of the Yamasee diet, according to current archaeological evidence.[20]

The terrestrial and aquatic life of the region offers numerous bivalves, gastropods, crustaceans, and fish for human consumption. Evidence demonstrates that the Yamasees ate marine mollusks, American oysters, and hardshell clams. Crustacea (crab and shrimp) are abundant today, but data indicates that only crabs were eaten by the Yamasees. The most common fish consumed by aboriginals were shark, marine catfish, sheepshead, black drum, and striped mullet. The Yamasees also sometimes ate alligators. Birds were part of the aboriginal diet; favorite species included ducks, common loons, double-crested cormorants, great blue herons, greater egrets, and turkey vultures.[21] Mammals were also consumed, especially the white-tailed deer. Black bear, dolphin, pygmy sperm whale, and the manatee appeared in the midden heaps. The wild turkey, opossum, raccoon, river otter, and cottontail inhabiting the areas were consumed only periodically.[22] Freshwater rivers entering the Atlantic Ocean created deltas along the coastal plain. Although delta water was fresh or only slightly brackish, such areas are of low relief, composed of sediments deposited in lagoons and offshore bar formations. These characteristics made Yamasee habitation in the delta area intermittent.[23] On the Atlantic shore, the larger rivers have often cut a bluff where they cross an old beach ridge before they enter the ocean, marking the start of the delta and the end of the pine barrens. The bluff is a part of the North and South Pleistocene terrace system which parallels the coastline. In contrast, the delta area is usually a swampy grassland. Seawater may intrude with the tides, or the riverine nature of the swamp may keep salt water out.[24]

The fauna of the section is also much like the lagoon and marsh section with wading birds nesting in the area. Anadromous fishes, including the American shad, glut herring, striped bass, and two species of sturgeon are found here. Essentially, the delta section is like the beach section since it provides little subsistence that would appeal to an aboriginal population.[25]

The pine barren region of Georgia and South Carolina is best defined by both vegetation and physiography. The vegetation can be characterized as vast expanses of longleaf pine forests. No botanically meaningful areas presently exist that can provide clues about these precolonial forests. Its destruction began with colonial settlement, and contemporary forest management practices continue to alter the area. Interestingly, the cultural significance of this forest has not been recognized by ethnohistorians and archaeologists. Those who work on problems of aboriginal culture in the Southeast have ignored the presence and significance of the forest because its destruction occurred before it was systematically investigated.[26]

The longleaf or yellow pine was the dominant species in this area due to its ability to adapt to fire. The forest possessed huge tracts of almost pure longleaf pine. The flowering dogwood and several scrub oak species, as well as the saw palmetto, occupy the first understory in restricted locales.[27] Along the river valleys that crossed the region were the floodplain forests where bald cypress, red maple, rattan vine, pecan, hackberry, water locust, several gums, and many oaks grew in profusion. In general, the physiography of the region is typified by an extensive, well-drained upland of gently rolling hills. The soils are sandy nearer the coast to sand clay in the higher regions. Over forty inches of rain in an average year leaches out large amounts of nitrogen and other soil nutrients.[28]

Few edible animals inhabited the longleaf pine forest. Most of the deer, the bear, raccoon, opossum, and other mammals common to the area lived in the floodplain forest, venturing out only when rivers were overflowing. The only plentiful source of food in the longleaf pine forest was the wild turkey. Most of the precolonial archaeological sites were associated with floodplain forest subsistence. Before the white contact period, the pine-barrens region supported few, if any, permanent aboriginal populations except along the riverine floodplains.[29]

The Yamasee Behavioral Environment

Yamasee attitudes, roles, philosophies, and emotional responses during the precontact period are not easy to assess. Most of the contemporary ethnology of Yamasees has largely been ignored by ethnohistorians, historians, and anthropologists. The Yamasee language is probably closely related to the Hitchiti dialect of the Muskogean linguistic group. Young boys were called *ticibane* until they were initiated into manhood. Then, each young man was given a name chosen because of an achievement or a special trait. A girl was called by family terms or named at birth after a meteorological occurrence or special event. Hernando de Soto observed that the Yamasees as a people were basically generous. At Cutha Fichique, about twenty-five miles south of the location of present-day Augusta, Georgia, De Soto met a female leader who stated: " . . . good wishes are to be valued more than all the treasures of the earth. . . . With sincerest and purest goodwill I tender you my person, my lands, my people, and make these small gifts."[30] The woman then gave a string of large pearls to De Soto. In general, early accounts portrayed the Yamasees as peaceful and loving people prone to mirth and dancing once daily work routines were done.

Yamasee philosophy and religion focused on a culture hero named Datha or Ocasta. Ocasta was God's helper, and he was a powerful giant. When he came to earth, he observed people killing animals with flint points. This frightened him so he picked up pieces of flint and made a stone coat to protect himself from humans. Ocasta's only magical power was the ability to disappear, but he could not do so in front of human beings. Legend claims that Ocasta was the source of evil. He made witches and other bad things and also traveled from village to village causing trouble. The people disliked his behavior and consequently devised a plan to get rid of him.[31]

They stationed seven nude, "moon-sick" (menstruating) women in the woods where Ocasta would pass. As he came down the path, Ocasta became very ill from seeing so many "moon-sick" women. When he fell down, the women picked some flint from his armor, then drove a stake into his heart to hold him down. All the men quickly gathered around Ocasta, and he promised to leave the earth. Before leaving, however, Ocasta taught the people songs and dances to please the Creator and to help them win wars and heal the sick. He also instructed the first medicine men. When his body began to burn, Ocasta's spirit rose singing. He had created both good and evil and had sacrificed himself to save the people from the evil he had made.[32] Thus, the story chronicles the origin of good and evil and the gift of medicines to treat evil.

One of the most important ceremonies was the Snake Dance. Members of the group assembled in a common area and after a period of dancing, they sat around the dance house. A medicine man would then appear carrying a poisonous snake. Each person would draw a small pictograph on a piece of bark representing his wishes for the year. Then the medicine man would walk slowly around the circle holding the snake's head so that it could see the pictographs. He would then release the snake in the woods to carry Yamasee wishes into the animal world.[33]

Another significant ritual to secure supernatural help was the use of the *sabia*, or crystals. According to Yamasee lore, these small crystals brought success in war, public speaking, courtship, hunting, and protection in emergencies. The crystals were kept in buckskin bundles, or pouches, and were used in conjunction with the "long song" to obtain special powers. Often a hunter would take his *sabia* pouch with him to hunt deer. Once he was a distance from the village, the hunter would open the pouch and then take a small amount of red paint placed in the bundle with the *sabia* and smear it on his cheek so that he would have little difficulty in locating and killing a deer. The source of the Yamasee *sabia* was the heart of a certain kind of rose, or Moon Flower. The crystals were obtained by burying the flower for a time and then digging it up again to find small crystals in the heart of the flower. Such roses were also considered sacred and venerated through a Yamasee ritual in the spring called the Dance of the Rose.[34] The *sabia* symbolized the rhythms and cycles of creation and the interrelatedness of the plant, animal, and mineral worlds. Through an understanding of its totality, great powers for good and evil could be obtained. For this reason, the knowledge of this ritual was only transferred to people who were well known to the person who possessed the power of the *sabia.*

Medicine objects like a Shadow Fighting Knife were also important in dealing with life-threatening situations and the afterlife. An old knowledgeable Yamasee, Stewart Shaffer, told the following story of its importance:

> *When a boy came of age, an aged relative of his, a man of some importance, would make him a knife of this sort from bone and paint it blue, the indigo type of blue. The knife would then be buried for thirteen cycles of the moon. Then it would be dug up, and the blue paint would be found to have turned black. The knife would be kept by the boy throughout his life, and he would carry it with him, together with other medicines, on war expeditions. At the time of the man's death, his bundle and the knife were burned so that he could use it on his journey to the afterworld.*[35]

Ceremonies for good weather and social dances, called stomp dances, were an integral part of social interaction. In general, the Yamasees sought to live in harmony with the environment and their neighbors. Ceremonies, dances, and games provided appropriate outlets for aggression. Fundamentally, the symbolic life of Yamasees involved reciprocity, harmony, and respect for creation, and their behavioral patterns did not appear significantly different from those of other southeastern groups.

Yamasee History and Demography

Our first records of historical contact with the Yamasees are from Spanish sources. In 1566, three Jesuit missionaries were sent from Spain to coastal Georgia. When the Jesuits landed on Cumberland Island, Father Pedro Martínez was killed by some Guales. By 1573, the Franciscans replaced the Jesuits. Under the Franciscans, missions and presidios were extended as far north of St. Augustine, Florida, as Santa Elena (present-day Port Royal, South Carolina).[36]

Spanish records describe Guale as a frontier province that experienced almost constant strife in its formative years. In 1586, the English adventurer Sir Francis Drake sacked and destroyed St. Augustine. The Spanish realized their defenses were overextended and withdrew from the Santa Elena presidio; Guale then became an isolated frontier outpost. There were only twelve soldiers stationed at each of six to eight remaining presidios. The entire Spanish military presence in the Southeast totaled only about four hundred men by the end of the sixteenth century.

In 1597, a Guale Indian leader known as Juanillo, "Little John," led a revolt against the Spanish missions. A Spanish Friar, Pedro Corpa, interfered with Juanillo's right to become a mico (chief) of Guale. On September 13, 1597, the rebels sequestered themselves in a church at Tolamato (MacIntosh County, Georgia) and killed Father Corpa when he came for his morning devotions. Three days later, Father Blas Rodríquez was captured at Tupique, a few miles north of Tolamato, and was executed. Several more Spanish priests were slain as the revolt swept up and down the coastal province of Guale. But at mission San Pedro on Cumberland Island, the Indians remained friendly, and it was the only mission to emerge unscathed from the revolt.

The Spanish governor led an expedition of 150 men from St. Augustine to put down the revolt in Guale. Spanish soldiers burned Indian villages and fields surrounding the mission, forced the Guale people inland to the pine barrens, and destroyed all their canoes. In spite of destruction all about them, the Guales suffered few casualties but were starved into submission. Loyalist Indians killed Juanillo at the last rebel stronghold in the interior and delivered his scalp to the Spanish at St. Augustine.[37]

For a while, Spanish authorities contemplated abandoning St. Augustine and the entire Southeast, but the governor was adamant in his belief that the mission system could be reestablished in Guale. Although Guale lacked agricultural potential, the Spaniards believed colonization would work. They were interested in developing the rich interior area beyond the pine barrens called Tama (central Georgia). The interior agricultural settlements could in turn support European-style defense settlements on the coast.[38]

For most of the early seventeenth century, the Spanish reasserted their presence in Guale through the gradual rebuilding of missions and presidios. No efforts were made to exploit the fertile lands of Tama, although all of the problems that beset the Spanish before Juanillo's revolt continued. Indian unrest and tensions between soldiers and missionaries jeopardized Spanish rule over the area. The missionaries felt that the soldiers were too few for protection during war, even though the friars believed that the soldiers corrupted the morals of the mission Indians. On the eve of English settlement, Spanish missionary zeal had waned, and Spanish control over Guale was nominal.[39]

When the English arrived at Charleston in 1670, the Spanish mission system lacked necessary resources to protect the Gualean missions from English and Creek attacks. Fifteen years later, the mission system collapsed. Consequently, most of the Guale Indians fled to Creek villages in Tama, or they sought the protection of the English at Charleston. Many Guales who left the Spanish missions in 1685 to join the English in Cusabo territory above the Savannah River returned to St. Augustine in 1715 as "Yamasees" when the Yamasee War broke out.[40]

As a result of the conflict between the English and the Spanish in the Southeast, the Savannah River Valley was almost devoid of native peoples by 1733. Only a small band of Yamacraws (mixed Guale and Creek) remained at Savannah. A few Yuchis and Yamasees lived farther up the Savannah River.

Birds-eye view of the city Pagus Hispanorum (St. Augustine), Florida, from Dapper's America, *1673.*

Many of the Creeks in Tama had fled almost as far west as the Chattahoochee River in western Georgia.

The drastic demographic change and the confusion over the term "Yamasee" have clouded our knowledge of the people bearing that name. The chief problems among contemporary ethnohistorians and their treatment of the Yamasees is twofold. First, many scholars ignore or give only passing attention to Spanish sources. Second, hardly any data from contemporary Yamasee informants is used despite the fact that this information was gathered and published a generation ago.[41]

Many contemporary scholars also use English-language sources uncritically. In the *Journals of the Commissioners of the Indian Trade 1710–1718* (colonial records of South Carolina), it is clear that "Yamasee Indians" was a general term. In one letter, the commissioners talk of "Nations of Yamasee Indians." At other times, the Palachocolas (Appalachees) and Yamasees are lumped together for administrative purposes. When complaints of Yamasee enslavement are brought to the commissioners, fine distinctions are made as to who was Yamasee and who was Appalachee. By the seventeenth century, most Yamasees and Appalachees shared a common Spanish foe and similar language. Both groups lived in close proximity, and intermarriage occurred.[42]

The population data on Yamasees is colored by the ambiguity regarding who should be included in the group. In 1685, Caleb Westbrook estimated that well over 1,000 Yamasees were seeking the protection of the English and had moved to the Savannah River area.[43] In 1715, South Carolina estimated the number of Yamasees to be 1,215; about half were children.[44] In 1719, after the Yamasee War 300 to 400 adult male Yamasees lived in the St. Augustine area in four or five villages.[45] This would indicate a total population of well over 1,000. In 1732, South Carolina estimated that 40 to 50 bowman (about 18 families or 200 people) of Yamasee and Creek descent were living on Yamacraw Bluff, the future site of Savannah. These Yamasees at the time of the founding of Georgia acknowledged affinity in language and culture to the Guales, Yamasees, and Creeks.[46]

These statistics indicate that the Gualean population of coastal Georgia remained fairly stable once they were identified as Yamasees in 1685, despite wrenching cultural and economic changes introduced by contact with Europeans. This population stability was probably the same under mission rule because Spanish control of the coastal region was always tenuous. Depopulation of the South Carolina coastal region occurred mainly during and after the Yamasee War. Unscrupulous traders who raped and murdered women and children and seized slaves for debts were major causes of the war. Arguments of ecological collapse accompanied by declining deer populations cannot be substantiated. After the Yamasee War, the English encouraged Creeks to engage in slave raiding among the Yamasees. This forced the Yamasees closer to St. Augustine or northward to Augusta, Georgia, where the remnants of the Yamasees live today. Yamasees and Yamacraws who moved to the Augusta area had to disguise their identities.[47]

Some scholars, such as Richard L. Haan, use dubious ecological assumptions about the coastal Southeast to argue that overhunting of deer populations forced the Yamasees into debt. Furthermore, it is claimed that domesticated animals such as cattle and pigs reduced the deer's browse and possibly introduced viruses or parasites that made the deer unhealthy. Rapid growth of rice plantations in coastal South Carolina also has been offered as evidence of ecological imbalance that threatened Yamasee existence.

These assumptions are based upon the belief that all Yamasees lived and hunted in South Carolina. Available evidence indicates, however, that the lower Yamasee towns were in coastal Georgia and along the Savannah River, where no white settlement occurred before 1715. The rich coastal section from the Savannah River to the St. Mary's River was still under Yamasee control at the outbreak of the Yamasee War.

The Yamasees had learned from the Spaniards to raise domesticated animals for food during the mission period. This became necessary because contemporary Yamasee informants report that the deer were infected with a moth that laid eggs in their nostrils. When the larvae grew, the deer sneezed blood and grew unhealthy. Modern Yamasee informants say this problem, which was a seasonal problem, still persists among deer in the region. The Yamasees refused to eat the deer and instead chose to subsist on wild turkey. Thus, the assumption that venison was a principal source of protein is dubious. Rumor has it that such venison was sold for consumption on the plantations! Contemporary informants say that the surviving Yamasees at Shellbluff Landing, Georgia, were originally "fish eaters" from the Atlantic Coast. The name of the groups were Tamathli, Tama, or Tolamato. (Tolamato was one of the lower Yamasee towns on the Altamaha River in coastal Georgia at the outbreak of the Yamasee War. Stewart R. Shaffer, a contemporary Yamasee, stated that the group moved inland and northward to the junction of the Oconee and Ocmulgee rivers after the Yamasee War. There deer were plentiful, but many of them harbored worms, so they were not eaten. Shaffer asserts that the Yamasees, beset by the problem of wormy deer, switched their protein preferences gradually to wild turkey, which ensured their survival in the pine barrens regions.[48]

In conclusion it can be stated that ecological assumptions cannot be separated from human behavior. Coastal Georgia has a rich marsh-lagoon area that supported about two thousand Gaules at the time of European contact. Precontact Yamasee subsistence centered on aquatic animal life and agriculture with some limited dependence on deer, opossums, and other land mammals. Beyond the marsh-lagoon area lay the pine barrens. Archaeological, ethnohistorical, ecological, and ethnological data indicate it was supportive of the longleaf pine and very little animal life except wild turkeys that foraged for grubs in the pine straw. Only a narrow strip of land suitable for livelihood existed along the banks of rivers in the pine barrens. Therefore, arguments that Yamasees occupied the pine barrens are misguided.

The Yamasees were a socially adaptable people. They practiced effective fertility management with families averaging two or three children, and were adept at resisting Spanish and English oppression. When the English deerskin trade became important, the Yamasees became involved quickly.

Long associations with the Spanish had made them aware of the complexities of commercial trade. Some Yamasees even moved to South Carolina to be closer to the trade, partially depopulating Guale (coastal Georgia). From 1685 to 1715, these upper towns in South Carolina became more dependent on the English. The role of adult men changed from subsistence hunter to commercial hunter. Yamasee women probably redirected a portion of their activities away from gathering to finishing deerskins for trade. Agriculture remained a stable pursuit for women because it was done in the warm months when hunting was not as important.

As the years passed, slave raiding, debts, and encroachment of white plantations forced the Yamasees in the upper towns in South Carolina to revolt. Rebellion was a time-honored Yamasee method of dealing with Spanish and English oppressors. Moreover, they knew that the sparsely populated area of Guale (coastal Georgia) as far south as St. Augustine was available for retreat. Hence, changes in Yamasee settlement due to war in South Carolina did not affect coastal Georgia.[49]

Thoroughly disgusted with English trade behavior, most Yamasees withdrew from the English sphere of economic influence after the Yamasee War, as they had earlier withdrawn from the Spanish. Some Yamasees retained a Spanish alliance however, while others chose neutrality. Yamasee power persisted in coastal Georgia as indicated by the fact that even after the English defeated them in 1715, the victors were unable to begin settlement of coastal Georgia until 1733. Even after the founding of Georgia, the first generation of colonial Georgians maintained a nonexpansionist, utopian-like colony for several decades. Meanwhile, the Yamasees pursued a conscious policy of peaceful coexistence. A few years after the founding of Georgia, the Yamacraws withdrew nonviolently from their settlement outside of Savannah. Perhaps those groups that had continuous contact with the English preferred to withdraw rather than go through the cycle of trade, exploitation, and violence that occurred earlier in the coastal Southeast.

In summary, ecological, historical, and archaeological evidence indicates that Yamasees inhabited the marsh-lagoon section of the Georgia coast as well as the floodplains of adjacent rivers. The basic ecological system remained unchanged until the founding of Georgia in 1733. After 1733, permanent white settlement led to a depletion of deer herds of the marshes and the riverine floodplain. Yamasees in South Carolina may also have experienced a decline in deer herds, but they were not the largest segment of the tribal population. Unscrupulous traders and fear of enslavement for debts caused the Yamasee War. Aboriginal depopulation of the coastal region occurred through immigration inland, immigration to Spanish Florida, and slave raiding of Yamasee settlements after the Yamasee War. Finally, generalizations about Yamasees should be tempered with the realization that they were essentially a group of Gualean Indians who left Florida missions to trade with the English in 1685. Therefore, attempts to locate the Yamasee people in the pine barrens of Georgia before 1733 are incorrect in light of the current ecological, ethnographic, historical, and archaeological evidence. Their relocation in the early eighteenth century to the pine barrens and subsequent heavy dependence on wild turkeys is an ecological adaptation to the process of European conquest in the Southeast.

Notes

1. See Michel Foucault, "Truth and Power," in *The Foucault Reader* (New York: Pantheon Books, 1984), 73.

2. Mary P. Andrews, Margaret M. Bubloz, and Beatrice Paolucci, "An Ecological Approach to the Family," *Marriage and Family Review*, 3, no. 3 (Summer 1980).

3. Ibid.

4. Uniformly, contemporary ethnohistorians ignore the existing Yamasee community in Shellbluff Landing, Georgia, ten miles south of Augusta, Georgia. For studies of modern Yamasees, see James H. Howard, "The Yamasee: A Supposedly Extinct Southeastern Tribe Rediscovered," *American Anthropologist* 62, no. 4 (August 1960): 681-83; and James H. Howard, "Altamaha Cherokee Folklore and Customs," *Journal of American Folklore* 72, no. 284 (Spring 1959): 134-38. In 1948, William H. Gilbert referred to the existing Yamasee

band in *Surviving Indian Groups of the Eastern United States*, Smithsonian Institute Annual Report (Washington, D.C.: Smithsonian Institution, 1948), 422. Instead of dealing with the corpus of ethnology and folklore on the Yamasees, most ethnohistorians depend uncritically upon John R. Swanton, *The Indian Tribes of North America*, Bureau of American Ethnology Bulletin No. 145 (Washington, D.C., Government Printing Office, 1952). On page 113, Swanton classifies the Tamathli as a Creek group. The ignoring of the Yamasees continues in *Southeastern Indians Since the Removal Era*, ed. Walter Williams (Athens: University of Georgia Press, 1979). Swanton's earlier work omits references to Yamasees also. See John R. Swanton, *Early History of the Creek Indians and Their Neighbors*, Bureau of American Ethnology Bulletin No. 73 (Washington, D.C.: Government Printing Office, 1922).

5. See Charles Hudson, *The Southeastern Indians* (Knoxville: University of Tennessee Press, 1976), Chapter 4; and Joseph R. Caldwell, Catherine McCann, and Frederick S. Hulse, *Irene Mound Site, Chatham County, Georgia* (Athens: University of Georgia Press, 1941), 60–73.

6. See Luis Geronimo de Ore, *The Martyrs of Florida* [1612], trans. Maynard Geiger, Franciscan Studies No. 18 (New York: Joseph F. Wagner, 1936), 40–44; and Peter Martyr D'Anghera, *De Orbe Novo* [1587], vol. 2 (New York: G. P. Putnam & Sons, 1912), 259–60.

7. Geronimo de Ore, *Martyrs*; and Hudson, *Southeastern Indians*, Chapter 4.

8. Martyr D'Anghere, *De Orbe Novo*, 258; and Caldwell et al., *Irene Mound*, 68.

9. Martyr D'Anghera, *De Orbe Novo*; and Jeanette T. Conner, ed., *Colonial Records of Spanish Florida, 1570–1577*, vol. 2 (Deland: The Florida State Historical Society, 1925), 239.

10. David I. Bushnell, Jr., *Native Villages and Village Sites East of the Mississippi*, Bureau of American Ethnology Bulletin No. 69 (Washington, D.C.: Government Printing Office, 1919), 84–87.

11. Caldwell et al., *Irene Mound*, 25–33; and Martyr D'Anghera, *De Orbe Novo*, 261–65.

12. For extensive archaeological data on the lifestyle of coastal Indians, see: Regina Flannery, "Some Notes on a Few Sites in Beaufort County, South Carolina," Bureau of American Ethnology Bulletin No. 133 (Washington, D.C.: Government Printing Office, 1943), 150; James B. Griffin, "An Analysis and Interpretation of the Ceramic Remains from Two Sites Near Beaufort, South Carolina," Bureau of American Ethnology Bulletin No. 133 (Washington, D.C.: Government Printing Office, 1943), 159; James B. Griffin, ed., *Archaeology of the Eastern United States* (Chicago: University of Chicago Press, 1952). For source of direct quotation and insights into fertility, see Robert Ferguson, *The*

Present State of Carolina with Advice to the Settlers (London: John Bringhurst, 1682), 14-15 in South Carolina Historical Society (hereafter SCHS); and Gene Waddell, *Indians of the South Carolina Low Country, 1562-1757* (Columbia: University of South Carolina Press, 1980), 1.

13. George Miliken-Johnson, *A Short Description of the Province of South Carolina . . .* (London: John Hinton, 1763), in SCHS.

14. J. F. D. Smyth, *A Tour of the United States*, vol. 1 (London: G. Robinson, J. Robson, and J. Sewell, 1784), 187-90, located in SCHS.

15. Gonzalo Fernandez de Oviedo, *Historia General y Natural de las Indias*, vols. 117-121 of *Bibloteca de Autores Españoles* (Madrid: Graficas Orbe, 1959), 120; 327-28.

16. Victor E. Shelford, *The Ecology of North America* (Urbana: University of Illinois Press, 1963), 78-80. The tragic experience of Jonathan Dickenson during the winter of 1696 to 1697 is testimony to the inhospitable nature of the coastal strand. See Evangeline W. Andrews and Charles M. Andrews, eds., *Jonathan Dickensen's Journal of God's Protecting Providence* (New Haven, Conn.: Yale University Press, 1945). For an interesting analysis of an aboriginal community near the beach, see Charles H. Fairbanks, "Gulf Complex Subsistence Economy," *Southeastern Archaeological Conference Bulletin*, 3: 57-62; and Preston Holder, "Excavations on Saint Simon's Island" (Winter 1936-1937), *Proceedings of the Society of Georgia Archaeology* 1, no. 1 (Spring 1938): 8-9. Furthermore, the historical accounts of early contacts (Cabeza de Vaca, Hernando de Soto, Jonathan Dickenson, and Jean Ribault) place aboriginal habitation in the lagoons and/or freshwater deltas of freshwater streams on the south Atlantic Coast.

17. William T. Penford and M. E. O'Neil, "The Vegetation of Cat Island, Mississippi," *Ecology* 15, no. 1 (Spring 1934): 1-13; Shelford, *The Ecology of North America* 78-80; and Henry J. Oosting, "Ecological Processes and Vegetation of the Maritime Strand in the Southeastern United States," *Botanical Review* 20, no. 3 (Summer 1954): 226-62.

18. Shelford, *Ecology of North America*, 79-80.

19. Shelford, *Ecology of North America*, 64-82.

20. Shelford, *Ecology of North America*, 64-82; and Lewis H. Larson, *Aboriginal Subsistence Technology on the Southeastern Coastal Plain During the Late Prehistoric Period* (Gainesville: University of Florida Presses, 1982), 13-20.

21. Shelford, *Ecology of North America*, 64-82; and Lewis H. Larson, *Aboriginal Subsistence Technology on the Southeastern Coastal Plain During the Late Prehistoric Period*, 13-20.

22. Shelford, *Ecology of North America*, 64-82; Larson, *Subsistence Technology*, 13-20; Dixon Hollingsworth, *Indians of the Savannah River* (Sylvania, Ga.: Partridge Pond Press, 1976), 22-25.

23. Shelford, *Ecology of North America*, 64–82.

24. Larson, *Subsistence Technology*, 21.

25. Ibid., 22.

26. Colonial observations of the longleaf pine forest of the Southeast are available. See Francis Harper, ed., *The Travels of William Bartram, Naturalist's Edition* (New Haven, Conn.: Yale University Press, 1958), 19.

27. See William G. Wahlenberg, *Longleaf Pine* (Washington, D.C.: U.S. Department of Agriculture, 1946) for an extensive discussion of fire and the longleaf pine. Also see H. H. Chapman, "Is the Longleaf Type a Climax?" *Ecology* 4 (Winter 1932): 328–34.

28. See Francis Harper, annotator, "Diary of a Journey through the Carolinas, Georgia and Florida, from July 1, 1765, to April 10, 1766," in *Transactions of the American Philosophical Society*, n.s., 23, no. 1: 15.

29. Larson, *Subsistence Technology*, 51–56.

30. Edward G. Bourne, ed., *Narrative of the Career of Hernando de Soto*, vol. 1 (New York: Allerton Books, 1904), 65–66; and Helen Todd, *Tomochichi* (Covington, Kent: Cherokee Publishing Company, 1977), Chapter 1.

31. Howard, *Altamaha Cherokee Folklore*, 136.

32. Ibid., 136–37.

33. Ibid.

34. James Shaffer and James H. Howard, "Medicine and Medicine Headdresses of the Yamasee," *American Indian Tradition* 8, no. 3 (1962): 125–26.

35. Ibid., 126.

36. Connor, *Records of Spanish Florida*, vol. 2, 225–27; and John Tate Lanning, *The Spanish Missions of Georgia* (Chapel Hill: University of North Carolina Press, 1935), 104–5.

37. For a more detailed discussion of the revolt, see Lanning, *Spanish Missions*, and Hollingsworth, *Indians*.

38. M. Serrano y Sanz, ed., *Documentos Historicos de la Florida y la Luisiana, Siglos XVI al SVII* (Madrid: Libreria Generai de Victoriano Swarex, 1913), 166–67; and Conner, *Records of Spanish Florida*, vol. 2, 225–27.

39. M. Serrano y Sanz, *Documentos*, 132–67; Lewis Hanke, *The Spanish Struggle for Justice in the Conquest of America* (Philadelphia: University of Pennsylvania Press, 1949), 83, 91–92, 173.

40. M. Serrano y Sanz, *Documentos*, 132; Hollingsworth, *Indians*, 23–26.

41. See Richard L. Haan, "The Trade Does Not Flourish as Formerly: The Ecological Origins of the Yamasee War of 1715," *Ethnohistory* 28, no. 4 (Fall 1982) as a good example of such works.

Haan argues that depletion of the deer on the coastal plain and the
decline of Yamasee slave raiding led to indebtedness and war in 1715.
Haan downplays the work of Verner Crane, *The Southern Frontier* (Ann
Arbor: University of Michigan Press, 1929), Chapman Milling, *Red
Carolinians* (Chapel Hill: University of North Carolina Press, 1940),
and M. Eugene Sirmons, *Colonial South Carolina* (Chapel Hill:
University of North Carolina Press, 1966) that emphasize trader abuse
as the main cause of the Yamasee War.

42. W. L. McDowell, ed., *Journals of the Commissioners of the Indian
Trade, September 20–August 29, 1718,* in *Colonial Records of South
Carolina,* series 2 (Columbia, S.C.: South Carolina Archives, 1955).

43. Caleb Westbrook to Deputy Governor of Carolina, February
21, 1685, Great Britain Public Records Office, vol. 2, 8–9.

44. Governor Johnson to the Lords of Trade, January 19 to February 1720, Great Britain Public Records Office, 1964, vol. 31, 302.

45. Address to the Lord's Commissioner for Trade and Assembly's
answers to their Lordship's Queries," January 29, 1919, in Coe Papers,
SCHS.

46. McDowell, ed., *Journals* [1736–1739], vol. 1, 153–54.

47. In 1900, an informal census placed 250 Yamasees in the
Savannah River Valley. In 1763, 89 Christianized Yamasees, under the
protection of the Spanish had been removed to the Yucatán peninsula
in Mexico. See also Howard, "Yamasees," ed. Hugh T. Lefler, *John
Lawson: A New Voyage to Carolina, 1709* (Chapel Hill: University of
North Carolina Press, 1967), 15, which documents that a hunting party
killed "two deers, which were very poor and their Maws fill of large
grubs . . ." On page 34, Lawson laments that ". . . fat turkeys began to
be loathsome to us, altho' we never wanting of a good appetite, yet a
continuance of one diet, made us very weary . . ." This ethnohistorical
evidence of conditions in coastal Carolina gives credence to the observation of contemporary Yamasee informants. For a detailed discussion
of this phenomenon in the deer population, see Robert M. Blair, *White-
tailed Deer in the Southern Forest Habitat* (Washington, D.C.: U.S.
Department of Agriculture, 1969). For a discussion of Indian slavery,
see Donald A. Grinde, Jr., "Native American Slavery in the Southern
Colonies," *Indian Historian* 10, no. 2 (Spring 1975): 38–42. See also
Robert Gold, "Conflict in San Carlos: Indian Immigrants in Eighteenth
Century Spain," *Ethnohistory* 17, no. 1 (Winter 1970): 1–10. The ongo-
ing debate with regards to the total population of the Western Hem-
isphere changed in the 1970s. See Chapter 1 in this book; Henry F.
Dobyns, *Native American Historical Demography* (Bloomington: Indiana
University Press, 1976); Alfred Crosby, Jr., *The Columbian Exchange*
(Greenwich, Conn.: Greenwood Press, 1972); and William M. Denevan,
ed., *The Native Population of the Americas in 1492* (Madison: University

of Wisconsin Press, 1972). Most of these works point to an upward revision of native populations of the Americas to about 90 million in 1492. Much of the depopulation seems due to disease.

48. See Howard, "Headdresses of the Yamasee," 126.

49. The activities of the Yamacraws should be taken into account, including both the current remnant group at Shellbluff Landing, Georgia, and the group of Yamasees that returned to St. Augustine. After the South Carolinians attracted and used a tribe like the Westos or the Yamasees for commercial reasons, they were discarded for a new group of Indians farther away. George Chicken's journey to the Cherokees to ask for aid in the Yamasee War signaled the increasing importance of the deerskin trade with the Cherokees. See: George Chicken, *Journal of George Chicken* [1715-1716] in *Yearbook of the City of Charlestown* (Charleston, S.C.: City of Charleston, 1894).

Navajo sheep flock on an Arizona sheep range, circa 1890. Photograph by Ben Wittick. Courtesy Museum of New Mexico. Neg. No. 16474.

Chapter Four

Navajo Ecology and Government Policy: How Many Sheep Are Too Many—and Why?

Ecology, as an idea, is defined relative to culture, like all concepts created by humankind. Like other theoretical concepts, humankind's relationship to its environment is constructed according to a given culture's intellectual and environmental experiences. Often, a dominant culture tries to impose its constructs on others. This chapter describes the human and ecological results of a conflict in ecological perceptions between the U.S. government, specifically the Bureau of Indian Affairs, and the people of the Navajo Nation.

Euro-American culture has asserted its dominance in many ways in Native America, even in a relatively "new" area such as environmental history. European intellectual dominance has been swift. The rationale for this intellectual aggressiveness is usually found in three assertions:

1) *The belief that Europe has been, and remains, the world's leading intellectual (as well as military) culture, an historical fact that has been ruthlessly driven home by five centuries of conquest in the Americas. Non-Western cultures and ideas are accorded less importance because they are said to be "primitive" and deserving of eradication in the "best interests" of the people who practice their ways.*

2) *Contemporary power relations are said to give the "conqueror" the right to impose the "winning" or "successful" mode of ideas upon the "losing" or "unsuccessful" cultures. This attitude reflects a latent form of the century-old Social Darwinism which rationalized the*

conquest of much of the world by European colonial powers.

3) The concept that the dominant culture's percep-tions will be useful to all people in all cultures. This belief assumes that all people behave and perceive things in basically the same way. The ideas of the dominant culture are said to require only minor refocusing in order to cover the "new facts or contents" of any culture.[1]

Some cultures perceive reality fundamentally differently from others. For example, Euro-American culture pursues knowledge in the academy through abstraction. That is, reali-ty is perceived through perceptual filters of science or reli-gion. Speculative philosophy often has been honed on the conflict of scientifically and religiously defined realities that were dominant at any given point in time. A society in which "science" and "religion" do not clash (as in many Native American cultures) does not suit the assumptions of Euro-pean thought.

Such an approach to reality is clearly reflected in the departmentalization of European society, from "department" stores to the university system, where disciplines are pack-aged in "departments," "schools," and "colleges," and where subjects such as history, biology, and literature are taught as separate and discrete areas of inquiry. Society is thus per-ceived in fragmented fashion, as comprised of categories such as church, state, business, education, and (in recent years) ecology.

Traditional American Indian (including Navajo) ways of perceiving the world contrast with the abstract conceptualiza-tions of Western thought. For Navajos and most other tribal peoples, reality is based on *experience*, not abstraction. Knowledge is not "compartmentalized." All ways of looking at the world (such as those that European thought defines as "science" and "religion") are regarded as mutually and per-petually informative. Visions, production of goods, observa-tion, and ritual constantly concretize human existence and connect it with nature (reality). Basically, all things, experiences, and ideas simultaneously reinforce that reality. This view is the characteristic "sacred hoop," or "circle," which defines the experience and traditions of many Native American people.

To sum up, if we juxtapose the two cultures, we find that the patterning of Western culture is based on planning, manipulation, predictability, competition, and power, while the Navajo way is based on reciprocation, response to situation, and cooperation.[2]

Navajo Ecological Perceptions

The Navajo conception of nature and Euro-American viewpoints on ecology have little in common. While "ecology" has become a relatively new abstract slice of reality in the Western mind, to Native Americans (including the Navajos) ecology was, and remains, an integral part of living and knowing. Such differences have produced conflict and confusion between the Navajos and the U.S. government. The basic value orientations of Navajo ecology are holistic and participative, while the theoretical underpinnings of Euro-American ecology are empirical, abstract, and narrowly defined. These differences, in a broad sense, have created a tension between the two societies because the U.S. government's definition of ecology often has been forced upon the Navajos with little sensitivity.[3]

A full explanation of Navajo ecology in linear and rational terms is virtually impossible because the Navajo view of the environment emphasizes participation and reciprocation. For instance, a moviemaker and an anthropologist recently gave some young Navajos cameras and asked them to make movies. One girl made a movie on Navajo weaving, supposedly a "technical" subject. But the forty-five-minute movie had only a few pictures of rugs and weaving. Most of the film depicted people herding sheep, riding horseback, shearing, and digging roots for dyes, as well as shots of the desert landscape. The entire film was a statement of the important factors to the Navajos in making rugs, that is, various forms of human interaction with nature. Human interaction with nature was far more important to the Navajo filmmaker than the mere "technique" of weaving. For the Navajos, weaving is an extension of the reciprocations embodied in a worldview. Needless to say reciprocity and balance are important factors in Navajo rug and fabric design as well.[4]

Reciprocity is central to the production of many other Navajo items. For instance, deer killed for food may be shot, but in the traditional Navajo way, deer killed for clothing must not have a punctured hide and thus cannot be shot. To obtain such a hide, a Navajo gathers pollen in a pouch, maneuvers the deer into open country, and jogs along behind it until the deer is exhausted. The deer is then thrown to the ground as gently as possible and smothered by the hunter with a handful of pollen so that it will die breathing a sacred substance. A ritual of apology explains the reason for taking the deer's life. The animal is then skinned in a ritual manner; disposal of the carcass is also attended by ritual. The deer hide is then tanned and dyed using herbs and parts of the deer. Moccasins are made by sewing the deer hide uppers to cowhide soles. Often, the moccasins are buried in wet sand until the person for whom they are intended comes by and puts them on. The person then wears them until they are dry. This creates a footprint in the sole so that the moccasins belong unmistakably to the person wearing them. In fact, the word *shi ke'*, "my shoes," is also the word for "my foot" in Navajo. The deerskin becomes a part of the wearer. Thus, moccasins, like rugs, are more than material artifacts. They are symbolic of the sacred human interaction with plants, animals, and the earth that is so central to Navajo reality and thus ecology.[5]

United States Bias in Land-use Patterns

American contact with the Navajos began at the outbreak of the Mexican War. When General Stephen Watts Kearny arrived in New Mexico with his Army of the West in May of 1846, he encountered a situation in which the Pueblos were

Mae Chee Castillo, a Navajo, herds her sheep near her hogan on the Navajo Nation. Photograph by Marcia Keegan, © 1986.

surrounded by Navajos, Apaches, and Comanches. The Navajos and other tribes raided the Pueblos continuously and had also kept their Mexican rulers at bay. Tension between Mexicans and Navajos was constant. Thus, one of Kearny's first official acts in New Mexico was to pledge protection for the white inhabitants from Apaches and Navajos. Kearny noted that the Mexican government had failed to provide this protection, a fact the Mexican government did not deny. The Mexican settlers and Pueblo villagers offered no resistance, and so New Mexico quickly passed into American hands.

However, Kearny was not successful in pacifying the Navajos before he moved on to California. Consequently, he ordered Colonel Alexander W. Doniphan, who had been left in New Mexico with a regiment, to make war on the Navajos and exact reprisals. Kearny also urged the Mexican and Pueblo people of the Rio Abajo area to raid the Navajos. The Navajos found it difficult to understand why they should be criticized for making war upon the same people that the United States was fighting. Colonel Doniphan stated to the Navajos that it was an American custom to treat those who had surrendered as friends.[6]

From the start, American policy was unconsciously biased in favor of the sedentary Pueblos versus the more mobile Navajos. Of course, the policy was also biased in favor of the white rather than the red race. By late 1846, temporary treaties were made with the Navajos and other Athabascan-speaking tribes. However, American overconfidence, Mexican intrigue, and Indian persistence led to the Taos Revolt of January 1847, in which the U.S. territorial governor and other U.S. officials were killed. As a result, American possession of New Mexico remained insecure until the summer of 1849, when James S. Calhoun, New Mexico's first Indian agent, arrived. Calhoun worked closely with Lieutenant Colonel John MacCrae Washington, the military commander and governor of New Mexico.[7]

In the autumn of 1849, Washington and Calhoun tried to impress upon the Navajos the power of the U.S. government and military, the right of the United States to assume jurisdiction over the area, and the right to build military garrisons on Navajo lands, if necessary. The council broke up when Washington tried to take a Navajo horse which a Mexican volunteer claimed had been stolen. Subsequently, Washington signed a treaty with a few minor Navajo chiefs that recognized U.S. jurisdiction, promised peace, sought to return captives, and asserted the U.S. government's right to determine the boundaries of Navajo lands. However, the treaty was meaningless to the major portion of the Navajo tribe, and warfare continued.

Calhoun believed that only brute force and separation of Navajos, Apaches, Comanches, and Utes on controlled reservations could stop conflict between the Athabascan-speaking tribes and the sedentary whites and Pueblo Indians. Thus, differences in land use and the accompanying ecological perceptions were among the first problems between Navajos and the U.S. government.

It is not surprising that Calhoun's approach to the resolution of conflict would be ecological. Calhoun stated that Navajos and other Athabascan-speaking tribes in the area would be made more pastoral and agricultural once settled upon a reservation. To Calhoun, the alternative was extermination. Agent Calhoun felt that the Pueblo Indians should be U.S. citizens because of their land-use characteristics. He also believed that the Pueblos could be used effectively to quell Navajo raids. Thus, U.S. government Indian policy was being based on the land-use practices of various Indian groups in New Mexico. Specifically, the Pueblos were being favored because their land-use practices more closely resembled those of the Euro-American settlers.[8]

Sheepherding and "Pacification"

In 1851, Colonel Edward V. Sumner arrived in New Mexico as the new military commander. Calhoun was made territorial governor in 1850 when New Mexico became a territory by virtue of the Compromise of 1850. After some debate, Sumner withdrew his troops from the towns and established two forts (Fort Union and Fort Defiance) in 1851. Fort Union was built on the Santa Fe Trail near Moro, and Fort Defiance was built in the heart of Navajo country as the name connotes. Fort Defiance was an attempt to assert U.S. military authority in Navajo lands and confine the Navajos and the other tribes. Seeds and farm implements were brought to these and new forts built to pursue this policy. Thus, the remedy to Navajo-American conflict was to alter the Navajos' economy, land-use, and ecological perceptions.

This policy was pursued with varying success for about a decade until the Civil War broke out and chaos enveloped the New Mexico territory. It was not until after 1864, when Kit Carson helped to round up the Navajos and take them on the Long Walk to Fort Sumner, that government attempts to fundamentally alter Navajo land use became more effective.[9]

In 1868, the government stepped up its policy of encouraging sheepherding among the Navajos. The Navajos had agreed by treaty to settle peacefully on the 3.5 million acres surrounding Fort Defiance, Arizona. At the time, they probably numbered about 15,000 people. After the Navajos' return from incarceration at Fort Sumner, the government issued them 34,000 sheep and goats. The idea was to make the Navajos self-sufficient sheepherders and thus pacify them. The program was a success. The reservation land base was expanded from 3.5 to 11.5 million acres by the 1920s. And by 1933, the population of the Navajo Nation had expanded to about 50,000 people.[10]

Outward appearances seemed to indicate that the Navajos had strengthened their pastoral economy and coupled it with a sound agricultural subsistence economy. In short, they had altered their land use in order to "survive." Governmental encouragement of pastoral pursuits had been overemphasized, however, with destructive ecological effects, such as soil erosion caused by overgrazing. Reservation traders also encouraged Navajos to exchange fleeces and rugs for cash that they used to buy hardware, coffee, and other foodstuffs, further encouraging the economy based on sheepherding and its negative ecological consequences.

The Stock Reduction Program:
Government Policy versus Navajo Ecology

Between 1910 and 1933, various governmental surveys analyzed soil erosion over most of the Navajo Reservation in Arizona, Utah, and New Mexico. By 1933, at least 2 million acres of grazing land was denuded and eroding. Various calculations indicated that between 37.5 and 60 percent of the silt in Lake Meade above Boulder Dam had flowed from the Navajo Reservation. To non-Indian environmentalists, Navajo range capital and the water supply of neighboring whites appeared threatened. The interests of the Navajos and the government conflicted. Moreover, the perceptions of the problem and its solutions were different for both the Navajo and the U.S. government.[11] The government's policies would prevail almost unchallenged (except for opposition on the reservation) over Navajo perceptions. This governmental paternalism and arrogance of power produced a social and economic disaster for the Navajo people.

In 1933, Secretary of the Interior Harold Ickes established a Soil Conservation Service that was to cooperate with the Public Works Administration to use federal funds earmarked for erosion control on the Navajo Reservation. In 1934, the Soil Conservation Service called for the reduction of Navajo livestock to about 50 percent of the number carried in 1933. Additionally, the Navajo Tribal Council set aside 50,000 acres for soil conservation experimentation in 1934. Using Public Works Administration funds, the Bureau of Indian Affairs (BIA) began to purchase and slaughter livestock in 1934.

To offset the impact of stock reduction, the BIA started a number of Works Progress Administration and Civilian Conservation Corps projects on the reservation. These projects were to provide wages to Navajos impoverished by stock reduction. The programs generally focused on soil conservation (dams and reseeding) and construction of roads and buildings. For several years about $2 million was spent annually on soil projects. Many Navajo traders encouraged this wage system because they could sell goods for cash instead of credit.

In 1935, the BIA centralized its administration of the Navajos at Window Rock, Arizona, superceding six separate agencies. Subsequently, the Navajo Reservation was divided into eighteen land-management districts. From 1935 to 1937, the Soil Conservation Service with the Navajo Service conducted surveys of the entire Navajo Reservation which documented the economy, climate, soil, vegetation, hydrology, population, and livestock problems of the Navajos.[12]

By 1937, the Navajo Service required every livestock owner on the reservation to register the total number of livestock owned at the time of the summer sheep-dipping. This registration was the basis for the issuance of grazing permits in accordance with the estimates of the Soil Conservation Service. In 1937, the Navajo Tribal Council drafted a set of grazing regulations that theoretically met the needs of the Navajos. After the secretary of the interior reviewed these regulations, the council approved them in 1938. At the same time, the council passed a resolution favoring elimination of nonproductive stock.[13] In 1939, the Arizona courts upheld the right of the interior department to regulate Navajo rangeland. In 1939, the Navajo tribal council also approved a program to reduce the horse population, which met with opposition.[14]

Grassroots Navajo opposition to the stock reduction program was organized, widespread, and critical. The nature of the opposition indicated radical differences between governmental and traditional Navajo perceptions regarding the environment and, thus, land use. According to traditional Navajo beliefs, sheep, rain, and land are related directly under an interlocking set of natural laws. The anthropologist David Aberle described the Navajo view of range management clearly:

> *Supernaturals gave sheep to the Navajos for their livelihood. When Navajos increase their flocks, the supernaturals see that the Navajos care for their gifts and bring rain. But when they use them improvidently or give them away the supernaturals respond by failing to bring rain. Hence reduction brings drought and damages the range.*[15]

This attitude is reflected in Navajo statements about live-stock reduction. Ernest Nelson, a Navajo who lived through the period, stated:

> *The reason why there is no grass is because of little rain. Before stock reduction it rained all the time. . . . Then, when John Collier put a blockade on livestock, the rain ceased altogether.*[16]

Another Navajo, Curly Mustache, observed that:

> *During the period before stock reduction you could see the big size of sheep and horses, and during that time, the rainfalls were never shy.*[17]

Thus, governmental and Navajo perceptions of the environment were still based on totally different views of the world, even though the Navajos had embraced sheepherding so successfully that their human population had increased between three and fourfold in six decades.

By the 1940s, livestock reduction had reduced many Navajos to poverty and more dependence on government programs. The number of grazing stock had been reduced to one-half its 1933 level. Although World War II provided some jobs for young Navajo men, overpopulation due to livestock reduction helped to justify the Navajo Indian relocation program of the 1950s. This program tore families apart and created further hardships. Stock reduction had broken the economic self-sufficiency of many Navajos.[18]

The Navajo view of the environment persists despite attacks by government policy. The basic problem is that U.S. government policy with regard to the Navajo environment has been manipulative, overly theoretical, and geared to solving "specific problems" (overgrazing, and so forth). By manipulating the Navajo natural environment, the government has produced a great deal of cultural and economic strife among the Navajos that goes untabulated in the government's theoretical equations. However, it appears that the Navajos and their governmental leadership still strive for bal-

ance with nature and mediation with the creative force to
ensure a harmonious relationship with nature.

Notes

1. See Vine Deloria, Jr., *God Is Red* (New York: Dell Publishing
Company, 1973). See also: Walter H. Capps, ed., *Seeing with a Native
Eye* (New York: Harper Forum Books, 1976), 1-8; Calvin Martin,
Keepers of the Game (Berkeley: University of California Press, 1978),
8-13; quotation from Donald A. Grinde, Jr., "Navajo Ecology and
Government Policy," in Kendall E. Bailes, ed., *Environmental History*
(Lanham, Maryl.: University of Geneva, 1985), 264; Ward Churchill,
"White Studies or Isolation: An Alternative Model for Native American
Studies Programs," unpublished paper at UCLA American Indian
Studies Conference, May 1980.

2. Christopher Vecsey and Robert W. Venables, eds., *American
Indian Environments* (Syracuse, N.Y.: Syracuse University Press,
1980), 1-37.

3. See Benjamin Lee Whorf, "An American Indian Model of the
Universe," in *Language, Thought, and Reality: Selected Writings of
Benjamin Lee Whorf*, ed. John M. Carroll (Cambridge, Mass.: MIT Press,
1956). See also Wilbur P. Jacobs, "Indians as Ecologists . . .," in
American Indian Environments, eds. Christopher Vecsey and Robert W.
Venables, 1-37, 46-64; and Barre Toelken, "Seeing with a Native Eye:
How Many Sheep Will It Hold?" in *Seeing with a Native Eye*, ed. Walter
H. Capps; *Navajo History*, ed. Ethelou Yazzie (Chinle, Ariz.: Navajo
Community College, 1971); Churchill, "White Studies or . . ." UCLA
conference paper.

4. Toelken, "Seeing with a Native Eye" in *Seeing with a Native Eye*,
ed. Walter H. Capps.

5. Ibid.

6. Roy A. Billington, *The Far Western Frontier 1830-1860* (New
York: Harper and Row, 1956), 179-80.

7. Wilcomb Washburn, *The Indian in America* (New York: Harper
and Row, 1975), 181-82.

8. For a fuller treatment of this policy, see Robert Anthony Tren-
nert, "The Far Western Indian Frontier and the Beginnings of the
Reservation System, 1846-1851" (Ph.D. diss., University of California,
Santa Barbara, 1969).

9. Jerry Kammer. *The Second Long Walk* (Albuquerque: University of New Mexico Press, 1980), 20-22.

10. U.S. Congress, House, Executive Document 263, 49th Cong., 1st sess., 15.

11. Edward Spicer, ed., *Human Problems in Technological Change* (New York: Russell Sage Foundation, 1952), 185-207.

12. Graham D. Taylor, *The New Deal and American Indian Tribalism* (Lincoln: University of Nebraska Press, 1980), 126-29; and Spicer, ed., *Human Problems*, 185-207.

13. Ruth Roessel, ed., *Navajo Livestock Reduction* (Chinle, Ariz.: Navajo Community College, 1975), Appendix.

14. Spicer, ed., *Human Problems*, 185-207.

15. David Aberle, *The Peyote Religion among the Navaho* (Chicago: University of Chicago Press, 1966), 87.

16. Roessel, ed., *Livestock Reduction*, 159.

17. Ibid., 172.

18. Spicer, ed., *Human Problems*, 185-207; and Peter Iverson, "The Evolving Navajo Nation: Diné Continuity Within Change" (Ph.D. diss., University of Wisconsin, 1975).

Emma Yazzie, Navajo-elder, stands at the bottom of a coal-strip mine near her home in Four Corners area of the Navajo Nation, 1976. Photograph by Bruce E. Johansen.

Chapter Five

The Navajos and National Sacrifice

As Emma Yazzie approached her hogan from Shiprock, New Mexico, on Highway 550, the sky gradually changed color from the familiar pastel turquoise blue of the surrounding countryside to a murky, hazy brown. Herding sheep up a hill below her hogan, Emma might have called the muddy sky above her a Chicago sky—if she had ever been to Chicago. But she has never even been as far as Tucson or Phoenix, the cities whose industries have been largely responsible for the deathly smoke that cloaks her home and sheep.

Emma Yazzie was nearly seventy years of age in 1976. Ever since she was two years old, Yazzie had lived here, where during the early 1960s four smokestacks near her hogan began to billow the smoke signals of death. The four smoke stacks belong to the Four Corners Power Plant, the largest single source of electric power—and pollution—in the western United States. After it was built, other power plants began to appear nearby, to sate the cities' growing appetite for electricity. By contrast, throughout her entire life, Yazzie's consumption of electricity has been constant—at zero.

Chiseled by the wind, Yazzie's kind and weathered face exudes a rugged strength, the result of countless days spent herding sheep in the blazing sun of summer and during the blizzards of winter. A smile etches valleys into it when she talks of the past of clear skies, fat sheep, and goats which gave milk. However, Yazzie's face turns somber when she describes the power plant. Her melodic Navajo words for the plant can be translated as: "This is the biggest, baddest disease ever visited on mankind." For thousands of years Yazzie's forebears woke up to a turquoise sky. Now, she wakes up to a brown sky smelling of burning dirty clothes and old tires. Some days the smoke funnels up the hill, over the poisoned lake and the chemical-coated grass, and into her hogan. She becomes sleepy and ill. A few hundred yards from the back of her home, a giant coal mining dragline scatters the bones of her ancestors, drawing from the earth the coal which feeds the plant's turbines and generators. In plush boardrooms in distant cities Yazzie's home is called a "national sacrifice area."

However, Yazzie will not move; she says that she will die here and that her bones will be returned to the earth, to join those of her ancestors. She does not say these things in a dramatic tone, to impress visitors. Rather, it is just the way things are done—the way of the creation. "The mother earth is very sacred to the Navajos . . . we replace what we take . . . we are born of the earth, and we return to rest," says Yazzie slowly and methodically.[1]

The draglines will not let the dead rest. Yazzie does not understand why people in the cities must use twice as much electricity as they did a generation ago. She has been to Shiprock, twenty miles to the southwest, and seen the artificial light, but she does not see much point to it. She is wise and dignified, and the Navajos listen to her. The power plant speaks a language of whistles and groans and mechanical voices, and it does not hear the wisdom of the earth nor the ages.

Yazzie speaks with her hands as she holds an imaginary lamb. "My sheep are dying. Their noses bleed. The baby goats do not grow up." She runs her left hand over the dusty earth, a foot above the surface, saying, "That's as big as they get now." Then Yazzie holds her hands an inch apart. "The wool is this thick now. It comes off in dirty brown balls. Before this disease—this thick." She holds her hands four inches apart. "And . . . I lose half the lambs. The ones which grow up are too skinny to sell. And the goats give no milk."[2] Before the power plant came, her lambs were fat, her sheep's wool was thick, and her goats gave milk. She lived relatively well, selling the wool or weaving rugs from it for the trading posts, producing lamb and mutton, and selling goat's milk. Now the sheep's thin, brown wool barely covers their skin. Before the year which the men at the power plant call 1963, Yazzie supported herself, but afterwards she got $80 a month from the government. The "free enterprise" system of rip-and-run resource exploitation has made her a "welfare Indian." When the government money runs out, she asks friends and relatives for food; when they are hungry, so is she.

While the affluent bask in electrically heated swimming pools in Phoenix, Yazzie goes hungry; ironically some of the coal which provides the electricity to heat the pools comes from the coal strip mine behind her hogan. She offers to take visitors into the huge, serpentine mine. "If you go alone, they will turn you back," she says. "They are afraid of me." Driving into the mine, Yazzie points to spots of brilliant green among the brown scrub land. "These are the reclaimed areas," she says. "Aren't they beautiful? But they won't last. They are drowned in water and fertilizer. And this kind of grass is not even native here. It will not survive." It is public relations grass, kept for touring government officials and television crews. At the bottom of the mine, Yazzie stands, her face to the sun, and points toward the dragline grabbing mouthfuls of earth. The shovel could hold several buses and cars. "That," she says, "is what I am fighting."[3]

Yazzie is shown standing at the bottom of one of the largest coal strip mines in the Western Hemisphere. Once the miners staked a road across her pasture for the trucks which rumble out of the mine toward the plant, without asking her permission. She pulled up the stakes, carried them to the mine manager's office, threw them on his immaculate desk, and raged: "You power plant people are watching us starve! You are making money off the coal in Navajo land, and you don't care for anything else! The earth is dying!" Occasionally Yazzie joined younger Navajos to protest coal development during lease negotiations in the tribal capital of Window Rock, Arizona. She smiles as she describes the bewildered expression on the faces of the riot police who confronted her.

Yazzie fought "progress," as defined by power plant developers and miners, whereby resources are mined from the earth, bought, sold, and used up. Plans in the middle 1970s called for at least three more coal-fired power plants in the Four Corners area. In addition, the developers wanted to build six coal-consuming plants which would make synthetic natural gas in the Burham area, a few miles south of Yazzie's hogan. By 1990, that anticipated pace of development had not been maintained, but there was still plenty of coal dust and air pollution in the area. The coal-gasification plants are so dirty that no one can live within thirteen miles of them, and so risky and expensive that banks would not finance them without government guarantees. The developers wanted billions of dollars from the federal government to build the plants during the energy crisis years of the 1970s.

Conversation in Yazzie's hogan does not center on energy policy, however. Nor does it center on the technology of power production, on conservation, or on solar, wind, or geo-thermal power. Yazzie talks about what she knows and what she sees—the smoke signals of death, resistance, and survival; dying lambs and poisoned water, and the rape of the sacred earth. The flicks of millions of urban light switches sing Yazzie's death song.

Mining the "Mother Mountain"

Across a mountain range from Yazzie's hogan the giant coal shovels dig into another strip mine on Black Mesa, the Mother Mountain of the Navajo spirit. If the harmony of the Mother Mountain is destroyed, it is said, the Navajos, who call themselves the *Diné*, will die: survival of a people is tied to survival of the land. Yazzie, by refusing to move from her land, stands with the traditionals, whose Mother Mountain is Black Mesa. For energy developers, however, Black Mesa has become a tabernacle to another religion: that of power, progress, and profit.

The coal which gives Black Mesa its dark color has the consistency of hard, dry dirt. Until technology was developed to crush the coal and combine it with water, forming a dirty sludge which could be transported away in pipelines, the coal companies saw little value in it. As this technology was being developed, coal strip mining was becoming cheaper for the companies than underground mining in the East. Machines were developed which didn't complain about wages or work-

Part of the Peabody Coal strip mining operation on Black Mesa on the Navajo Nation, 1970. In addition to making the land unusable, it pollutes aquifers, poisoning the Navajos' water. Strip mining operations on a massive scale have often been carried out within a few hundred yards of Navajo homes. Photograph by Marcia Keegan, © 1970.

ing conditions, machines which never demanded pensions, went on strike, or got black lung disease. The western coal rush had begun; the companies were enticed westward not by the exhaustion of coal in the East but by the profit potential of open-pit mines in the West. The huge draglines float above the tabletop of the mesa, giraffelike, their necks reaching three hundred feet into the air; their wheels propelling gigantic digging machines. The signs around the mine give the name of the company, Peabody. The coal becomes coal slurry, which, transported to giant smokestack-crowned monoliths in the desert, becomes electricity, which is carried in high-voltage transmission lines across the Navajo Reservation to Los Angeles, Phoenix, Tucson, and many other places outside the land of the *Diné*. The spidery, steel superstructures carrying the high-voltage lines stand in rank order, their cargo of kilowatts buzzing over Navajo homes, most of which have no electricity.

Across the countless ridges of mountains, across the plateaus and the deserts, in California the doctors of consumption have been at work developing new ways for people to use the power which comes out of the breast of the Mother Mountain. For example, the taste and waste makers have been test-marketing an electric toilet seat. Rusco American Bidet Corporation advertises that for a mere $175 to $195 its electric bidet will substitute for toilet paper a jet of electrically heated water and further claims that the bidet is "environmental," because it saves trees that would otherwise be used for toilet paper.[4] Of course, the inventors of such products do not seem concerned about where the electricity to run them comes from and the consequences of obtaining it. Those who are made to sacrifice so that such energy can be produced are seldom able to make use of such products. A majority of Navajo homes are automatically out of the market for the electric toilet seat because they have no running water. Most Navajo homes could also not make use of another California dream, the Mobot. The ultimate lawn mowing convenience sold for $700 in 1976, or slightly less than what the average Navajo earned that year.[5] Of course, most Navajos do not have lawns as Californians know them anyway, and the

Navajos have been using automatic lawn mowers for centuries—they call them sheep.

In order to justify more production, the developers told the Navajos that there was an energy crisis—in the United States that per capita consumption of electricity had doubled between 1963 and 1975. Many of the energy developers complained that the grassroots Navajos just did not understand the energy crisis, but in about half the homes of the Navajo Nation, energy consumption remained constant: twice zero is zero.

To many Navajos, digging coal is sacrilegious and a form of energy colonialism. To them, the coal rush is only a transmutation of the gold rushes and land rushes which drove many Indians off their lands. It is an old story: the developers want the resources, and the Indians are in the way. The lure of profits demands growth, what Edward Abbey called "the ideology of the cancer cell."[6] That ideology puts the doctors of consumption to work, seeking more and more ways for the Alices in this technological Wonderland to consume electric power. The Navajos—their land, their heritage, their lives—are being consumed. The National Academy of Sciences ruefully calls their lands "national sacrifice areas."[7]

Everywhere the missionaries of power development go they promise to be "good neighbors," but the character of strip mining and power plants makes that promise impossible. Power development is as good a neighbor as an agitated skunk in close quarters, but with a difference: the damage it does is permanent. The National Academy of Sciences reports that no land has ever been successfully reclaimed after being strip-mined in the arid West; true reclamation takes centuries.[8] The conditions that Emma Yazzie lives with today are being prescribed as the future for many Navajos—all in the "national interest."

The "national interest" has paralleled the financial interests of some powerful Navajos, a select class which has been inculcated with a reverence for the yellow metal which drives white men crazy. Peter MacDonald, Navajo tribal chairman during much of the 1970s and 1980s, promoted resource development. The rents and royalties paid by the coal mining

Peabody Coal Mine operation on Black Mesa on the Navajo Reservation.
Photographs © 1970 Marcia Keegan.

companies flowed directly to his tribal government. He was a businessman. The grassroots Navajos through whose hogans the dirty smoke flows, called him "MacDollar." He lived in a luxurious ranch house, drove a Lincoln Continental, and drew a $30,000 annual salary as chairman of the Navajo Nation, where the average per capita income was about $900 in the late 1970s. In June 1976, tribal chairman MacDonald also assumed the presidency and controlling interest in Denay Insurance, a Window Rock-based company.

The Navajo tribal government is made up of a central administration (in Window Rock) and a tribal council, composed of members from 102 "chapters," or local governments. In the late 1970s, the tribal government system, which replaced traditional governance for the Navajos (and many other Indian nations) unfortunately attracted a group of Navajos with a taste for the kind of green that sheep do not eat. Art Arviso, assistant to MacDonald, was convicted of embezzlement; David Jackson, manager of the Navajo tribal fair, also was convicted of embezzlement. The list goes on: Larry Wilson, assistant manager of the fair, convicted of embezzlement; Stanley K. Smith, manager of Piñon Credit Union, convicted of embezzlement; Ernie Shorey, license examiner for the state of Arizona, convicted of embezzlement; Pat Chee Miller, director, Navajo Housing Authority, convicted of conspiracy to defraud; Mervin Schaffer, vice president, Jusco Construction Company, convicted of fraud; Regina Henderson, Navajo welfare worker, convicted of embezzlement; Doris McLancer, tribal court clerk, convicted of embezzlement; Laurita Williams, Navajo Election Board clerk, convicted of embezzlement; Ross Roll, tribal employee, convicted of embezzlement.[9]

Although MacDonald was relatively popular when he was first elected to head the tribal government, soon afterward he joined the ranks of the native elite in a very decisive way; he lived rather lavishly and promoted energy development—provided the price was right. Opposition to his policies began to grow, especially among the grassroots Navajos and on the northeastern quarter of the reservation, where much of the proposed energy development was to take place.

The Navajo Liberation Front

The Coalition for Navajo Liberation was born in 1974 and became most active in and near Shiprock. Navajo traditionalists from that area led a demonstration of about six hundred people on May 18, 1976, in Window Rock, the tribal capital. The marchers demanded MacDonald's resignation, and eighteen people were arrested. On August 25, 1976, traditionalists assembled again in Window Rock during a tribal council meeting where a coal strip-mine lease with El Paso Natural Gas and Consolidation Coal, a subsidiary of Continental Oil, was being negotiated. The majority of the demonstrators were from the Shiprock-Burnham area of the reservation, where most of the energy development was planned. Many of them stood to lose at least their land, probably their livelihoods, and perhaps their lives. At the Burnham chapter house residents voted 228 to 0 against coal gasification in 1976; in the same year the Shiprock Chapter rejected gasification proposals 129 to 0. The power to negotiate leases and mining plans, however, resided with the central tribal council and MacDonald, and thus the Shiprock Chapter voted 255 to 6 to demand MacDonald's resignation.

Opposition to gasification and the coal mining that it requires was so strong in the Burnham area that one tribal council member from the chapter offered to resign under pressure from area residents after he had supported a El Paso Natural Gas lease proposal during a debate held in August 1976. The closer to the grassroots level an energy development proposal came, the more strongly it was opposed. The tribal council itself has tended to support strip-mining leases while opposing the gasification and power plants which are inevitably proposed to consume the coal. In a letter to Congress written in 1976, 41 of the tribal council's 76 members opposed federal loan guarantees for gasification plant construction. The same council, however, approved the El Paso coal lease by 49 to 11 during August of the same year. MacDonald bragged that the El Paso coal lease was the best of its kind ever negotiated by an Indian nation or tribe. It was the best in terms of monetary value; the 55¢ a ton that was promised the Navajos was almost three times as much as the Crows and Northern Cheyennes had been offered on leases which later were suspended.

However, to traditional Navajos, especially those near Shiprock and Burnham, a lease was still a lease, even though the terms were good. To them, such leasing was a repeat of history, a trade of land and resources for money, an exchange which has almost always ended in Indian losses. Their opposition to the coal and uranium leases, as well as to the construction of electricity and gasification plants, was more than spiritual; it was a matter of economics, and ultimately a matter of life or death. Energy development would destroy the land and life that the Navajos had sustained for hundreds of years.

The Department of the Interior, which must approve all plans for energy development on Indian lands after tribal councils negotiate contracts, held hearings on the El Paso coal lease in March 1977. Cecilia Bitsui, a resident of the Burnham Chapter reflected the beliefs of many of her neighbors when she said the following:

> Do we have to wait until the whole land is destroyed before the tribal council says "enough"? The people in Window Rock are only concerned with money. But no cash payment will replace what my family will lose. My children will not be able to herd sheep in Burnham and learn the ways of the Navajo as I did.[10]

The resistance to energy development runs long and deep. Fred Johnson, one of the founding members and early leaders of the Coalition for Navajo Liberation, told the U.S. Civil Rights Commission in 1974:

> Our clean waters are clouded with silt and the wastes of the white man; Mother Earth is being ravaged and squandered. To the Navajo people it seems as if these Europeans hate everything in nature—the grass, the birds, the beasts, the water, the soil, and the air. We refuse to abandon our beautiful land. To Navajos, land

was something no one could possess, any more than he could possess the air. Land is sacred to the Navajos; it is part of the Almighty's design for life . . . "Mother Earth," because it is the mother of all living. To the whites, this is paganism as well as communistic, and it has to be eradicated. All the laws and federal regulations in existence cannot justify the criminal acts of tribal officials who knowingly deceive those who have placed their trust in them. . . . To protest is to speak out against, to let it be known that you don't like a certain action . . . To protest is an act of intellectual commitment. To protest is to hate the inhumanity of another. To resist, we believe, is to stop inhumanity and affirm our own humanity. . . . The Coalition for Navajo Liberation intends to stop the land robberies known as the gasification plants, the T.G.&E. power line, the Black Mesa destruction of land, the Four Corners power plants and the Exxon uranium deal.[11]

Johnson, who was killed in the mysterious crash of a small airplane in early 1976, spoke forcefully about the dangers of strip mining and power generation, which could turn large areas of Navajo land into wastelands unreclaimable for perhaps hundreds of years. True reclamation involves more than simply filling in the mines and planting grass to cover the scars; it involves restoring the entire ecological community of plants and animals. A National Academy of Sciences (NAS) report states bluntly that this cannot be done in areas with less than ten inches of rainfall a year; the rainfall over most of the Navajo Reservation ranges from six to ten inches a year. The NAS suggests that such areas be spared development or honestly labeled "national sacrifice areas."[12]

Is "Reclamation" a Sham?

The amount of money a coal mining company spends on reclamation is not the crucial factor, asserts the National Academy of Sciences report. Nor are state or federal reclamation laws.[13] Reclamation is simply not possible until nature heals its wounds over several centuries.

Strip mining does more than scar the land. It also disrupts underground water flow and poisons the water itself. Coal seams in the arid West also act as aquifers—they carry water just as some metals conduct electricity. Underground water is a vital consideration in sparsely populated dry areas of the Navajo Reservation where a majority of Navajos rely on well water. Much of the soil in the Southwest (as well as on the northern plains) is high in alkaline salts. Usually the salts are leached out of the surface layers of soil and are concentrated below the topsoil. However, strip mining mixes the soil, resulting in high salt levels at the surface—which kill many plants. The process escalates as rain or irrigation water at the surface carries the freed salts into the aquifers, which feed wells and rivers. Every living thing then suffers from salty water. Strip mining also loosens surface soil, which is carried by rainfall and irrigation as silt and mud into rivers and wells.

No amount of corporate goodwill, no amount of money and effort, and no combination of reclamation laws will resolve the fundamental incompatibility of coal strip mining and nature in the arid Southwest.

Generation of electricity or natural gas from the coal only compounds the problems, which amount to a sentence of death for the land and a way of life. Fly ash, produced by burning coal, pollutes the air and water. Even if much of the fly ash is removed from power plant stacks before reaching the air, it is usually dumped in nearby landfills, where rainfall leaches chemicals into the groundwater.[14] Already the clouds of pollution sometimes obscure the turquoise sky around majestic Shiprock, which gives the Navajo town its name; more power plants will merely make the pollution denser. Between one hundred and two hundred pounds of fly ash can be released by the burning of a single ton of coal.[15] The burning of coal also releases sulfur dioxide, which is poisonous to people, plants, and animals. The sulfur dioxide reacts with water vapor in the atmosphere to form sulfuric acid, which returns to the earth as highly acidic rainfall. In addition, coal burning releases nitrogen oxide, which combines with ozone and carbon in the air to produce smog. The pollution potential of coal gasification exceeds that of burning coal. According to research done by the National Indian Youth Council (NIYC):

> *There will be at least two toxic air pollutants (lead and mercury) emitted from those [gasification] plants in such uncontrolled quantities that [they] may inflict permanent damage to all animal, plant and human life in the immediate vicinity of the plants. Expert testimony from a National Aeronautics and Space Administration physicist at recent environmental hearings revealed that all persons living within a 13-mile radius of the plants will have to be evacuated due to the dangerously high levels of lead and mercury around these plants. In fact, it is predicted that all workers in and around the plants will have to wear protective face masks for health and safety reasons. Another toxic emission (boron) is greatly feared by the planners of the Navajo Nation Irrigation Project because it could easily wipe out all of the crops grown there.*[16]

The dangers to people, plants, and animals, as well as to the earth itself do not end with the generation of electricity. The transmission lines which ride atop the spidery steel towers across the mountains to consumers carry so much electricity that they create a force field beneath them. Extra-high-voltage (EHV) transmission lines of the size planned for the Indian coal lands have given several people in Ohio severe shocks. One woman was knocked from her horse by such a force field; and a man working in his yard was knocked unconscious. The power company which owns the line advised the man to wear chains around his ankles to ground the current. Twelve of eighteen persons living near the Ohio EHV lines also have reported strong electrical shocks.[17] In addition, the transmission lines may create their own smog; electricity seeping from the lines combines with elements in the atmosphere to form ozone.[18]

Squandering Water in an Arid Land

Energy development also requires massive amounts of water from the arid lands of the Navajos. The use of water begins with the mining of the flaky coal of Black Mesa to form the coal slurry which is transported through pipelines. Water consumption continues with power generation, especially in coal gasification. One coal gasification plant requires about 10,000 acre-feet of water a year.[19] About 28 cubic feet of water per second, or 20,270 acre-feet a year, are required to cool the generating equipment of a 1,000 megawatt, coal-fired electricity plant. All of the water used in gasification is hydrolyzed into hydrogen and oxygen and lost to the arid Southwest. Some of the water used in electricity generation also evaporates; the remainder is returned to its source 10 to 15 degrees Fahrenheit warmer than it was before entering the plant.

To add insult to injury, the water demands and pollution generated by energy development pose a dual threat to an irrigation project which was included in the Navajo treaty of 1868. The first stages of the 110,000-acre project, near Burnham, began operating in 1976. If completed, the irrigation project could provide employment in the fields or in food-processing and marketing industries for 30,000 Navajos. However, the pollution and water demands of strip mining and of the gasification and coal-fired electricity plants may kill or severely damage the crops. The irrigation project has long been a dream of the traditional Navajos; its survival was a major reason why energy development was so bitterly opposed. The water required for the irrigation system, as well as for energy development, comes from the shallow, muddy brown San Juan River, which flows through Shiprock. The two projects are not environmentally compatible, and there is simply not enough water for both.[20] The Navajo Indian Irrigation Project could provide the beginning of a totally Indian-owned and controlled economic base. Instead of always having to sacrifice their land and resources, Navajo people could develop and utilize their own land and resources in ways that would not destroy their homeland.

Another factor in the water demand equation is the roughly 50,000 people who were imported to build and operate the complex of strip mines and power plants in and near the Navajo Reservation. Many brought with them habits of squandering water that they acquired in less arid climates. In the middle 1970s, Gerald Wilkinson, director of the National Indian Youth Council, said that those Navajos worried about the harm of uncontrolled strip mining are not totally against resource use. They want development to take place in a manner which does not disrupt the earth, human life, traditions, or the irrigation project. Wilkinson suggested that coal should be mined underground, using room-and-pillar techniques, if it is mined at all, and that the coal, once mined, ought to be transported away from the Navajo Reservation for power generation. The Navajo Nation should also be a joint partner in any energy project, Wilkinson suggested. Only in this way could Navajo coal be mined without the penalties of energy colonization or the devastation implied by the designation "national sacrifice area."

The developers did not agree to such terms because they did not migrate to the Southwest (and to the West in general) merely to mine coal. They came to strip-mine coal. If the coal companies wanted to mine coal underground, there was plenty of it in the East and the Midwest, much of it in abandoned underground mines. At present rates of consumption, enough coal remains in mines already opened to last the United States seventy-five years. Converging trends in labor relations and technology, not scarcity of coal, have propelled the coal companies westward. A corporate policy based on bottom-line profit, instead of ecological and human needs or scarcity of coal, has brought coal miners to the West, where a million tons of coal a year can be mined with newly developed draglines using only twenty-five mine workers. A large force of underground miners paid at prevailing union rates would be much more expensive.

Nor have the miners of coal come to the West for the low-sulfur coal only because it will reduce pollution. While it is true that western coal is generally lower in sulfur content than eastern coal, it is also lower in heat value. More of it must be burned to produce the same amount of heat than eastern coal.[21] In addition, western coal acts as an aquifer, and so when removed from the ground it holds much more water than eastern coal. The water must be removed from the coal; the remaining product is lighter and, therefore, even higher in sulfur content. Consequently, by the time it is burned, western coal contains no less sulfur per pound than eastern coal.

In the long run, the energy the coal companies might provide by strip-mining the Navajo Reservation and much of the rest of the West may not even be necessary. It is probable that if people were not manipulated through advertising to use more energy, and conservation was promoted aggressively, per capita energy consumption from coal might stabilize or decline. Future coal needs could then be met from already opened mines or from careful underground mining in the East.

As for natural gas, several experiments are under way which may furnish substantial amounts of ersatz gas generated from methane, a clean-burning gas produced by the decomposition of organic matter.[22] For example, at Bay St. Louis, Mississippi, the National Aeronautics and Space Administration has harvested water hyacinths for distillation into methane. The hyacinths are one of nature's fastest growing plants. They thrive on raw sewage and have until now been considered a problem because they clog waterways in the South. Similarly, off the southern California coast scientists from the Naval Undersea Center and the California Institute of Technology have experimented with ocean farms of giant California kelp to be harvested, dried, and converted into methane. Ocean farms measuring 470 miles on each side could have supplied all of the United States's 1976 demand for natural gas, according to Dr. Harold Wilcox, director of the project.[23] Both of these projects utilize a renewable resource to produce a clean-burning form of energy; they are ecological, in harmony a Navajo might say, with the "Right Way." Many other environmentally compatible energy resources could also be utilized, including solar power, wind power, and tidal power. There is no energy shortage; there is a shortage of will and imagination in dealing with an energy production system now wedded to fossil fuels.

Gasification: Corporate Welfare?

In 1976, a bill providing $6 billion in loan guarantees for synthetic fuels—80 percent of that for gasification—was narrowly defeated in Congress. "Because of the large capital investment requirements of the coal-gasification project, it will be difficult if not impossible for our industry to finance these plants by the conventional means of issuing stocks and bonds. Some form of financial federal guarantees will be required," an El Paso Natural Gas spokesman said two weeks after the 1976 version of the bill (House Resolution 12112) was defeated by a vote of 193 to 192.[24] The bid for corporate welfare appeared again in 1977 as Senate bills 429 and 430.

New Mexico's political elite lined up behind the loan guarantees, believing that gasification would bring economic growth to the state. Bob Duke, the *Albuquerque Journal's* Washington correspondent, warned, "If Congress [does not approve], New Mexico's coal-gasification projects and Colorado's oil-shale development are virtually certain to be shelved permanently."[25] The NIYC celebrated after the 1976 bill was defeated—but not unreservedly. Its members knew the importance of the fight and that it would resume. John Redhouse said, "In every sense of the word, we are engaged in a life- and death- duel. We have no other choice but to carry on with this struggle so that someday our children, their children, and generations yet unborn will in their own time all walk in beauty."[26]

John Redhouse, associate director of NIYC, told the American Indian Policy Review Commission on February 9, 1976: "This [coal gasification] is only a small part of a larger governmental and corporate conspiracy to steal Indian land and resources. During the past hundred years, the methods may have changed, but the sordid cast of characters and ulterior motives remain the same."[27] The developers were coming to take land and resources and promising to be "good neighbors," telling the Indians they were doing them a favor. The ulterior motive was private aggrandizement. It was an old, old story for the Indians:

Where will we all be 20 or 25 years from now when the coal is all consumed and the companies operating these gasification plants have cleaned up all the resources and moved away? There will be nothing; they will be working elsewhere and we will be sitting on top of a bunch of ashes with nothing to live on.[28]

The story now had ramifications for far more people than the American Indians:

The margin has critically narrowed for both [American] Indians and world survival. The Indians are on the edge of and may eventually be drawn into the resource exploitation machine—the mining, production and consumption machine of modern society that transforms and exhausts the earth's resources in response to its own unseeing drives and compulsions. The managers of the machine must plan and guide it to provide the maximum wealth and power for its corporate components. The owners who provide the needed investment put their money where the highest and most secure rewards are offered. The workers have no role except to keep up production. Finally, the machine itself creates the consumption ethic—the pleasure of purchasing and the success motivation geared to material wealth—which, in turn, keeps it going.[29]

Two years after the Coalition for Navajo Liberation and the MacDonald administration faced off with riot police between them in Window Rock, there were some indications that the message of the traditional *Diné* was beginning to be heard more strongly inside the tribal council. As the House of Representatives and the Senate passed (after a half-decade of pressure) a multimillion-dollar loan-guarantee program for synthetic fuels, including coal gasification, the Navajo council was moving toward rejecting a WESCO plan for gasification plants near Burnham. James Abourezk, one of the few consistent defenders in the Senate of Indian treaty rights during this period, said that the loan guarantees were a government subsidy to multinational energy companies, which desired to extend their grip on fossil fuel resources as domestic oil and gas were depleted.[30] Navajo traditionalists called the loan guarantees only the latest form of Manifest Destiny.

Lobbyists for the fuel-development subsidies had their own historical perspective. "The federal government helped build the nuclear industry," said William Gribeaut, government research manager for the American Gas Association, a pipeline and distributors' trade group. "Now, the synthetic fuels industry needs the same kind of help." He compared the subsidies passed for synthetic fuels to the gifts of land made to the railroads a century ago.[31] While Gribeaut thought of this as a positive comparison, many native people were reminded of the role the railroads played in bringing about the destruction of a self-sufficient lifestyle which had existed for centuries.

On February 1, 1978, the Navajo Tribal Council rejected the WESCO proposal, which included four commercial gasification plants. The vote was 48 to 8. MacDonald said WESCO's proposal was not a good business deal; WESCO wanted the tribe to come up with $200 million to invest in the plant. "Gasification has not proved itself," MacDonald also said. However, WESCO indicated that it would try again. The *Navajo Times* commented, "Many WESCO officials feel, according to a WESCO spokesman, that the upcoming tribal elections may have been the reason the council turned down the proposal and that once the [tribal] elections are over the council will be more receptive to the idea."[32]

At about the same time, the National Indian Youth Council, allied with residents of the Shiprock-Burnham area, refused to agree with what MacDonald called the best Indian coal lease ever signed—the one passed in August 1976 which allowed the Navajo Nation 55¢ a ton or 8 percent of the market price of the coal. Interior Secretary Cecil Andrus told the Navajos that the minimum coal royalty rate, following amendments to the Federal Coal Leasing Act of 1975, was 12.5 percent, a good indication of where the "best Indian coal lease ever signed" stood outside the energy colony.

Like residents of many Third World countries, the Navajos gained more awareness of how their land was being exploited and began to take more concrete action. A tax on sulfur emissions was passed along with a business tax aimed at energy companies. The tax, which assesses the gross receipts of a business at 5 percent, exempted traditional livestock and farming enterprises.[33] The targets of the sulfur tax, the owners of two reservation power plants, filed suit during October 1977 in federal court seeking relief. The levy was officially called a "fee," since the contracts the BIA had persuaded the tribe to sign more than a decade ago with the two companies forbade the levying of taxes.[34]

During the same period, many grassroots Navajos who had been forced off their land and into employment in power plants or oil refineries went on strike. The strikes sparked occupations of some work places, as community residents often joined the workers. For example, a Texaco oil refinery in Aneth, Utah, on the northern edge of the reservation, was occupied by workers and their families during April 1978. The occupants demanded that Texaco agree to keep its white employees from bringing alcoholic beverages onto the reservation, dismiss employees found carrying side arms on the reservation, reclaim land damaged by oil drilling, compensate Navajo families who suffered losses due to oil drilling (including water wells which had been damaged), preserve Navajo burial sites, and give Navajo people preference in hiring at drilling sites.

To resist expropriation of Navajo resources under cover of a domestic energy crisis, the growing grassroots resistance in Navajo country expanded into a large popular movement during the 1970s; local residents who did not want their livelihood and traditional culture destroyed by uranium and coal mining, or by coal-fired power and gasification plant development, were coming together.

The situation which developed at Crownpoint, New Mexico, was typical of the situations the Navajos were forced to face in many other areas of the Navajo Reservation. When a U.S. Geological Survey report showed that the water table there would drop a thousand feet as a result of uranium mining, the local residents rose up in protest. The report further indicated that the water table would not return to its former levels for thirty to fifty years after the mines closed. On top of that, much of the water could be polluted by uranium residues. "If the water supply is depleted, then this will become a ghost town," said Joe Gmusca, a Navajo attorney. "The only people left here will be the ones who come to work in the mines."[35] The choice that the Navajos were being forced to face at Crownpoint was not a new one: accommodate to the requirements of the encroaching culture or starve.

At the end of the twentieth century, the shadow of death in a waterless future was facing the Hopis, as well as the Navajos. When they signed a coal lease that allowed Peabody Company to mine coal from their sacred Black Mesa in the late 1960s, Hopi leaders were told that a coal slurry pipeline wouldn't use much water, "like taking a cup, and dipping it into the sea," recalled Vernon Masayesva, Hopi Tribal Chairman in the early 1990s.[36] Instead, the coal slurry pipeline swallowed more than a billion gallons of water a year, so much that the Hopis' sacred springs, which have nourished them for at least a thousand years, began to dry up. In the arid Hopi homeland, underground water means life, culture, and survival. After a quarter century of mining, Peabody's spin doctors deny that the company is taking too much water, but for Masayesva and the Hopis, "If it's a choice between money and water, we'll take the water."[37] The Hopis may have to make that choice by the turn of the century; in the quarter century since the Peabody mine opened, its royalties have swelled to 80 percent of the Hopis' tribal budget, another not-so-subtle form of colonialism that began with the first Spanish incursions and has never ceased.

Notes

1. Interview, Bruce E. Johansen with Emma Yazzie, at her home, eastern Navajo Reservation, August 14, 1976.

2. Ibid.

3. Ibid.

4. *Seattle Post-Intelligencer*, August 29, 1976, B-6.

5. "Gasification," *Akwesasne Notes* (Autumn 1976): 10.

6. Edward Abbey, *The Journey Home* (New York: Dutton, 1977), 183.

7. Thadis Box et al., *Rehabilitation Potential of Western Coal Lands* (Cambridge, Mass.: Ballinger Publishing Co., 1974), 85.

8. Ibid., 2.

9. *Navajo Times*, March 31, 1977.

10. Copy of remarks in the archives of the National Indian Youth Council, Albuquerque, New Mexico.

11. Speech of Fred Johnson to the U. S. Civil Rights Commission, archives, National Indian Youth Council, Albuquerque, New Mexico.

12. Box et al., *Rehabilitation Potential*, 85.

13. Ibid., 2.

14. James Cannon, *Leased and Lost: A Study of Public and Indian Coal Leasing in the West* (New York: Council on Economic Priorities, 1974), 17. Cannon's conclusions were confirmed in a follow-up report released by the council in 1978.

15. Ibid.

16. National Indian Youth Council, *What Is Coal Gasification?* (Albuquerque, N.M.: NIYC, 1976), 4.

17. Cannon, *Leased and Lost*, 18.

18. Ibid.

19. Ibid., 16. An acre-foot is the amount of water which will cover one acre a foot deep, or 326,000 gallons.

20. National Indian Youth Council, *Coal Gassification*, 4.

21. Western coals provide an average of 6,100 to 9,500 British Thermal Units per pound, compared with an average of 13,000 for eastern coals.

22. *Capturing the Energy of the Sun*, proceedings from the National Conference on Bioconversion as an Energy Resource, March 11–33, 1976, 249.

23. *Energy of the Sun*, 255.

24. *Albuquerque Journal*, October 6, 1976.

25. Ibid.

26. National Indian Youth Council, *Annual Report* (Albuquerque, N.M.: NIYC, 1976), 2.

27. Mimeographed copy in archives of National Indian Youth Council, Albuquerque, New Mexico.

28. Lucy Keeswood, Coalition for Navajo Liberation, cited in U. S. Commission on Civil Rights, *The Farmington Report* (Washington, D.C: Government Printing Office, July 1975), 128.

29. "Mother Earth, Father Sky and Indian Survival," *The Nation*, March 29, 1975, 359.

30. "James Abourezk vs. COAC Gasification Loans," *New York Times*, October 9, 1977.

31. William Gribeaut, "American Gas Association Synthetic Fuels 'Need Help,'" *The Wall Street Journal*, January 24, 1978, 31.

32. *Navajo Times*, June 22, 1978.

33. *Navajo Times*, May 4, 1978, 21.

34. *Navajo Times*, September 1, 1977.

35. *Navajo Times*, June 15, 1978.

36. "Hopi Tribe Fears for Its Future," San Francisco *Chronicle* in Omaha *World-Herald*, December 18, 1993, 10.

37. Ibid.

Native fishermen haul in salmon during a 1966 "fish-in" on the Nisqually River in Olympia, Washington. Courtesy of UPI/Bettman.

Chapter Six

Fishing Rights: The Usual and Accustomed Places

When the Romans colonized Gaul about the time of the birth of Christ, they found a fish-eating people. Soon the demand for the pink-fleshed fish they named *salmo*, "the climber," rose in Roman markets. As a result, the waters were over-fished until in the ensuing centuries the salmon became extinct in many European rivers.[1]

The taste for salmon traveled with the European colonists to the New World. In 1654, Jesuit fathers Le Moyne and Le Mercier, riding the cutting edge of conquest on a diplomatic mission to the Onondagas for the French government, noticed that there were so many fish in Lake Ontario that they could be speared or clubbed with paddles. The last salmon to be caught in that body of water was taken during 1896.[2] Wherever a civilization became established which allowed predatory profit without regard for the needs of nature, the salmon died.

By the turn of the century, the descendants of the fishermen who had feasted on salmon in Europe before cattle and sheep were domesticated found the same fish in many streams of the Pacific Northwest.[3] In that area, it was said, one could walk across the backs of the salmon from one stream bank to another when the whites first set eyes on the area during the last century. Fifty thousand Indians took 18 million pounds of salmon a year from the Columbia River watershed before "civilization" began to deplete the runs.[4]

Salmon as a Way of Life

To the Northwest Indian nations the salmon was as central to the economy as the buffalo was to the tribes of the Great

Plains; for example, 80 to 90 percent of the Puyallup diet consisted of fish.[5] The salmon represented more than food; it was the center of a culture. A festival accompanied the first salmon caught in the yearly run. The fish was barbecued over an open fire and bits of its flesh parceled out to all. The bones were saved intact, to be carried by a torch-bearing, singing, dancing, and chanting procession back to the river, where they were placed in the water with the head pointing upstream—symbolic of the spawning fish, to assure that there would be runs in the future.[6]

The ceremony showed an extraordinary respect for the salmon and a desire to maintain runs for future generations with techniques honed by centuries of experience, without the careless industrialism that led to the damming, polluting, and overfishing of rivers. Indian fishermen sustained an average annual catch of 18 million pounds, which is higher than the present annual catch for the entire state of Washington.

Euro-Americans began to settle in what is now Washington in large numbers during the 1850s; their primary vocation was cutting timber and growing food for the swelling population of California, where gold had been discovered in 1848. The first settlers were predominantly interested in acquiring land, not fish. So when the Indians agreed to give up large amounts of land in exchange for the treaty right to fish at their "usual and accustomed places," the federal government signed. Like the gold of the Black Hills, the salmon of the Northwest did not become valuable in the eyes of entrepreneurs or industry until after the treaties were signed.

Washington became a territory of the United States on March 2, 1853, with no consent from the Indians who occupied most of the land. Isaac Stevens was appointed governor and superintendent of Indian affairs for the territory. As governor, Stevens wished to build the economic base of the territory; this required the attraction of a proposed transcontinental railroad, which, in turn, required peace with the Indians.[7] Stevens worked with remarkable speed; in 1854 and 1855 alone, he negotiated five treaties with six thousand Indian people west of the Cascades.

During these years, Governor Stevens wrested from the Indians most of the land of the present-day states of Montana and Idaho, as well as that of eastern Washington. In all the treaties Stevens drove an extremely tough bargain, but the Indians would not relent on one point: the continued right to fish. After signing the Medicine Creek Treaty on December 26, 1854, Stevens said: "It was also thought necessary to allow them to fish at all accustomed places, since this would not in any manner interfere with the rights of citizens and was necessary for the Indians to obtain a subsistence."[8] The treaty, signed on a small island surrounded by salt marshes not far from the present-day state capital, Olympia, guaranteed the Indians the right to fish at their usual and accustomed places "in common with" citizens of the territory. By signing the treaty, the Indians ceded to the United States 2,240,000 acres of land, an immense sacrifice for the right to fish.[9]

More Fishermen, Fewer Fish

During the seventy years after the signing of the Medicine Creek Treaty and other treaties in western Washington, the non-Indian population increased considerably. As the salmon were fished and polluted to extinction along much of the American and European Atlantic shoreline, fishermen began to move to the Northwest. By the turn of the century, Washington was ignoring the treaties and arresting Indian fishermen who were taking salmon in accordance with them. State police arrested Indians for fishing as early as 1913.[10] By 1929, the state had decided to deny the Quinaults their fishing rights and to lease these rights to Bakers Bay, a private company, for $36,000.[11]

At the same time that non-Indian fishermen were increasing their catch, the encroachment of Euro-American settlement was reducing the salmon runs. Around 1914, 16 million fish were caught annually; by the 1920s annual catches had declined to an average of 6 million. In the late 1930s, following construction of several large hydroelectric dams on the Columbia River and its tributaries, the annual catch had fallen as low as 3 million, about one-sixth of what native peoples alone had been harvesting a century earlier. By the 1970s, with more aggressive conservation measures in place, including construction of fish ladders at most major dams, the annual catch rose to 4 to 6 million, just short of a third of the precontact harvest.

Salmon are migratory fish; they spawn at the headwaters of rivers and streams, travel downstream as smolts, or fry, to the open ocean, and then—three, four, or five years after they have hatched—return to their birthplaces to spawn again. Dams severely alter this migratory cycle, although the damage has been partly remedied by construction of fish ladders and artificial hatcheries. However, salmon are so sensitive to changes in water temperature, oxygen content, and turbidity that logging and industrial development have destroyed many of their breeding grounds.

By 1960, the number of non-Indian fishermen, many of whom had migrated from Scandinavia, was rising rapidly, competing for diminishing fish runs. Between 1947 and 1976 the number of commercial gillnetters rose from 428 to 1,659.[12] Between 1965 and 1974 the number of commercial fishing licenses issued by the state more than doubled, feeding money into a state fish-and-game bureaucracy which grew into an antitreaty police force.[13]

Native peoples who had signed the Medicine Creek Treaty and other treaties were having a more difficult time harvesting enough fish to survive. Problems resulting from the huge increase in the number of fishermen and the decrease in runs were compounded by changes in the nature of fishing. Indian fishermen traditionally took their catch from the mouths of rivers, using nets, wires, and small boats. Non-Indian fishermen, on the other hand, used much more costly open-water fishing gear, including sonar, to get the fish before they returned to the streams to spawn.

The cost and energy effectiveness of the Indian fishery led University of Washington professor Russel Barsh to conclude that open-water fishing should be banned.[14] A root of the problem, wrote Barsh, is that the fish are regarded as a common good in a capitalistic economy. The fish belong to whomever catches them. The common-good nature of the resource has caused too many fishermen to spend too much energy chasing immature fish across the ocean with expensive gear, to catch them before anyone else. Instead of addressing this problem, Barsh wrote, state regulatory agencies used the Indians as scapegoats. Indians were being accused of "overfishing" in the late 1950s when they took less than 1 percent of the total state harvest.[15]

By the early 1960s, state fisheries police were conducting wholesale arrests of Indians, confiscating their boats and nets. Indians took their treaty-rights case to state courts and found them solidly in support of non-Indian commercial interests. In 1962, the Washington State Supreme Court ruled against a Swinomish Indian who had asserted fishing rights under the 1855 Treaty of Point Elliott. The court held that the state had the right to subject Indians to "reasonable and necessary regulations" for conservation.[16] It was a rather hypocritical ruling, considering that the Indians had not built the dams, logged the forests, or constructed the pulp mills which (without regard for the biological needs of the fish) had helped to reduce the runs by three-quarters within fifty years. The ruling, however, was not out of character for a state supreme court which had held in 1916 that

> *at no time did our ancestors in getting title to this continent ever regard the Aborigines as other than mere occupants, and incompetent occupants of the soil. Neither Rome nor sagacious Britain ever dealt more liberally with their subject races than we with these savage tribes whom it was generally tempting and always easy to destroy and whom we have so often permitted to squander vast areas of fertile land before our eyes.[17]*

Denied justice in the state courts, the tribes pursued their claim at the federal level. During the 1960s and early 1970s, they also militantly protected their rights in the face of raids by state fisheries authorities. A nucleus of fishing-rights activists from Franks Landing, living only a few miles from the site at which the Medicine Creek Treaty had been signed, continued to fish on the basis of the treaty, which gave them the right to fish as long as the rivers run.[18] Day by day the rivers ran, the Indians fished, and the state fishery police descended on them as the legal battle continued in the courts. Vigilante sports fishermen joined state fisheries in policing and harassing the Indians, stealing their boats and slashing their nets, and sometimes shooting at them. Everyone, including the elders and women, stood alongside the young men, Hank Adams, Sid Mills, and others. Maisel and Al Bridges, mother and father, fished beside their daughters, Suzette Mills, Valerie and Allison Bridges.

Supporters from Seattle joined the Indians in their confrontation with the police, the vigilantes, and the cold rain. Chicanos from Seattle's El Centro de la Raza also took an active part in these early battles, as did the National Indian Youth Council of Albuquerque, New Mexico.[19] Marlon Brando, Dick Gregory, and Jane Fonda stopped by to hoist nets and spread the aura of national celebrity, making the Northwest conflict over fish the first widely publicized treaty-rights defense of the late twentieth century. In addition, many other treaty struggles were surfacing at this time, particularly in the North and West, where subjugation was little more than a century in the past.

The Road to Rerecognition of the Treaties

By 1965, the U.S. Supreme Court had ruled that Indians had a right to fish at their "usual and accustomed places" but that the state had the right, through its courts, to regulate Indian fishing. That ruling, and a few federal court rulings after it had little practical effect as long as the state, whose fishery managers were adamantly opposed to any Indian fishing at all, held enforcement power.

Billy Frank, Jr., a Nisqually, grew up amidst the "fishing wars." By the early 1990s, Frank, in his fifties, had become chairman of the Northwest Indian Fish Commission and a leading spokesman for environmentalism in the Pacific Northwest. He recalled:

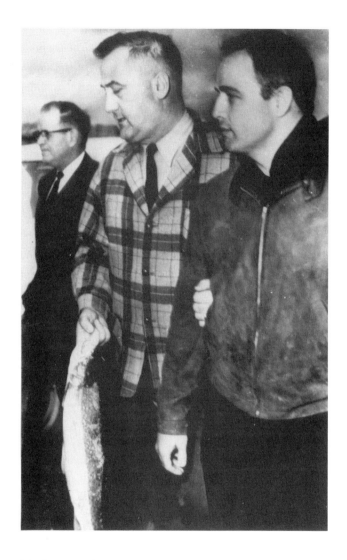

Marlon Brando is led away from a "fish-in" during 1964 on the Puyallup River near Tacoma, after his arrest by state fisheries officer Ellsworth Sawyer. Courtesy of AP/Wide World Photos.

I went to jail when I was fourteen years old. That was the first time I ever went to jail for treaty rights. The State of Washington said I couldn't fish on the Nisqually River. So, at fourteen, I went to jail. Ninety times I went back to jail. The State of Washington said "you can't go on that river and go fishing anymore." That's what they told us Indians. "If you go on that river, you're going to jail." We went back fishing and we went to jail over and over until 1974.[20]

The fish-ins continued until February 12, 1974, when U.S. District Court Judge George Boldt ruled that Indians were entitled to an opportunity to catch as many as half the fish returning to off-reservation sites which had been the "usual and accustomed places" when the treaties were signed. Boldt had put three years into the case; he used two hundred pages to interpret one sentence of the treaty in an opinion which some legal scholars say was "the most carefully researched, thoroughly analyzed ever handed down in an Indian fishing-rights case."[21] The nucleus of Boldt's decision had to do with nineteenth-century dictionaries' definitions of "in common with." Boldt said the word meant shared equally. During the next three years the Ninth Circuit Court of Appeals upheld Boldt's ruling, and the U.S. Supreme Court twice let it stand by refusing to hear it.

Judge Boldt's ruling had a profound effect not only on who would be allowed to catch salmon in Puget Sound but on white-Indian relations generally:

The relative powerlessness of the Indian communities left non-Indians unprepared for the sudden turn of events brought about by the Boldt decision, and the shocked white community reacted immediately. Non-Indians, who had long come to regard the salmon harvest as virtually their own, were suddenly faced with the possible prospect of being forced out of the fishing industry, or [of] facing large reductions in their catch. Hostility became so serious that Indians armed their fish camps after enduring attacks on themselves and their *equipment. Many whites displayed their reaction to the decision with bumper stickers proclaiming "Can Judge Boldt" on their cars. A widely held view was that the Boldt decision had given an <u>unfair advantage</u> to Indians in the fisheries.*[22]

State officials and the fishermen whose interests they represented were furious at Boldt. Rumors circulated about the sanity of the seventy-five-year-old judge. It was said that he had taken bribes of free fish and had an Indian mistress, neither of which was true. Judge Boldt was hung in effigy by angry non-Indian fishermen, who on other occasions formed "convoys" with their boats and rammed Coast Guard vessels which had been dispatched to enforce the court's orders. At least <u>one Coastguardsman was shot</u>. State Senator August Mardesich, himself a commercial fisherman, proposed that the state withhold social services from Indians who failed to comply with the state fishing laws that conflicted with Boldt's ruling.[23] Lost in the fray were a number of small, landless western Washington tribes that were not "recognized" by the federal government and therefore not entitled to participate in the federally mandated solution. A few such tribes, such as the Upper Skagits and Sauk-Suiattles, were recognized after the decision. A number of others remained in legal limbo, as non-persons with no fishing rights under federal law.[24] While the <u>commercial interests raged</u>, the <u>Indians were catching nothing close to the 50 percent allowed by the Boldt ruling</u>. In <u>1974 they caught between 7 and 8 percent</u>, in 1975 between <u>11 and 12 percent</u>, in 1976 between <u>13 and 25</u> percent, and in <u>1977 17 percent</u>, depending on who did the counting—the Indians or the state.[25]

Among state officials during the middle and late 1970s a backlash to Indian rights formed, which would become the nucleus for a <u>nationwide non-Indian campaign to abrogate the treaties</u>. Washington State Attorney General (later U.S. senator) Slade Gorton called Indians "supercitizens" with <u>"special rights"</u> and proposed that constitutional equilibrium be reestablished not by open state violation of the treaties (Boldt had outlawed that) but by <u>purchasing the Indians'</u>

fishing rights. The tribes, which had been listening to offers of money for Indian resources for a century, flatly refused Gorton's offer. To them, the selling of fishing rights would have been tantamount to termination.

Advocates of treaty abrogation anticipated another court case, popularly tagged "Phase II," a continuation of the cases which began with Boldt's 1974 ruling. In this part of the case Indians sought a voice in matters such as antipollution and zoning regulations, as well as building permits, which affected the size and health of salmon runs which passed through their "usual and accustomed places." The economic stakes of Phase II greatly overshadowed those of Judge Boldt's first fishing ruling. Among those who would need to consider Indian viewpoints under such a ruling would be land developers, including power companies and other industries which desired plant sites near rivers and streams. As if to foreshadow the case, the tribes of the Skagit Valley (north of Seattle) in June 1978 asked to intervene in federal hearings on two nuclear power plants which Puget Sound Power and Light wanted to build. The tribes were concerned about the salmon runs in the Skagit River and the threat that could be posed by the nuclear plants, which would use river water for cooling and then discharge it back into the river several degrees warmer than when it was taken out—thus affecting the salmon. The position of the Skagit Valley tribes was in some ways similar to that of the Northern Cheyennes, who sought protection under the Clean Air Act in the face of power plant development near their reservation in eastern Montana. The basic rationale was that native nations should have a voice in developments which might degrade the environment of their reservations or the livelihood of tribal members.

As the treaty tribes of Washington moved to implement Judge Boldt's ruling during the late 1970s, the state's resistance stiffened again. Since the state would not implement his ruling fully, Judge Boldt assumed the state's management power over the fishery himself, piece by piece. On April 25, 1978, however, Judge Boldt withdrew from the second phase of the case but said he would continue to oversee the first phase as much as his health allowed. He had just undergone major surgery. After Boldt withdrew from the second phase of the case, the Ninth Circuit Court of Appeals in San Francisco upheld Boldt's assumption of the state's fishery management, including allocation of salmon between Indians and non-Indians.

As legal maneuvering continued, non-Indian fishermen disobeyed the Boldt ruling in force; several dozen were cited during 1977 and 1978. U.S. Magistrate Robert Cooper, who had taken Judge Boldt's place on the bench while the judge recuperated, said that there had been increasing difficulty since 1974 in enforcing Indian treaty rights.[26] The non-Indian fishermen replied that the Boldt ruling was unconstitutional, although no federal court had agreed with them. Judge Boldt totally withdrew from the case on February 7, 1979. A day later, Boldt said he was shocked by the violent tactics non-Indian fishermen had used to resist his ruling. "It came as a shock to me to discover that the vast majority of Washington residents, at least those who fish, don't give a damn about Indian rights," Judge Boldt stated. The judge said he had great confidence in the Supreme Court, which had agreed to hear an appeal brought by the state of Washington on February 28, 1979.

The evolving state-federal court conflict over Washington treaty fishing rights shared some legal ground with the Cherokee cases which had led to the Trail of Tears. In both cases state agencies and courts were being used by non-Indian special interest groups to wrest control of a resource guaranteed by treaty—the Cherokees' land, the Northwest tribes' fish. In both cases federal courts generally interpreted the treaties as favoring the Indians, and in both cases the federal executive bowed in with a plan to circumvent the treaties. President Jimmy Carter's plan, which paralleled that of Andrew Jackson, another southern semipopulist Democrat, came veiled in the skilled public relations of the twentieth century, as Jackson's had been shrouded in the rationalizations of the nineteenth century.

The vehicle for twentieth-century treaty abrogation was a Federal Task Force on Washington State Fisheries. After more than a year of investigation, this task force issued a settlement proposal, to be forwarded to Congress, which, according to the plan, would legislate a solution to the "fishing war" to supersede the Boldt decision. A new congressional act could also be used in court as evidence that a new agreement had been reached between the federal government and the tribes. It could not be called a treaty (Congress had ended treaty-making in 1871) but could be used to supersede the agreements of 1854 and 1855, upon which the Boldt rulings had been based.

The proposal of the Federal Task Force on Washington State Fisheries recommended that management of state waters be returned to the state Department of Fisheries—the agency that had evaded treaty rights for years before Judge Boldt himself assumed control of the fishery. A tribal commission would be formed under the proposal to manage smaller zones. Steelhead trout management would be returned to the state Department of Game, which for decades before the Boldt ruling had attempted to reserve this agile fish for non-Indian sports activity. Most western Washington tribes would have been forced to give up their steelhead catch. The plan proposed to allow treaty fishermen up to 40 percent of the catch, instead of 50 percent under the Boldt ruling.

As a concession, the plan proposed a reduction in the size of the non-Indian fishing fleet and $15.4 million to increase the size and efficiency of the Indian fleet. A keystone of the proposal was an "enhancement program," involving $121.6 million budgeted to construct new artificial hatcheries to build the salmon runs back to 1914 levels, or approximately the level which would allow 15 million fish to be caught each year. Under the plan, the majority of the new hatcheries would be managed by the state. This was the plan as it would be proposed to Congress, where representatives addled by non-Indian majorities would have a chance to build it (as Congress built the General Allotment Act of 1887) into a device by which to abrogate the treaties.

By the time the final proposal was issued in mid-1978, some Indian tribes questioned the assumption that more hatcheries would automatically produce more harvestable fish; the assumption of a technological fix, without full knowledge of natural mechanisms, could fail, they said. Fisheries biologists for the Quinault Indian Nation provided statistics which indicated that if the state really wanted to double the hatchery-bred runs, it could do so by applying better feeding and breeding standards to existing hatcheries. At the University of Washington, for example, where highly refined feeding and nurturing methods were being used, 160,000 salmon were released during 1972; of those, 2,461 returned to the hatchery, or 1.5 percent. An estimated 1 to 2 percent were caught before returning, giving an estimated survival rate of 2.5 to 3.5 percent. Comparable survival rates for the university hatchery fish released during 1973 were between 3 and 4 percent. For fish released during 1974 the rate was between 5 and 6 percent.

State hatcheries, by comparison, had return rates one-fifth to one-tenth or less than that of the University of Washington hatchery. During 1972, for example, 533,177 tagged fish were released from hatcheries operated by the state at Green River, Minter Creek, and Puyallup (all streams that empty into Puget Sound). The return rate—1,329 were caught or returned—was 0.25 percent. The following year 639,491 tagged fish were released from three state hatcheries, which, like the University of Washington's are located on Puget Sound rivers and streams. The return rate was 0.18 percent. During 1974, the state's return rate for 202,729 fish released from the Green River Hatchery was 0.67 percent.

The differences in survival rates indicate that if scientific breeding and feeding were to be applied to state hatcheries, the surviving runs could be doubled, or more, while spending a fraction of what was proposed for new hatcheries. The spread of hatcheries also raised other biological questions, such as: Do carelessly raised hatchery fish spread disease among the natural runs? Do the large numbers of hatchery-bred fry and smolts which eventually die crowd hardier fish from natural runs out of feeding areas, decreasing the overall return rate? These questions had to be answered on a scientific level. On a political level, the Federal Task Force on Washington State Fisheries seemed to have taken one step toward repressing the exercise of treaty

158 Ecocide of Native America

rights that state agencies had long ignored and harassed treaty lndians for practicing—until Indian militance forced a clarification of the issue from the federal courts.

The Antitreaty Backlash

On an economic level, resistance to Phase II of the Boldt decision was becoming more organized among Washington State business leaders who comprised the Washington Water Resource Committee. Membership on the committee cost each business a $10,000 donation, much of which went into a legal fund to hire Vocal and Gates, a well-known Seattle law firm, which drew up an *amicus* brief in the Ninth Circuit Court of Appeals, San Francisco, in an effort to overturn the Boldt decision's Phase II.

Billy Frank, Jr., and other fishing rights activists decided to boycott Seattle-First National Bank, a member of the Water Resource Committee; they discussed the idea with friends at El Centro de la Raza, a Seattle social service agency. All a-greed they had a good idea, with one flaw. They did not have enough money in the bank to make a boycott effective.

After a few weeks, however, they began to talk to other people. Frank recalled:

> We got the Colvilles to pull out sixteen million. . . .
> Then, the Washington State University kids started
> pulling their money out and the Teamsters Union, and
> other local people. . . . Then I flew up to Alaska to our
> native friends up there. . . . They passed a resolution
> and pulled out eighty million dollars.[27]

By this time, the boycott had drawn notice at Sea-First:

> At that time, Mike Barry was the president of Sea-First.
> He called me up and he said, "Bill, before I jump out of
> the seventeenth floor of the Sea-First bank, we got to
> have a meeting." So, I brought in all my tribal leaders
> again. . . . He asked: "What do you want us to do?" He

said fly back to Alaska and tell the Natives to put that money back in the bank because that was only the beginning. They had another hundred fifty million that they were going to pull out.[28]

"We know who the boss is in this country. It sure as hell isn't us," said Frank.[29] Nevertheless, the boycott was pinching the bank, the region's largest at that time, before mismanaged oil investments caused its near bankruptcy. The Indians refused to restore their deposits unless Sea-First and other businesses called off their attack on the Boldt decision.

The Washington State offensive was one part of a nationwide backlash which emerged against treaty rights during the middle and late 1970s. This movement was fueled, as expropriation of Indian resources have always been, by non-native economic interests. During the 1980s, the battle over who would harvest how many fish continued in western Washington and spread to other states, such as Wisconsin and Minnesota, where treaties had reserved Indians' rights to harvest fish.

The Anishinabes (Chippewas) in the upper Great Lakes Region retained the right to hunt, fish, and gather on lands they sold through treaties to the U.S. government in the mid-1800s. The U.S. Constitution states that "treaties are the supreme law of the land," meaning that states may not interfere with such treaties since they are based on the notion that Indian nations are sovereign and thus have rights to self-determination and self-government.

In the early 1980s, the Chippewas began to reassert their aboriginal rights to hunt, fish, and gather in areas specified in treaties negotiated in the nineteenth century—resulting in legal disputes. On January 25, 1983, the U.S. Court of Appeals for the Seventh Circuit agreed with the Lake Superior Chippewas that hunting, fishing, and gathering rights still were protected in Chippewa treaties, a ruling known as the Voight decision.[30] Later, the U.S. Supreme Court refused to hear the appeal of the Voight decision by the state of Wisconsin, but the three-judge panel of the Seventh Circuit did return the case to Federal District Court to "determine the scope of state regulation." Subsequent decisions defined the scope of Chippewa hunting, fishing, and gathering rights in Wisconsin so they have rights to the following:

1. to harvest and sell hunting, fishing, and gathering products;
2. to exercise these rights on private land if necessary to produce a modest living;
3. to harvest a quantity sufficient to produce a modest living.

In addition, portions of game and forest products (excluding commercial timber) available to the Chippewas through their treaty rights have been quantified in court rulings since the Voight decision. In 1991, the rulings in the Federal District Court implementing the Voight decision were allowed to stand since neither the Chippewas nor the state of Wisconsin appealed them by the deadline of May 1991. On May 20, 1991, the Chippewas announced their decision not to appeal with the following message:

The . . . Lake Superior Chippewa . . . have preserved . . . [their hunting, fishing, and gathering] rights for generations to come, [and they] . . . have this day foregone their right to further appeal. . . . They do this as a gesture of peace and friendship towards the people of Wisconsin, in a spirit they hope may be reciprocated on the part of the general citizenry and officials of this state.[31]

The path to resolution of the issue of Chippewa fishing rights was littered with racial conflict. During the Indian spearfishing seasons in the late 1980s, Chippewas were subjected to violent harassment and racial slurs by non-Indians while attempting to exercise their treaty rights. Antispearfishing slogans included: "Save a walleye; spear a squaw" and "Custer had the right idea." A suit filed by the American Civil Liberties Union on behalf of the Chippewas served to deter some of the more ardent anti-Indian violent protests by

Members of the American Indian Movement lent support to the Saint Croix band of Chippawa Indians in assertion of their fishing rights. Courtesy of UPI/Bettman.

the 1990 fishing season.[32] Recently, the Chippewas also have been exercising their sovereignty by establishing gambling halls on their reservations.

In 1988, Dean Crist, a Wisconsin antitreaty activist and head of Stop Treaty Abuse, began selling "Treaty Beer" as a promotional and fund-raising device in his campaign to abrogate treaties across the United States. When Crist tried to market his political brew in Washington State, however, he ran into a solid wall of opposition from native people and their non-Indian allies (including several church groups). With the conflict over fishing being rather successfully managed by the bureaucracy that had evolved out of the many federal court rulings following the Boldt decision, most people in Washington did not want to return to the old days of armed conflict on the rivers and streams of the state. U.S. Senator Dan Evans joined the opposition to the marketing of Treaty Beer in Washington. Both of Seattle's daily newspapers, the *Seattle Times* and the *Seattle Post-Intelligencer*, condemned the marketing ploy, as did Governor Booth Gardner and many environmental activists.

Even the usually antitreaty Steelhead and Salmon Protection Association for Washington Now (S/SPAWN), a group of sports fishermen, came out against Treaty Beer. Crist had offended his potential allies in S/SPAWN by claiming its support without the group's consent. Ellis Lind, speaking for S/SPAWN, told the *Seattle Times* that the claim of support was "an absolute lie. We don't want any part of this garbage."[33] Crist did get support from the state gillnetter's association, which represented about half of Washington's commercial fishermen.

Treaty Beer was variously called "a very hateful brew . . . [and] a dreadful, sick joke" (by the *Seattle Times*), "the Klan in a Can" (by William B. Cate of the Church Council of Greater Seattle), and "a particular brand of toxic waste" (by the Washington Environmental Council). Senator Dan Evans, who was vice chairman of the Senate Select Committee on Indian Affairs at the time, decried Crist as an "outside agitator [who sees] our state as fertile ground for their message of hate."[34] In the face of such opposition, Crist's distributor refused to carry the beer in Washington. Instead, public opinion and formerly antagonistic groups in the state seemed to now be more united behind plans to preserve and enhance salmon runs.

David Sohappy's Vigil

Although the Boldt decision restored recognition of treaty rights west of the Cascades, at least regarding salmon, during the 1980s the fishing-rights battle continued east of the Cascades in a form that reminded many people of the Frank's Landing "fish-ins" of the 1960s. Many native people along the Columbia River and its tributaries fished for a livelihood long before Euro-Americans migrated to their land, but no treaties protected their right to do so.

David Sohappy of the Wanapam Band, for example, had erected his riverbank shelter and fished in the traditional manner for years. His name came from the Wanapam word *souiehappie*, meaning "shoving something under a ledge,"[35] and his ancestors had traded fish with members of the Lewis and Clark expedition. The Wanapams had never signed a treaty, wishing only to be left in peace to live as they had for hundreds, if not thousands, of years. By the early 1940s, Sohappy's family was pushed off its ancestral homeland at Priest Rapids and White Bluffs, an area which became part of the Hanford Nuclear Reservation, in the middle of a desert that Lewis and Clark characterized as the most barren piece of land that they saw between St. Louis and the Pacific Ocean. Still, David Sohappy fished, even as his father, Jim Sohappy, warned him that if he continued to live in the old ways, "the white man is going to put you in jail someday."[36]

During the 1950s, development devastated Celilo Falls, one of the richest Indian fishing grounds in North America. Most of the people who had fished there gave up their traditional livelihood and moved to the nearby Yakima Reservation, or into urban areas. David Sohappy and his wife Myra moved to a sliver of federal land called Cook's Landing, just above the first of several dams along the Columbia and its tributaries. There they built a small longhouse with a dirt floor. As the "fish-ins" of the 1960s attracted nationwide publicity, Sohappy fished in silence, using fishing traps he had built from driftwood, until state game and fishing officials raided his camp, beat family members, and, in 1968, put Sohappy in jail on charges of illegal fishing. He then brought legal action, and the case, *Sohappy v. Smith*, produced a landmark federal ruling that was supposed to prevent the states of Washington and Oregon from interfering with Indian fishing, except for conservation purposes.

The reaction of the state to the *Sohappy v. Smith* ruling reminded some people of President Andrew Jackson's reaction to the Supreme Court's 1832 ruling in *Worcester v. Georgia.* The state ignored the ruling and continued to harass Sohappy and his family. Usually under cover of darkness, state agents sunk their boats and slashed their nets. In 1981 and 1982, the states of Washington and Oregon successfully (but quietly) lobbied into law a federal provision that made the interstate sale of fish taken in violation of state law a felony—an act aimed squarely at Sohappy. Eight months before the law was signed by President Reagan, the state enlisted federal undercover agents in a fish-buying sting that the press called "Salmonscam," to entrap Sohappy, who was later convicted in Los Angeles (the trial had been moved from the local jurisdiction because of racial prejudice against Indians). Sohappy was convicted of taking 317 fish and sentenced to five years in prison. During the trial, testimony about Sohappy's religion and the practice of conservation was not allowed.[37]

Sohappy became a symbol of native rights across the United States. Myra Sohappy sought support from the U.N. Commission on Human Rights to have her husband tried by a jury of his peers in the Yakima Nation's Tribal Court. The new trial was arranged with the help of Sen. Daniel K. Inouye, chairman of the Senate Select Committee on Indian affairs. The Yakima court found that the federal prosecution had interfered with Sohappy's practice of his Seven Drum religion.[38]

Released after twenty months in prison, Sohappy had

David Sohappy, Sr. (left), and his son David Sohappy, Jr. (center, back-ground), pause on the steps of the Federal Courthouse in Los Angeles dur-ing their 1983 trial for illegal fishing on the Columbia River. Bruce Jim (right) and his wife Barbara (center, foreground) also were among sixteen Native Americans charged with being part of a fish-poaching ring. Courtesy of AP/Wide World Photos.

aged rapidly; confinement and the prison diet had sapped his strength. He had suffered several strokes during the months in prison, when he was even denied the use of an eagle prayer feather for comfort (it was rejected as "contraband" by prison officials). Back at Cook's Landing, Sohappy found that vindictive federal officials had tacked an eviction notice to his small house. Sohappy took the eviction notice to court and beat the government for what turned out to be his last time. He died in a nursing home in Hood River, Oregon, on May 6, 1991.

A few days later Sohappy was buried, as his Wanapam relatives gathered in an old graveyard. They sang traditional songs as they lowered his body into the earth, having wrapped it in a Pendleton blanket. He was placed so that the early morning sun would warm his head, facing west toward Mount Adams. Tom Keefe, Jr., an attorney who had been instrumental in securing Sohappy's release from prison, stood by the grave and remembered:

> *And while the sun chased a crescent moon across the Yakima Valley, I thanked David Sohappy for the time we had spent together, and I wondered how the salmon he had fought to protect would fare in his absence. Now he is gone, and the natural runs of Chinook that fed his family since time immemorial are headed for the Endangered Species Act list. "Be glad for my dad," David Sohappy, Jr., told the mourners. "He is free now, he doesn't need any tears."*[39]

Ironically, as state and federal officials hounded David Sohappy into his grave on the eastern side of the Cascades, their counterparts in the Puget Sound area, site of battles over fishing rights a generation earlier, were preparing a peace offering. They released one of many fishing boats confiscated from western Washington native fishermen and returned the boat to its owner. Billy Frank, Jr., of Franks Landing, one of the "fish-in" leaders, was older and gray around the temples in 1992. He has become a nationally recognized leader in the cooperative effort to restore salmon runs of the eastern Pacific. Frank installed the old cedar dugout canoe at a spot of honor alongside the riverbank where his quest to fish in accordance with the treaties had begun. Respect comes slowly. The struggle continues, Frank would sometimes say, in other places for the same reasons.

By 1993, the question of fishing rights had become entwined with broader ecological issues, as tests revealed potentially toxic levels of dioxin in fish at several sites east and west of the Cascades. Surveys by the Environmental Protection Agency also indicated that Native Americans in the Northwest consume a dozen times as much fish as most other Americans, placing them at greater risk of contamination.[40] It was no longer enough to enjoy the right to fish, if the catch could kill you. Northwest tribal environmentalists began searching federal law for ways to reduce or eliminate toxin levels in their catch. Salmon were not as much at risk (they spend most of their lives at sea) as bottom fish and shellfish, which often reside in polluted areas and build levels of toxins in their bodies. Northwest tribes were looking for legal justifications under the Clean Water Act to enforce tough and potentially expensive controls on sources of toxic effluent upstream from their usual and accustomed fishing grounds—the next stage in a fight for survival that reaches back to early warnings by Chief Seal'th of the Duwamish that those who foul their own nests will drown in their own wastes. Today, the valley that Chief Seal'th's Duwamish vacated in the 1850s to make way for the growing village of Seattle is a hive of industrial activity. The Duwamish River, which once sustained Chief Seal'th's band, often is closed to fishing because of pollution, even as thousands of people continue to move into the once-pristine Northwest, searching for a corner of paradise.

Notes

1. Anthony Netboy, *The Atlantic Salmon: A Vanishing Species* (Boston: Houghton Mifflin, 1968), 23–26.
2. Ibid., 331.
3. Ibid., 387.

4. Department of the Interior, Bureau of Reclamation, *Columbia River Comprehensive Report on Development* (Washington, D.C.: Government Printing Office, 1947), 353.

5. U.S. Senate, Committee on Interior and Insular Affairs, Subcommittee on Indian Affairs, *Indian Fishing Rights: Hearings on S.J.R. 170 and 171*, 88th Cong., 2nd sess., August 5-6, 1964 (statement of Frank Wright, chairman of the Puyallup), 105.

6. Ibid.

7. American Friends Service Committee, comp., *Uncommon Controversy: A Report on the Fishing Rights of the Muckleshoot, Puyallup and Nisqually Indians* (Seattle and London: University of Washington Press, 1970), 19-23.

8. Ibid., 23. Indians generally were not classified by the U.S. government as citizens until 1924.

9. Ibid., 27.

10. William Meyer, *Native Americans: The New Indian Resistance* (New York: International Publishers, 1971), 70.

11. Ibid.

12. Bruce Brown, "A Long Look at the Boldt Decision," *Argus* (Seattle), December 3, 1976, 4.

13. U.S. Federal Task Force on Washington State Fisheries Settlement Plan for Washington State Salmon and Steelhead Fisheries, mimeographed, June 1978, 232.

14. Russel L. Barsh. *The Washington Fishing Rights Controversy: An Economic Critique* (Seattle: University of Washington School of Business Administration, 1977).

15. Ibid., 21.

16. Brown, "The Boldt Decision," 5.

17. Fred Brack, "Fishing Rights: Who Is Entitled to Northwest Salmon?" *Seattle Post-Intelligencer Northwest Magazine*, January 16, 1977, 6.

18. An excellent film entitled *As Long as the Rivers Run* was produced by the Survival of American Indians Association, which grew out of the fishing-rights struggle in 1968.

19. The Chicanos were recognizing their own Indian ancestry, as well as the fact that the United States had signed, and broken, the Treaty of Guadalupe Hidalgo after the conclusion of the Mexican-American War in 1848.

20. Billy Frank, Jr., in Kurt Russo, ed., *Our People, Our Land: Perspectives on the Columbus Quincentenary* (Bellingham, Wash.: Lummi Tribe and Kluckhohn Center, 1992), 55.

21. Brack, "Fishing Rights," 4.

22. Bruce J. Miller, "The Press, the Boldt Decision, and Indian-White Relations," *American Indian Culture and Research Journal* 17, no. 2 (1993): 77.

23. Brack, "Fishing Rights," 7.

24. Miller, "The Press, the Boldt Decision," 78.

25. Brack, "Fishing Rights," 8.

26. *Wassaja*, May 1978, 1.

27. Frank in *Our People, Our Land*, ed. Russo, 56.

28. Ibid.

29. Ibid.

30. Lac Courte Oreilles vs. Wisconsin (LCO I), 653 F. Supp. 1420 (W.D. Wis. 1987).

31. *A Guide to Understanding Chippewa Treaty Rights* (Odanah, Wisc.: Great Lakes Indian Fish and Wildlife Commission, 1991), 18.

32. Ibid., 11; and *Los Angeles Times*, November 7, 1993.

33. See Bruce E. Johansen, "The Klan in a Can," *The Progressive* (July 1988), 13.

34. Ibid.

35. Tom Keefe, Jr., "A Tribute to David Sohappy," *Native Nations*, June/July, 1991, 4.

36. Ibid.

37. Ibid., 6.

38. Ibid.

39. Ibid.

40. *Seattle Post-Intelligencer*, September 7, 1993, A-1, A-8.

A freeway overpass looms over Mohawk children at play near Schoharie Creek in 1957. Their parents were camped on the creek to assert Mohawk land rights to 8,000 acres nearby. Courtesy of AP/Wide World Photos.

Chapter Seven
Akwesasne's Toxic Turtles

For three millennia of human occupancy, the site the Mohawks call Akwesasne was a natural wonderland: well watered, thickly forested with white pine, oak, elm, hickory, and ash, home to deer, elk, and other game animals. The rich soil of the bottomlands allowed farming to flourish. The very name that the Akwesasne Mohawks gave their land when permanent occupancy began about 1755, near the site of a Jesuit mission, testifies to the richness of game there. In Mohawk, Akwesasne means "land where the partridge drums," after the distinctive sound that a male ruffled grouse, or partridge, makes during its spring courtship rituals. The area, which lies at the confluence of the Saint Lawrence, Saint Regis, Racquette, Grasse, and Salmon rivers, once had some of the largest runs of sturgeon, bass, and walleyed pike in eastern North America.

In two generations, this land of natural wonders has become a place so poisoned that it is not safe to eat the fish or game. In some locations, it is not safe even to drink the water, while in others, people have been told not to till the soil. Akwesasne has become the most polluted native reserve in Canada and one of the most severely poisoned sections of earth in the United States. Instead of a sustaining river to which the Mohawks traditionally offer thanksgiving prayers, late-twentieth century capitalism has offered gambling and smuggling, along with proposed incinerators and dumps for medical waste, all operated free from state and federal law under so-called "Indians sovereignty."

In just two generations, the land where the partridge drums has become a toxic dumping ground, a place where any partridge still alive is no doubt more concerned about its heartbeat than its drumbeat. These environmental circumstances have descended on a people whose entire way of life

After construction of the Saint Lawrence Seaway, Iroquois lands came into demand for industrialization and urbanization. Tuscarora activist Wallace "Mad Bear" Anderson burns a New York State injunction prohibiting demonstrations against construction to add a lane to Route 31 through the Onondaga Reservation. Courtesy of UPI/Bettmann.

had been enmeshed with the natural world, in a place where the Iroquois origin story says the world took shape on a gigantic turtle's back. Today, environmental pathologists are finding turtles at Akwesasne that qualify as toxic waste.

The rapidity and manner with which Akwesasne has been transformed from a natural paradise to an environmental hell makes it a metaphor for environmental degradation. A once-pristine landscape of rivers and forests has been turned into a chemical dump where unsuspecting children played on piles of dirt laced with polychlorinated biphenyls (PCBs) dumped by a nearby General Motors foundry. PCBs, chemicals used to insulate electrical equipment before they were banned by the federal government during the 1970s, are highly stable molecules of two conjoined hexagonal rings of varying numbers of chlorine atoms. The number of such atoms determines the degree of toxicity. In some of its forms, PCBs cause liver damage and several types of cancer.

The Mohawks of Akwesasne are not "New Age" converts to environmental consciousness. For many generations, they have watched and protested the degradation of their homeland. As early as 1834, their chiefs told Canadian officials that control structures built to channel the flow of the Saint Lawrence River near Barnhart Island were destroying important fish spawning grounds. However, environmental degradation at Akwesasne took a quantum leap after the late 1950s when the Saint Lawrence Seaway opened up bountiful, cheap power. Access to power drew heavy industry that soon turned large segments of this magnificent river into open sewers.

The Worst Place in the World to Be a Duck

Ward Stone, a wildlife pathologist for the New York State Department of Environmental Conservation believes that Akwesasne is "the worst place in the world to be a duck"[1] which is not much of an exaggeration. A duck might be as bad off in certain areas of the Mediterranean Sea, where the Cetacean Society, a group of Italian scientists, has found dolphins contaminated by up to 1,400 times the amounts of DDT and PCBs considered safe, or perhaps a duck sitting downwind of Union Carbide's Bhopal plant in India might have been worse off during a couple of days in early December 1984, when a chemical leak killed at least 2,500 people and injured 200,000 others. However, it is clear that the environment of Akwesasne today punishes any living organism.

When Stone began examining animals at Akwesasne, he found that the PCBs, insecticides, and other toxins were not being contained in designated dumps. After years of use, the dump sites had leaked, and the toxins had gotten into the food chain of human beings and nearly every other species of animal in the area. The Mohawks' traditional economy, based on hunting, fishing, and agriculture, had been literally poisoned out of existence.

Pollution in Iroquois country is not limited to Akwesasne, but it is most acute there. Onondaga Lake, for example, is so polluted that its fish are inedible. The lake that once supplied the firekeepers of the Iroquois Confederacy with food is today dominated by the skyline of Syracuse. The waters of Akwesasne are so laced with PCBs that people whose ancestors subsisted on fish for thousands of years can no longer eat them. "We are still lonesome for those fish," says Tom Porter, one of nine Akwesasne Mohawk Nation Council chiefs. Porter, whose Mohawk name is Sakowkenonkwas, lives at Racquette Point with his Choctaw wife and six children in a house with no electricity that Porter, a carpenter by trade, built by hand many years ago. Until fifteen years ago, when they were warned against eating fish from the waters around Akwesasne, Porter's family, like many Mohawk families, took sturgeon, bullhead, bass, trout, and other fish from nearby rivers in their nets, eating what they needed and keeping extra fish for visitors in submerged boxes. Their fishing nets have since rotted, symbolic of the destruction of a way of life as a result of PCBs, Mirex, mercury, and other contaminants.

The Porters now worry not only about the fish but also about the produce they raise in gardens around their house; even the health of the Belgian horses that Porter raises is at risk.

The rivers of Akwesasne mean more to the Mohawks than

fish for eating. They are the center of a way of life that has been destroyed. As with the native harvesters of salmon in the Pacific Northwest, the people of Akwesasne did not just catch and eat fish. They gave thanks to the fish for allowing themselves to be caught and eaten, and to nature and the spirit world for providing sustenance.

The pollution at Akwesasne (and at other points along the Saint Lawrence River) is so acute and widespread it has affected the food chain into the Atlantic Ocean. Sea creatures feeding on fish from the Saint Lawrence River, such as beluga whales, suffer from various forms of cancer, reproductive problems, and immune-system deficiencies. More than 500 environmental contaminants have been measured in autopsies of the wildlife in and near Akwesasne, 125 of them in the fish, with PCBs being only the most prominent. Industrial plants, including the General Motors foundry, give the area a skyline of spewing smokestacks that popular imagery might associate with New Jersey or Delaware, rather than upstate New York; however, industrial plants that located here were not concerned with aesthetics but with access to international shipping facilities and cheap hydroelectric power.

The scope of the environmental disaster at Akwesasne began to unfold in the early 1980s, as environmental scientists initiated more intensive testing of the area. While environmental scientists were just discovering Akwesasne's problems, farmers in the area had been suffering for years. Lloyd Benedict, a former chief on the Mohawk Council of Akwesasne, living on Cornwall Island, said that the number of cattle on the island declined from about 500 to less than 200 during the 1960s because of fluoride poisoning; the cattle were dying, and "the farmers just couldn't keep up with replacing [them] all the time."[3]

A study by Cornell University indicated that smokestack effluvia from a Reynolds Metals factory also was destroying once-profitable cattle and dairy farms in Cornwall, on the Ontario side of Akwesasne. The study linked fluorides to the demise of cattle as early as 1978. Many of the cattle, as well as fish, suffered from fluoride poisoning that weakened their bones and decayed their teeth. Ernest Benedict's Herefords died while giving birth, while Noah Point's cattle lost their teeth, and Mohawk fishermen landed perch and bass with deformed spines and large ulcers on their skins. The fluoride was a by-product of a large aluminum smelter in Massena, New York, that routinely fills the air with yellowish gray fumes smelling of acid and metal. Another plant in the same area manufactures caustic soda and chlorine, while another produces pulp and paper.

The Cornell University study provided an early glimpse of PCB poisoning at Akwesasne. Subsequently, the Mohawk Council of Akwesasne filed a $150 million lawsuit against another company, Alcoa, but settled for $650,000. The council spent so much on lawyers' fees that it nearly went bankrupt. Although Reynolds Metals, owner of the aluminum smelter, cut its fluoride emissions from 300 pounds an hour in 1959 to 75 pounds per hour in 1980, the few cattle still feeding in the area continued to die of fluoride poisoning. The pollution of Akwesasne is accentuated by the fact that most of the plants emitting toxins are located west of there, upstream, and often upwind.

The Saint Lawrence River at Akwesasne also carries pollutants dumped into it from the Great Lakes system as it moves downstream toward the Atlantic Ocean. Akwesasne lies downstream not only from the General Motors foundry and other polluters but also downstream from other infamous toxic areas, such as the Love Canal.

In 1981, the Mohawk Council of Akwesasne and the Canadian Ministry of Health requested a study of exposure to fluorides, mercury, Mirex, and PCBs by the Environmental Sciences Laboratory at the Mt. Sinai School of Medicine. By December 1981, brief reports alleged the presence of PCBs around the General Motors foundry. The reports were practically on the rumor level at the time. There was no precise information on the degree of PCB contamination or its location. This information was vital to Mohawks in Racquette Point, some of whom lived less than a thousand yards from the General Motors' dump site, as well as people whose water intake from the Saint Lawrence River was only a half-mile from the plant.

At about the same time, almost two years before General Motors officially acknowledged that a problem existed, the New York Department of Environmental Conservation (DEC) rejected the company's cleanup plan, which would have merely closed and capped the waste sites, with none of the expensive but environmentally necessary remedial work that would stop the deadly spread of PCBs, which already had leached out of the foundry's dump.

By the early 1980s, John Wilson of the DEC indicated that the department had learned of possible PCB contamination at Akwesasne. Preliminary tests had shown the area to be the worst PCB contamination site in Franklin County, with "widespread contamination of groundwater."[4] Wilson went on to say that "there was no reversal practical"[5] a statement that was terrifying to residents of Akwesasne. Wilson also made a statement that angered many Mohawks, saying, "The Indians have not been notified," despite the fact that they had many shallow wells that might suffer from groundwater seepage. Robert Hendrichs, manager of the General Motors foundry, said that the company was preparing its final cleanup proposal, and that the company was working harmoniously with state environmental officials. Furthermore, Hendrichs also said that PCB-laden materials had been used at the foundry since 1972, when such use became illegal, and that other toxic wastes were being shipped to a federally approved waste disposal site. However, he left a few questions unanswered: When did the contamination begin? What concentration of PCBs had been re-leased? How far into the environment had they spread and with what effects?

For a time early in 1982, it seemed as if concern over PCB contamination at Akwesasne had been one of the shortest pollution scares on record, as General Motors and the DEC assured the Mohawks that there was little to worry about. As the state Department of Health began testing wells in the Racquette Point area, a DEC water quality expert "explained that the hazardous waste dumps on the General Motors property were separated from the reservation by geographical and geological barriers unlikely to permit the spread of the pollutants."[6] No PCBs were found in the first well water sample at Racquette Point.[7]

When researchers tested the water itself, they were unable to find traces of PCBs, since they are not water soluble. By mid-January, however, body-fat analyses were beginning to come in from Mt. Sinai, and they told another story. Traces of PCBs had been found in the bodies of several St. Regis residents. While the Mt. Sinai study did not link the PCB contamination directly to the General Motors dump, Dr. Stephen Levin, an environmental specialist at the hospital, said that "the initial results suggest there is a local source of PCB contamination."[8] A week later, a test was reported that had found PCBs in one well at St. Regis. The well was not close to the General Motors plant, however, and no connection was suggested.[9]

Little action seems to have been taken regarding early reports of scattered PCB contamination at Akwesasne. In April of 1982, the DEC criticized a General Motors plan to use "scavenger wells" meant to keep groundwater below the level of lagoons tainted with waste from the dump. In March 1983, the state Health Department and St. Regis Tribal Council set up a well-sampling schedule. In July, the tests produced indications of cancer-causing pollutants such as benzene and trichloroethylene in groundwater below homes at Akwesasne. A public relations spokesman for General Motors said that neither chemical was being used at the foundry.[10]

In mid-July 1983, St. Regis Tribal Council environmental technician Jim Ransom complained that General Motors was being less than forthcoming with information. "We don't know exactly what's in the dump," he said.[11] In August, General Motors officials declined to attend a meeting of New York State, Canadian, and tribal environmental officials. General Motors said it knew of no evidence showing that its landfill was causing health problems. At the meeting, DEC officials disclosed that they had asked the Environmental Protection Agency (EPA) to put the General Motors dumps on the Superfund list. At that time, the EPA estimated that the area contained 800,000 cubic yards of sediments contaminated with PCBs. Residents were warned not to eat vegetables from their gardens.

Despite General Motors' attempts to downplay the problem, Berton Mead, a DEC engineer, said on August 18 that "there are a number of areas . . . with high levels of PCB-contaminated groundwater. . . It does violate the groundwater standards."[12] At the time, however, General Motors had done no testing of its own property. The company said it did not have enough information to develop a remedial plan. Mead also said that the DEC did not have enough information "to make an intelligent decision" about how the PCB problem at Akwesasne should be corrected.[13]

In October 1983, the EPA fined General Motors $507,000, charging the company with seventeen counts of illegal PCB disposal. The fine was the largest the agency had levied in a PCB-related case to that time. The EPA also made Superfund money available to help dredge sediments laced with PCBs from the bed of the Saint Lawrence River and other waterways. During the same month, the United Auto Workers disclosed that in 1982 it had threatened a strike at the foundry over PCB exposure on the job. To avoid the strike, the company complied with union demands to clean the interior of the plant. The Mohawks outside, with no such leverage, were not so lucky, however.

In November 1983, the *Watertown Daily Times* obtained internal DEC memos dated 1981 to 1983 which revealed that there may have been PCB contamination in the area during that period (General Motors had said that no PCBs were dumped there after 1972). There may also have been PCB leakage at General Motors in addition to that disclosed by the company for the Superfund list. The newspaper also reported that General Motors had not complied with DEC requests for information. While many Mohawks and other local people had criticized the DEC for foot-dragging on the issue, the internal memos indicated that the agency had tried to do its job while General Motors had done its best to stall.

The memo obtained by the newspaper indicated that Robert McCarty, a site investigation supervisor, had suggested possible contamination of the reservation and the Saint

Lawrence River. Darrell Sweredoski, a DEC engineer, commented that "groundwater contamination is evident in all wells and at all elevations along the eastern boundary with the reservation . . . I can only conclude from this information the contamination from one or both of the sludge deposits has indeed migrated off-site to the east."[14] Apparently unaware of Sweredoski's findings, J. L. Jeffrey of General Motors wrote to the DEC the following May 6: "Since there is no proof that the Indians are affected by the sludge deposits, there is no purpose to involving them in the closure planning."[15]

By 1983, *Indian Time*, a newspaper published for Akwesasne residents, was carrying detailed reports on the effects of PCB contamination as far away as Japan. One article, published in early July, focused on the chemistry and industrial uses of the chemicals. The July 27 issue of *Indian Time* described the effects of PCB poisoning based on exposure in Yusho, Japan, where a heat exchanger leaked PCBs that contaminated a shipment of rice oil during 1968. It stated: "Toxic effects in human beings include an acne-like skin eruption called chloracne, pigmentation of the skin and nails, distinctive hair follicles, excessive eye discharge, swelling of the eyelids, headache, fatigue, nausea and vomiting, digestive disorders, and liver dysfunction."[16] Symptoms persisted in some cases for several months after workers left the source of contamination, which also caused some cases of impotence and hematuria (blood in the urine).

More than a thousand Japanese who consumed some of the contaminated rice oil were tested afterwards; the concentration of toxicity in the rice oil was 2,000 to 3,000 parts per million, a level of contamination that would become very familiar to environmental scientists testing animals at Akwesasne during the next few years. Of thirteen Japanese women who were pregnant when they consumed the toxic rice oil . . . two had still births. Live births were characterized by grayish brown skin pigmentation, discolored nails, and abnormally large amounts of eye discharge. In addition, some of the babies had abnormally shaped skulls and protruding eyeballs. Such evidence convinced researchers, according to *Indian Time*, that "PCBs were transferred to the fetus through the placenta."[17] Some babies seemed to be getting a double dose, because PCBs also had contaminated their mothers' milk.

In January 1984, *Indian Time* reported that Environment Canada was preparing to test for mercury, PCBs, and Mirex contamination on Cornwall Island. The article reported that Akwesasne had been accorded an "A-1" rating by Canadian environmental officials because of a history of open dumping on the island. In February 1985, *Indian Time* began publishing acid rain readings indicating that precipitation falling on the reservation had an average acidity (Ph) ranging from 4.06 to 5.11, considerably more acid than the 5.6 considered the usual minimum Ph factor of natural precipitation.

In July 1984, General Motors disclosed in a report required by the EPA that PCBs and other toxic wastes such as solvents, degreasers, trichloroethylene, and formaldehyde had been dumped in the Akwesasne area since 1959, when the plant opened. From 1968 through 1973, PCBs were used inside the foundry to protect against fire and thermal degradation in the searing heat of its die-casting machines. At that time, the company had no idea how much had been disposed of over the years (that figure was later estimated to be 823,000 cubic yards). In the sanitized language of the corporation, some of that waste was "not containerized." In plain English, the toxins were dumped on the open ground in a number of sites, the North Disposal Area, the East Disposal Area, the Industrial Landfill, and four sludge lagoons, most of which were close enough to contaminate both Akwesasne and the Saint Lawrence River. The company also admitted that its dumping grounds were unlined and uncapped and that the sludge lagoons had overflowed into the Saint Lawrence at least seven times between January and September 1982. As a result, the Saint Lawrence River now contained "hot spots" of PCB contamination more than 50 parts per million.

Hugh Kaufman, assistant director of EPA's Hazardous Waste Site Control Division, said in October 1983 at a Clarkson University conference on "Managing Environmental Risk" that while technology existed to avoid many toxic-dump problems, the government and industry were not putting in the necessary time and money to use it and that General Motors could easily have contained toxic leakage from its dumps. The toxic plague that scientists were beginning to piece together at Akwesasne also could have been contained if the Reagan administration had been more interested in prosecuting violations of environmental laws, said Kaufman.

Moreover, Kaufman said that of 18,000 toxic-waste "candidate sites" around the United States, only 8,000 had even been subject to inspection. Of those, 800 had been "identified for national action," of which the Superfund at present had funds to clean up only 115—less than 1 per cent of the toxic-waste sites that might need it. "We don't have the resources," Kaufman said. "It's a brand-new program. The EPA lost three years thanks to Mrs. Buford, thanks to Rita Lavell [agency supervisors appointed by President Reagan] . . . You are talking about a situation that will take you through the next century just to stabilize."[18]

According to Kaufman, special-interest groups were preventing the government from issuing effective regulations to prevent the creation of new waste dumps, as the EPA struggled to deal with decades of neglected effluvia. He also said that lobbyists had been very effective on Capitol Hill in delaying the cleanup of existing sites, so costly and embarrassing to companies such as General Motors which, for so long, had disposed of their toxic wastes the easiest and least expensive way possible, with little regard for environmental consequences.

Referring specifically to the General Motors dumps near Akwesasne, Kaufman said that General Motors did not have to dump its toxic waste in lagoons: "If it's PCB-contaminated waste oils, a mobile incinerator can be set up at the site. Those materials can be destroyed by the company tomorrow, no problem. . . . PCB-contaminated waste oils are one of the easiest waste streams to destroy." Kaufman indicated that perhaps General Motors was more willing to pay fines than to install costly new technology. If that was the case, he said, the EPA should install the technology and charge the company three times the damages. "Certainly," Kaufman said, "General Motors cannot complain that they cannot afford a half-million dollars to set up an incinerator there." Kaufman then implied that the company was using its inability to come to an agreement on cleanup with the state as a delaying tactic: "Have they [General Motors], in their plan, requested a mobile incinerator to destroy those materials, or have they just said they are going to dump some kitty litter in it and put a clay cap on it?"[19] Kaufman continued:

> *The longer that those waste materials remain in that lagoon, the more toxic material is going to continue to leak into the groundwater. . . . Under immediate removal or emergency action, [the EPA] can go in and destroy those waste oils and PCBs. . . . It's a simple case, but there are two different issues. One issue is dealing with stopping the leak. . . . [The] second issue is the long-term issue of documenting the movement of contamination from the site.*[20]

General Motors spokesman Bill O'Neill replied that the company "has been working with state and federal agencies to remedy that situation." O'Neill reiterated the company's position that the EPA should not be involved in the "site solution." Said O'Neill: "The site is ours, and . . . if there is any action that is necessary . . . we will be responsible for it and we will take care of it." He said the company "had a method" to deal with the problem but didn't specify what it was.[21]

Toxic Turtles at Contaminant Cove

At Akwesasne, environmental bills were coming due with amazing swiftness. The degree of crisis at Akwesasne seemed to expand with the number and intensity of studies conducted to measure it. As Kaufman spoke, only the bare outline of the problem at Akwesasne had become officially visible. By the mid-1980s, Ward Stone had begun to piece together evidence indicating that Akwesasne had become one of the

Mohawk ecologist Ken Jock removes a dead pike from "Contaminant Cove" at Akwesasne. Attawa Citizen staff photo by Lynn Ball.

worst pollution sites in New York State and possibly one of the worst in North America.

The Mohawks started Stone's environmental tour of Akwesasne with a visit to one of the General Motors waste lagoons, a place called "unnamed tributary cove" on some maps. Stone gave it the name "contaminant cove" because of the amount of toxic pollution in it. "When I first went there in 1985, there were Indian children playing barefoot [in the cove]. They were walking in hazardous waste. There was so much PCBs and other contaminants in the sediment of that cove, that the cove bottom was actually hazardous waste."[22]

One day in 1985, at contaminant cove, the environmental crisis at Akwesasne assumed a whole new foreboding shape. The New York State Department of Conservation caught a female snapping turtle that contained 835 parts per million of PCBs. While no federal standards exist for PCBs in turtles, the federal standard for edible poultry is 3 parts per million, or about one-third of 1 percent of the concentration in the snapping turtle. The federal standard for edible fish is 2 parts per million. In soil, on a dry-weight basis, 50 parts per million is considered hazardous waste, so the turtle contained roughly fifteen times the concentration of PCBs necessary, by federal standards, to qualify its body as toxic waste. In the fall of 1987, Stone found another snapping turtle, a male, containing 3,067 parts per million in its body fat—a thousand times the concentration allowed in domestic chicken, and sixty times the minimum standard for hazardous waste. Contamination was lower in female turtles because they shed some of their own contamination by laying eggs, while the males stored more of what they ingested.

The turtle carries a special significance among the Iroquois, whose creation story describes how the world took shape on a turtle's back. To this day, many Iroquois call North America Turtle Island. "To the Mohawks, and to me, it appeared that if turtles were being sickened by pollutants, it might indicate that the very underpinnings of the earth were coming apart," said Stone.[23] Now, at Akwesasne, the turtle had assumed a new status as harbinger of death by pollution.

The contamination also threatened a struggling caviar industry in the area and shut down many fishing camps that used to draw anglers from around the northeastern United States and Canada. One fishing camp operator, Tony Barnes, was forced to leave his nets to rot in 1985. His only remaining source of livelihood, and the only use for his boats, became ferrying environmental investigators across the river. Other former fishermen got occasional work collecting water and soil samples.

The Mohawks and Stone continued to find contaminated animals at Akwesasne. In 1985, Stone, working in close cooperation with the Mohawks, found a masked shrew that somehow had managed to survive in spite of a PCB level of 11,522 parts per million in its body, the highest concentration that Stone had ever seen in a living creature, 250 times the minimum standard to qualify as hazardous waste! Using these samples, and others, Stone and the Mohawks established Akwesasne as one of the worst PCB-pollution sites in North America. Then in the fall of 1987, they found young ducks in an area once called Reynolds Cove that contained PCBs in their body fat at 300 parts per million. The ducks were too young to fly, so environmental inspectors could be sure that the PCBs had been ingested locally. Stone remarked:

> *In the fall of 1987, Mohawk biologist Ken Jock and I went to that cove, and there was a ravine with a stream coming down with a lot of white, foamy water on it, and a strong, chemical odor coming off of that water. We sampled the stream for several thousand feet up to the fence line of Reynolds. And I found that it had high levels of PCBs in the water and high levels in the sediment, for a depth of about eight inches. So they had been going in there and layering [waste] for many years.*[24]

After these initial discoveries, Stone had trouble getting others to investigate Reynolds, which used PCBs in a heat transfer system that heated pitch. According to Stone, the system experienced explosions, as well as fires, and leaked thousands of gallons of PCBs, especially when it was being refilled.

The Politics of PCB Testing

As Stone compiled data at Akwesasne, he also became a subject of investigation himself:

> *I got investigated for about six months as to whether my science was correct. Reynolds said the river was polluting them, [that] the river was putting pollutants into their plant in coolant water, and [that] they were not polluting the river. That . . . was garbage. Our data has held up. They are not only polluting the Saint Lawrence River, but the Racquette River as well. And it's going to cost tens of millions of dollars to clean the river and to control the pollutants from Reynolds.*[25]

Stone, an employee of New York's state environmental agency for twenty-two years, said that some of the delay in diagnosing the scope of the environmental disaster at Akwesasne came from the DEC itself:

> *I counted thirteen people from DEC who went to study that plant [Reynolds] looking for PCBs. No one made a diagnosis. It was about a one-and-a-half hour situation for me, taking samples to make the diagnosis. A couple thousand dollars worth of chemistry. It was mere child's play. If pollution can be missed at Reynolds, it can be missed anywhere. . . . This should have been detected and cut off at least a decade ago.*[26]

In 1986, under pressure from the state as well as the Mohawks, however, General Motors closed one of its waste sites, the industrial landfill.

The Akwesasne area was home to many trappers before construction of the Saint Lawrence Seaway devastated the trapping areas and wetlands. To speed the melting of ice in the spring, the level of the river is raised and dropped very quickly; air pockets caught in the water pulverize the ice. The swirling, crushing action of water, ice, and air also floods muskrat and beaver hutches, killing their occupants. The animals have drowned en masse, destroying the traditional trapping industry in the area. In a similar vein, logging and acid rain have destroyed many stands of the black asp that Mohawk people use to make baskets and other crafts. Chief Benedict said:

> *A lot of these things all contributed to a community that was sensitive to its natural surroundings and depending on its natural surroundings. Then, all of a sudden, the rug is pulled out from under you. Then we're expected to survive. But we don't have the tools to survive in this contemporary time.*[27]

Jim Ransom outlined his own proposal for cleanup of the General Motors waste sites:

> *The contaminated sediments need to be excavated and treated on site. The reservation soils need to be removed and treated onsite. Clean soils should be brought in to replace the soils taken out. The [General Motors] industrial landfill needs to be permanently treated by excavating and treating the contaminated soils. General Motors could be given time to find an in-place treatment technology for the landfill. An interim cap should be placed on the landfill immediately to isolate it, as it is still an active source of PCBs [leaking] into the Saint Lawrence River. Other permanent treatment technologies need to be looked at in addition to incineration and biological treatment. The risks of incineration are potentially high, and biological treatment is not proven for a site this size.*[28]

Studies also found that drinking water at Racquette Point, directly downstream from the General Motors plant, was contaminated with PCBs. The main intake for the tribe's community water system was two miles downstream from the foundry and its gaggle of waste sites. General Motors then began supplying people in the area with bottled water, including students at the Akwesasne Freedom School.

Don't Drink the Water, Don't Eat the Fish

In 1986, pregnant women were advised not to eat fish from the Saint Lawrence, historically the Mohawks' main source of protein. Until the 1950s, Akwesasne had been home to more than 100 commercial fishermen and about 120 farmers. By 1990, less than 10 commercial fishermen and 20 farmers remained. The rest had been put out of business by pollution, which has devastated the Mohawks' traditional economy, sending many of them to search for employment in casinos and cigarette stores—or off the reservation—to survive. Other people were advised to limit their consumption of Saint Lawrence fish to half a pound a week. By 1990, the state was warning residents not to eat any fish at all, if they had been caught in certain areas of the reservation.

Pollution also may be related to an increase in birth defects among Akwesasne Mohawks. Katsi Cook, a Mohawk midwife on the reservation, said that she never wanted to become an environmental activist, but the role was forced on her as she found more and more infants at Akwesasne being born with cleft palates, deafness, and intestinal abnormalities. She then began to study PCB contamination in mothers' milk at Akwesasne.

One mother at Akwesasne, Sherry Skidders, began to cry as she described how she, her husband Richard, and their seven children learned that they and their land were being poisoned. One day, a man showed up to test the water. Another day, Stone took one of their ducks to test the level of PCBs in its body fat. A little later, another environmental scientist noted that she was breast-feeding her youngest child and suggested that she have her milk tested. Although Sherry was repelled by the thought, she had her breast milk tested anyway and discovered it was laced with PCBs. She had been poisoning her own children. "Now, you have to wonder every time you take a breath," she said.[29] From the Skidders' farm, the family can see the large water tower that stands atop the General Motors plant. The setting sun sometimes throws the stark shadow of General Motors' water tower across the land that used to sustain the Skid-

Mohawk midwife Katsi Cook talks with Akwesasne Mohawk mother Karla Ransom about PCBs in the breast milk of nursing mothers on the Mohawk Reservation in Hoganburg, N.Y. Courtesy of AP/Wide World Photos.

ders and other Mohawks, a visual reminder of responsibility for the land's demise.

In place of the native economy, the government offered food stamps, just enough to buy a fatty diet of macaroni and potatoes. The few Mohawks who could afford fish were buying them from New England vendors who visited the reservation in refrigerated trucks. After the Mohawks' intake of native fish was restricted by pollution, the rate of adult-onset diabetes—a problem afflicting many Native American communities—began to soar at Akwesasne. By 1990, half the people living at Akwesasne over the age of forty were diabetic. Health problems developed hand in hand with destruction of the traditional economic base. By 1990, 80 percent of the adults on the reservation were unemployed or underemployed, and 70 percent were drawing public assistance. This was the environmental context in which gambling and smuggling developed as Akwesasne's main industries.

The Struggle over Cleanup

In early October 1989, the Environmental Protection Agency ordered the Alcoa and Reynolds plants, whose 2,500 employees form the economic backbone of Massena, to determine the degree to which their effluent (especially PCBs, organic toxins, and metals) had polluted the rivers around Akwesasne. The two companies also were instructed to design a system to clean up the river sediments containing pollutants, including possible dredging, along with other, more sophisticated alternatives. As a final step, the EPA ordered implementation of that system. The order did not give a final deadline for completion nor estimate a final cost, but the companies could be fined $25,000 a day if the EPA thought they were stalling. In early January 1991, Alcoa announced that it would take a $90 million charge against earnings to "settle its environmental obligations" at the plant in Massena.

The EPA released its Superfund cleanup plan for the General Motors foundry during March of 1990. The cleanup was estimated to cost $138 million, making the General

Motors dumps near Akwesasne the costliest Superfund clean-up job in the United States, number one on the EPA's "most-wanted" list as the United States' worst toxic dump. By 1991, the cost was scaled down to $78 million, but the General Motors dumps were still ranked as the most expensive toxic cleanup. The plan covered much of the PCB cleanup from the plant but not the industrial landfill. Cleanup of that area could cost an additional $202 million, according to the EPA report. The EPA was proposing first to dredge and clean the Saint Lawrence River, then to excavate, incinerate, or biologically treat polluted soil at the plant and some of its dump sites, as well as on some areas of Akwesasne. The EPA estimated that the whole process would take seven to ten years. General Motors' counterproposal, estimated to cost $37 million, would have encapsulated the waste sites and monitored them to assure that toxic wastes were not migrating.[30]

As the people of Akwesasne learned the scope of their poisoning, other corporate suitors appeared on the reservation with proposals for municipal waste and medical incinerators, among other things. Terry Peterson, owner of now-defunct United Scientific Associates of Nashua, New Hampshire, told the Mohawks that "They're sitting on a gold mine for themselves up there."[31] The "gold mine" he referred to was his proposal to build a large complex to gasify municipal solid waste, a medical-waste incinerator, and a huge landfill. Ron LaFrance, a Mohawk Nation Council subchief, director of Cornell University's American Indian Program, and a man widely known around Mohawk country for his love of a good meal, sarcastically told one purveyor of waste-plant-fueled dreams after the man had treated LaFrance to a very expensive lunch, "Why *do* you want to go into an Indian community? Is there some sort of compassion from your company to 'save' the Indian?"[32] The Mohawks' response to nearly all these self-described "friends of the Indian" was a swift and emphatic "no thanks!"

In December 1989, however, Mohawk Nation Council subchief Edward Gray was given permission by the Mohawk Nation Council of Chiefs to build a recycling plant for construction debris with consulting advice from a New Hampshire "waste broker." The new plan was called C & D Recycling. After heavy trucks invaded the reservation, a popular outcry caused cancellation of the plan. The Akwesasne Task Force on the Environment asked that the plant be terminated, after Warriors, with broad community support, refused to let waste-laden trucks pass onto the site of the proposed dump in February 1990.

Residents had learned that some of the trucks were hauling debris contaminated with PCBs, the very carcinogens that had done so much to debase their land and water during the previous four decades. Some of the construction waste also contained lead-based paint, asbestos, wood preservatives, and insecticides. Some of the debris caught fire even before it was unloaded. Dana Leigh, one opponent of the new recycling operation, said it was hypocritical for the Mohawks to allow dumping of potentially hazardous waste on the reservation while they criticized local industrial plants for fouling their land, water, and air.

Gray also learned that the trucking firm that was hauling debris to his recycling plant was under investigation in Massachusetts for illegal dumping. This was one reason it may have decided to buddy up with the Mohawks, who quickly unified to fight a new environmental threat, even as factional violence related to gambling continued to explode. Even in this time of profound division, both supporters and opponents of commercial gaming heeded Ward Stone's warning that as environmental laws tightened outside native lands, promoters would be seeking new dumping grounds. As had happened so often in the past, Akwesasne got it first. All Mohawks did not speak with the same voice on the pollution front, however. After the Warriors' outcry against the proposed dump, some Akwesasne residents also asked when they would raise similar protests against pollution caused by some of the casinos. Sewage seepage at Tony Vegas International was mentioned most often.

As the people of Akwesasne turned thumbs down on a stream of new disposal proposals, the Environmental Protection Agency in March 1991 filed complaints seeking $35.4

million in fines not only from General Motors but also against the two largest U.S. waste management companies. Both had helped General Motors dispose of its PCB-laden wastes on and near the reservation. By making haulers of toxic waste liable for their cargo, the EPA was attempting to force them to police their loads more strictly. This was the first time that the EPA had extended liability to haulers of toxic wastes.

"We're insisting they look beyond just the truck that appears on their doorstep, so they don't become an active party in circumventing the law," Michael J. Walker, EPA associate counsel for toxic substances, said.[33] Environmental spokesmen for the two hauling companies, Browning-Ferris Industries and Waste Management, complained that the EPA placed an unfair burden on them. "They're asking a disposal company to become an arm of law enforcement," said Peter Tarnawskyj, manager of environmental compliance at Niagara Falls-based Browning-Ferris.[34]

The EPA's case contended that both hauling companies illegally diluted PCBs dumped near the General Motors foundry, a move that the auto maker had believed would excuse it from having to incinerate, rather than bury, its effluent. Incineration is environmentally more sound but up to ten times more expensive than the burial of wastes. The EPA contended that at least 31,000 tons of PCB-contaminated waste was diluted in order to avoid the standard requiring incineration. The two hauling companies said that by the time the waste in question arrived at their dumps it was solid, not liquid. This is one way to get around the indictment that applies only to liquid wastes. General Motors reduced the case to a dispute over semantics: "a disagreement over sampling and analysis." The EPA was seeking $14.2 million from General Motors, the same amount from Browning-Ferris, and $7.1 million from Waste Management.

The Hard Road to Recovery

In August 1990, Ward Stone said that enforcing agencies were dealing with environmental problems at Akwesasne too slowly, as if they were engaging the offending corporations in a sort of bureaucratic pantomime.

> *As I speak, Alcoa is still putting PCBs into the Grasse River. And they are going into the nearby Saint Lawrence into Indian waters adjacent to Cornwall Island, a main part of the fishing and hunting area of Akwesasne. . . . Reynolds Metals is heavily hitting the [Saint Lawrence] River with PCBs, fluorides, aluminum, a wide variety of pollutants right now. It's ongoing. The water is still being degraded.*
>
> *When I arrived in June 1985, the United States Environmental Protection Agency was involved at General Motors. . . . We still have a pollution problem more than five years later. The river is not cleaned up. [The EPA] didn't identify Reynolds. It was pathology DEC that identified that, and the Mohawks. And so, the EPA is involved, but exceedingly slowly. And it's quite questionable whether or not their standards of cleanup will be sufficient to bring the river back—we think that it won't—to a place where the Mohawks will once again be able to utilize the fish and wildlife for food.*[35]

By December 20, 1990, General Motors officials were complaining they could not meet the 1 part per million standard for PCBs in river sediment, nor even the 10 parts per million required by the EPA on the plant grounds itself. "It's going to be hard for us to agree to a standard we don't think is technically possible," said David L. Lippert, media manager for General Motors' automotive components group in Detroit.[36] The EPA estimated that its cleanup plan for the foundry would cost $78 million and would include removal of soil contaminated with PCBs from the reservation, dredging and treatment of contaminated sediments from the riverbeds of the Saint Lawrence and Racquette Point, removal of polluted soils from two General Motors disposal sites, and treatment of waste water before it was released into the Saint Lawrence River. The company also threatened to close its foundry if the EPA forced it to close down and clean up its active waste lagoons. Additionally, General Motors argued that to dredge the river would stir up more PCB residue than would be released if the area were simply left alone. For the seventh year since the General Motors site had been placed on the EPA Superfund list, the company and the government continued to dicker over just how to clean up this corner of Mohawk country. As they did, the PCBs continued to spread. Such was the nature of natural life, and death, as 1991 opened in the land of the toxic turtle.

Six months later, in July 1991, Alcoa suddenly agreed to pay $7.5 million in civil and criminal penalties in connection with the dumping of PCBs and other pollutants at its Massena plant. The $3.75 million criminal penalty alone was the largest ever assessed in U.S. history for a hazardous-waste violation. After the company pled guilty to state pollution charges, its chairman, Paul O'Neill, said: "Alcoa has a clear environmental policy which was not followed in this instance."[37] More bluntly, the company had continued to dump PCBs and other hazardous wastes long after they became illegal. A state investigation had found that during 1989 the company had excavated thirty-three railroad carloads of PCB-contaminated soil while it prepared to install a drainage system. The soil was left piled for more than ninety days, after which some of it was hauled away by train. The company also pleaded guilty to illegally dumping caustic and acidic waste down manholes at its plant in Massena. Alcoa pleaded guilty to four very expensive misdemeanors. The $3.75 million in additional civil penalties were levied because the company failed to report (or underreported) unauthorized discharges of hazardous wastes on approximately 2,000 occasions since 1985.

Alcoa's guilty plea was hailed as an environmental victory. After the euphoria faded, many at Akwesasne remembered that it was only one small step in the long road to restoring an environment that could once again sustain life in their homeland. The size of the fines merely indicated how great the damage had been and continues to be. Mark Narsisian, who lives in a small cabin near the General Motors foundry, said, "People have the false sense that money will even things out. If I can't plant in the ground anymore, what good is it? If I plant my coins in the ground, [will] corn grow?"[38] Narsisian's comments underlie a timeless dilemma for American Indians who have exchanged their land and resources for money: without land and a healthy environment, money is worthless.

The people at Akwesasne disagreed vehemently on whether their homeland should be opened to gambling, but nearly everyone living there deplores the environmental degradation of the area. Loran Thompson, a spokesman for the Warriors said that he had had to plow under his garden because pollution from the General Motors foundry had poisoned the soil. Moreover, he described a lagoon near the Saint Lawrence River where he remembered that, in his youth, one could practically walk on the back of the fish. Now, there are no fish, he said, and the lagoon is a backwash of thick, black sludge: "The family lived off that pond. Muskrat, ducks, geese, fish. We used to swim there, too. I get so depressed just to think about it. . . . You should have seen it here when I was a kid—beautiful, clean, crystal-clear water. We used to come here for our drinking water."[39] Now, said Thompson, who lives an eighth of a mile from one of General Motors' dumps,

> *I have a hard time explaining to people why I live here. Some days you can hardly breathe, from the stryene that comes out of their [General Motors'] smokestack. It's all gone now. Progress took it all away. Progress? We go backwards.[40] My father raised us with gardens and animals. That's what I was going to do. I had two beautiful gardens. I was raising pigs; [I] was going to get horses and cows. . . . I got rid of the pigs. I got rid of the gardens. People are afraid to start anything here.[41]*

Thompson's wife died of cancer a few years ago, just as he was finding that his dream of having a farm had died because of the PCB-laced soil. Thompson's family was the fourth generation to farm land now unsuitable for raising any kind of food. They cannot raise crops on it, hunt animals that fed on it, nor fish from water bordering it without poisoning themselves. Despite this, Thompson says he will never move. By his reasoning, he and the rest of the Mohawks were on this land first, before industry spoiled it. "I've lived here all my life," said Thompson, "and I'm going to stay here, even if it kills me."[42]

The environmental crisis at Akwesasne had become so acute by mid-1990 that in the midst of the violence over gambling, Mohawk leaders called a press conference to remind people that the biggest problem they faced was environmental pollution, not the gambling feud. The press conference was convened at New York's Five Rivers wildlife preserve, in a joint presentation with Greenpeace, the Sierra Club, New York Public Interest Research Group, and other environmental-advocacy groups.

"If we are to heal the divisions and the crisis at Akwesasne, we first must deal with the environment," elected chief Harold Tarbell said May 30, three days before his opposition to gambling cost him his seat on the St. Regis Tribal Council.[43] Ward Stone said that General Motors, Reynolds, and Alcoa had polluted the area for decades. "The PCBs are flowing out of the GM plant right now," he said, contradicting company assertions that direct pollution had stopped.[44]

We can't try to meet the challenges with the meager resources we have, said Henry Lickers, a Seneca who is employed by the Mohawk Council at Akwesasne and who has been a mentor to today's younger environmentalists at Akwesasne. Lickers has also been a leader in the fight against fluoride emissions from the Reynolds plant. "The next ten years will be a cleanup time for us, even without the money,"[45] said Lickers.

The destruction of Akwesasne's environment is credited by Lickers with being the catalyst that spawned the Mohawks' deadly battle over high-stakes gambling and smuggling. "A desperation sets in when year after year you see the decimation of the philosophical center of your society," he said.[46] "It's heinous," he added. "You have a people whose philosophy is intrinsically linked to nature, and they can't use the environment. This is a crime against the whole community, a crime against humanity."[47] Many of gambling's most ardent supporters assert that the contamination of Akwesasne made gaming necessary for economic survival, since people there can no longer live off the land. The destruction of a natural world that once fed, housed, and clothed the Mohawks has made it impossible for them to make a living in their traditional manner.

Maurice Hinchey, chairman of the New York Assembly's Environmental Conservation Committee, said that he would continue to press in Albany for action on Akwesasne's environmental crisis. He said that there are few places where so many destructive forces have had as much impact as at Akwesasne. The Mohawks are not alone, however. Increasingly, restrictive environmental regulations enacted by states and cities are bringing polluters to native reservations. "Indian tribes across America are grappling with some of the worst of its pollution: uranium tailings, chemical lagoons, and illegal dumps. Nowhere has it been more troublesome than at . . . Akwesasne," wrote one observer.[48]

Notes

1. Rupert Tomsho, "Dumping Grounds: Indian Tribes Contend with Some of the Worst of America's Pollution," *Wall Street Journal,* November 29, 1990, A-1, A-6.
2. Associated Press, in the Syracuse *Herald-American,* July 15, 1990.
3. Lloyd Benedict, New York State Assembly Hearings, *Crisis at Akwesasne,* Day I (Ft. Covington, New York), July 24, 1990, transcript 289-92.
4. Massena *Observer,* December 8, 1981; cited in Cornell University American Indian Program, "Significant Dates, Events, and Findings in the Akwesasne-General Motors Environmental Situation," n.d., 5. Transcript in Cornell AIP files.
5. Ibid.
6. Syracuse *Post-Standard,* December 21, 1981.
7. Cornwall *Standard-Freeholder,* January 7, 1982.
8. Watertown *Daily Times,* January 12, 1982.

9. Syracuse *Post-Standard*, January 19, 1982.

10. Massena *Observer*, July 21, 1983.

11. *Advance News* (Ogdensburg, New York), July 17, 1983.

12. Massena *Observer*, August 18, 1983.

13. Ibid.

14. Watertown *Daily Times*, November 28, 1983. The memo was dated February 2, 1982.

15. Ibid.

16. *Indian Time*, July 27, 1983.

17. Ibid.

18. October 10, 1984, WSLU-FM, public radio at St. Lawrence University, Canton, New York, broadcast report. Transcript in Cornell AIP files.

19. Ibid.

20. Ibid.

21. Ibid.

22. Tomsho, "Dumping Grounds," *Wall Street Journal*, November 29, 1990.

23. Ward Stone, New York State Assembly Hearings, *Crisis at Akwesasne*, Day II (Albany, New York), August 2, 1990, transcript, 295.

24. Ibid., 288.

25. Ibid., 289.

26. Ibid.

27. Lloyd Benedict, New York State Assembly Hearings, *Crisis at Akwesasne*, Day I, transcript, 289.

28. Jim Ransom, letter to the editor. Massena *Courier-Observer*, November 3, 1990.

29. Jeff Jones, "A Nation Divided," *Metroland*, June 7–13, 1990, 1.

30. The General Motors ruling was mentioned in the context of a hearing being held December 13 in Saratoga Springs, New York, to determine whether General Electric would be forced to spend $270 million cleaning up PCBs along the Hudson River north of Albany, near Fort Edward. General Electric claimed that the cleanup was unnecessary because a specialized group of microorganisms in the riverbed could degrade the PCBs. This form of "bioremediation," said to be under development by General Electric and biotechnology concerns, employs cylinders six feet across and sixteen feet long, which are sunk into river bottoms containing some of the 209 varieties of PCBs. The cylinders release bacteria related to those commonly used in sewage-treatment plants and to clean up oil spills. The *Journal* also reported that the hearing would have a bearing on PCB cleanups in rivers and streams of upstate New York by Reynolds Metals Company and Aluminum Company of America. While General Electric said it is spending $50 million on bioremediation technology, some environ-

mental advocates believe that the research is a public-relations stunt designed to get the company out from under more costly dredging to clean up PBC-laden river bottoms.

31. *Wall Street Journal,* November 29, 1990.

32. Interview, Ron LaFrance with Bruce E. Johansen, Akwesasne, August 4, 1991.

33. Jeff Bailey, "EPA Complaint against Waste Haulers May Widen Responsibility in Disposal," *Wall Street Journal,* April 8, 1991, A-6.

34. Ibid.

35. Ward Stone, New York State Assembly Hearings, *Crisis at Akwesasne,* Day II, transcript, 288.

36. Syracuse *Post-Standard,* December 20, 1990.

37. "Alcoa to Pay $7.5 Million Fine for Hazardous Waste Violation," Rochester *Democrat and Chronicle,* July 12, 1991, B-6.

38. Tomsho, "Dumping Grounds," *Wall Street Journal,* November 29, 1990.

39. Mane Villan, "Man Who Remembers Good Days to Remain," Syracuse *Herald-American,* June 30, 1991.

40. Ibid.

41. Ibid.

42. Ibid.

43. "Mohawks Seek Help on Environment," Syracuse *Post-Standard,* May 31, 1990.

44. Ward Stone, New York State Assembly GHearings, *Crisis at Akwesasne,* Day II, transcript, 288.

45. "Mohawks Seek Help on Environment," Syracuse *Post-Standard,* May 31, 1990.

46. Michael Hill, "Pollution Ravages St. Regis Reservation," Associated Press, in Syracuse *Herald-American,* July 15, 1990.

47. Quoted in John E. Milich, "Contaminant Cove: Where Polluters Defile Mohawk Land, *The Progressive* (January 1989): 25.

48. Tomsho, "Dumping Grounds."

This horse died from drinking water contaminated by the nuclear spill into the Rio Puerco, 1979. Photograph by Dan Budnick © 1979.

Chapter Eight

The High Cost of Uranium

When Native Americans in the western United States were as-signed reservations in the late nineteenth century, many were sent to land thought nearly worthless for mining or agricul-ture. The year 1871, when treaty-making stopped, was a time before sophisticated irrigation and before dry-land farming techniques had been developed. Industrialization was only beginning to transform the cities of the eastern seaboard, and the demand for oil, gas, and even coal was trivial by pre-sent-day standards. And in 1871, Madame Marie Curie had not yet isolated radium. Before 1900, there was little interest in locating or mining uranium, which later became the dri-ving energy force of the nuclear age.

In a century and a quarter, the circumstances of industri-alization and technological change have made many of these treaty-guaranteed lands very valuable, in large part because under their often barren surface lies a significant share of the country's remaining fossil fuel and uranium resources.

Nationwide, the Indians' greatest mineral wealth is prob-ably in uranium. According to a Federal Trade Commission (FTC) Report of October 1975, an estimated 16 percent of the United States' uranium reserves that were recoverable at market prices were on reservation lands; this was about two-thirds of the uranium on land under the legal jurisdic-tion of the U.S. government. There were almost four hundred uranium leases on these lands, according to the FTC, and between 1 million and 2 million tons of uranium ore a year, about 20 percent of the national total, was being mined on reservation land.

Moreover, if to the uranium reserves on reservation land are added those estimated on land guaranteed to Indian nations by treaty, the Indians' share of uranium reserves within the United States rises to nearly 60 percent; the Coun-cil of Energy Resource Tribes places the figure at 75 percent

to 80 percent. About two-thirds of the 150 million acres guaranteed to Indians by treaty has been alienated from them—
by allotment, other means of sale, or by seizure without compensation. Some of these areas, notably the Black Hills of
South Dakota, underwent a uranium mining boom during
the 1970s, even though legal title to the land is still clouded.
Sioux leaders have refused to settle with the United States for
the land, despite a price tag that had grown to $351 million
principal and interest by 1993. Assertion of treaty claims to
the Black Hills, as well as to other uranium-rich treaty lands,
has forged strong links in the West among groups supporting
treaty rights and those opposing nuclear power and weapons
development. Lakota Indian activists have worked with
numerous antinuclear groups to help them "stop the poison
at the source."

The Black Hills Uranium Rush

Black Elk, a Lakota (Sioux) medicine man, was eleven years
old during the summer of 1874 when, by his account (published in *Black Elk Speaks*, an expedition under Gen. George
Armstrong Custer invaded the *Paha Sapa* ("hills that are
black"), the holy land of the Lakota. The Black Hills had
been guaranteed to the Lakota "in perpetuity" by the Fort
Laramie Treaty of 1868. Custer's expedition was on a geological mission, not a military one. Custer was looking for gold,
and he found it. In his wake, several thousand gold seekers
poured into the sacred Black Hills, ignoring the treaty.

In the words of Black Elk, the Lakotas and Cheyennes
"painted their faces black"—went to war—to regain the Black
Hills. The result was Custer's Last Stand, one of the best-
remembered debacles in U.S. military history, during which
an overconfident Custer led his march-weary men and horses
into a Lakota and Cheyenne encampment that was twice the
size his scouts had estimated. The Black Hills never were
ceded by treaty; the Lakotas have never accepted the United
States' offer of $17.5 million (plus roughly $330 million
interest) for their land. Mt. Rushmore still stands on Lakota

land, surrounded by gaudy tourist traps, including glittering new gambling establishments. Even actor and director Kevin Costner, of *Dances with Wolves*, has proposed building an eighty-five-acre resort and casino there, without asking the Lakota people. According to the 1868 Fort Lar-amie Treaty, three-quarters of the adult members of the signatory tribes must accept any settlement.

In January 1977, another group of government employees followed General Custer's footsteps into the Black Hills and emerged from their geological errand bearing news of urani-um-bearing Precambrian rock formations near Nemo, southwest of Rapid City. The news ignited another rush for claims, which again ignored the question of Lakota title. Between February 15 and April 15, 1977, more than 1,200 location certificates were filed in the area, many of them by large companies such as Johns-Manville, American Copper & Nickel, and Homestake Mining. Homestake Mining had grown rich on the Custer strike, earning profits which later helped to buy William Randolph Hearst a newspaper empire.

Other large companies had joined the uranium rush elsewhere in the Black Hills. The Tennessee Valley Authority (TVA), looking to fuel the seventeen nuclear power plants for which it had licenses, acquired leases on 65,000 Black Hills acres and on 35,000 more acres just west of the Wyoming border. TVA officials said that two mining methods were being considered: stripmining and underground mining in which a chemical solution would be injected into the ground to dissolve the uranium before a radium-rich slush is drawn to the surface. Because the Black Hills is a watershed for much of western South Dakota, native people, as well as local ranchers and farmers, objected because such solution mining could pollute the underground water on which ranchers and farmers rely.

Uranium Mining and the American Indian Movement

The uranium rush in the Black Hills began at the same time that the American Indian Movement (AIM) became the target of an FBI campaign along COINTELPRO lines on and near the Pine Ridge Reservation. The FBI's attention had been drawn to the area by the occupation of Wounded Knee in 1973. Following the shooting deaths of two FBI agents on the reservation, the FBI made Pine Ridge its national focus in mid-1975. The FBI's "Operation Resmurs" (reservation murders) climaxed in 1977 with the conviction in the Fargo, North Dakota, Federal District Court of Leonard Peltier, an AIM activist, for killing the two FBI agents. Many AIM leaders suggested that mineral resources, and especially uranium, were a major reason why so much attention had been paid to their activities during the mid-1970s. Peltier wrote:

> *In the late 19th century, land was stolen for economic reasons. We were left with what was believed to be worthless land. Still, we managed to live and defy the wish to exterminate us. Today, what was once called worthless land suddenly becomes valuable as the technology of white society advances. . . . [That society] would now like to push us off our reservations because beneath the barren land lie valuable mineral resources.*[1]

Uranium Mining on Navajo Land

About half the recoverable uranium within the United States lies in New Mexico—and about half of that is on the Navajo Reservation. As the Indian tribes have in South Dakota, many Navajos have come to oppose the mining, joining forces with non-Indians who regard nuclear power plants and arms proliferation as a twofold menace.

Uranium has been mined on Navajo land since the late 1940s; the Indians dug the ore that started the United States' stockpile of nuclear weapons. For thirty years after the first atomic explosions in New Mexico, uranium was mined much like any other mineral. More than 99 percent of the product of the mines was waste, cast aside as tailings near mine sites after the uranium had been extracted. One of the mesa-like waste piles grew to be a mile long and seventy feet high. On

Navajos at the Kerr-McGee mine removed uranium ore from the earth much as if it were coal in this photograph, taken in 1953. Courtesy of AP/Wide World Photos.

windy days, dust from the tailings blew into local communities, filling the air and settling on the water supplies. The Atomic Energy Commission assured worried local residents that the dust was harmless.

In February 1978, however, the Department of Energy released a Nuclear Waste Management Task Force report that said that people living near the tailings ran twice the risk of lung cancer than the general population. The *Navajo Times* carried reports of a Public Health Service study asserting that one in six uranium miners had died, or would die prematurely, of lung cancer. For some, the news came too late. Esther Keeswood, a member of the Coalition for Navajo Liberation from Shiprock, New Mexico, a reservation city near tailings piles, said in 1978 that the Coalition for Navajo Liberation had documented the deaths of at least fifty residents (including uranium miners) from lung cancer and related diseases.[2]

The Kerr-McGee Company, the first corporation to mine uranium on Navaio Nation lands (beginning in 1948) found the reservation location extremely lucrative—there were no taxes at the time, and labor was cheap. There were no health, safety, or pollution regulations, and few other jobs for the many Navajos recently home from service in World War II. The first uranium miners in the area, almost all of them Navajos, remember being sent into shallow tunnels within minutes after blasting. They loaded the radioactive ore into wheelbarrows and emerged from the mines spitting black mucus from the dust and coughing so hard it gave many of them headaches, according to Tom Barry, energy writer for the *Navajo Times*, who interviewed the miners. Such mining practices exposed the Navajos who worked for Kerr-McGee to between one hundred and one thousand times the limit later considered safe for exposure to radon gas. Officials for the Public Health Service have estimated these levels of exposure; no one was monitoring the Navajo miners' health in the late 1940s.

Thirty years after mining began, an increasing number of deaths from lung cancer made evident the fact that Kerr-McGee had considered miners' lives as cheaply as their labor.

As Navajo miners continued to die, children who played in water that had flowed over or through abandoned mines and tailing piles came home with burning sores.

Even *if* the tailings were to be buried—a staggering task—radioactive pollution could leak into the surrounding water table. A 1976 Environmental Protection Agency report found radioactive contamination of drinking water on the Navajo Reservation in the Grants, New Mexico, area near a uranium mining and milling facility. Doris Bunting of Citizens Against Nuclear Threats, a predominately white group that joined with The Coalition for Navajo Liberation (CNL) and the National Indian Youth Council to oppose uranium mining, supplied data indicating that radium-bearing sediments had spread into the Colorado River basin, from which water is drawn for much of the Southwest. Through the opposition to uranium mining in the area, among Indians and non-Indians alike, runs a deep concern for the long-term poisoning of land, air, and water by low-level radiation. It has produced demands from Indian and white groups for a moratorium on all uranium mining, exploration, and milling until the issues of untreated radioactive tailings and other waste-disposal problems are faced and solved.

The threat of death which haunted the Navajos came at what company public-relations specialists might have deemed an inappropriate time; the same rush for uranium that had filled the Black Hills with speculators was coming to the Southwest, as arms stockpiling and the anticipated needs of nuclear power plants drove up demand, and the price, for the mineral. By late 1978, more than 700,000 acres of Indian land were under lease for uranium exploration and development in an area centering on Shiprock and Crownpoint, New Mexico, both on the Navajo Reservation. Atlantic Richfield, Continental Oil, Exxon, Humble Oil, Homestake Mining, Kerr-McGee, Mobil Oil, Pioneer Nuclear, and United Nuclear were among the companies exploring, planning to mine, or already extracting ore.[3] During the 1980s the mining frenzy subsided somewhat as recession and a slowing of the nuclear arms race reduced demand. Some ore was still being mined, but most of it lay in the ground, waiting for the next upward spike in the market.

As a result of mining for uranium and other materials, the U.S. Geological Survey predicted that the water table at Crownpoint would drop a thousand feet and that it would return to present levels thirty to fifty years after the mining ceased. Much of what water remained could be polluted by uranium residue, the report indicated.[4]

Local residents rose in anger and found themselves neatly ambushed by the white man's law. The Indians owned the surface rights; the mineral rights in the area are owned by private companies such as the Santa Fe Railroad. "If the water supply is depleted, then this [Crownpoint] will become a ghost town," said Joe Gmusea, a Navajo attorney. "The only people left will be the ones who come to work in the mines."[5] John Redhouse, associate director of the Albuquerque-based National Indian Youth Council, said that the uranium boom is "an issue of spiritual and physical genocide."[6] "We are not isolated in our struggle against uranium development," Redhouse said. "Many Indian people are now supporting the struggles of the Australian Aborigines and the Black indigenous peoples of Namibia [Southwest Africa] against similar uranium developments. We have recognized that we are facing the same international beast."[7]

The uranium boom has put the residents of Crownpoint in a position not unlike that faced by their ancestors who were driven up the sides of Canyon de Chelly not far away, as cavalry troops circled below. The choice offered the Indians then, as now, was to assimilate—accommodate the white man's wishes—or starve. The Indian opposition to uranium mining is an attempt to get off this modern-day mesa—and to do it by reaching out to others who are concerned more with the needs of future generations than with the immediate price tags of the international supermarket.

With the growing energy development in the Rocky Mountains area (uranium included) has spread a recognition that parts of the region, including areas other than Indian reservations, are slated for devastation to provide power to the energy consumers of the East and West coasts, and profits to the companies that stoke that demand for energy. Again, as a century ago, people who stand to lose their livelihoods to invaders are "painting their faces black." The historic twist is that, while a century ago Custer had Indian scouts, this time the Indians' allies are white. Winona La Duke, of the International Indian Treaty Council, may have been speaking for more people than Indians when, at an antinuclear demonstration near Grants, New Mexico, she said: "Indian people refuse to become the silent martyrs of the nuclear industry. We stand fighting in our homelands for a future free of the threat of genocide for our children."[8]

The Largest Nuclear Accident in the United States

Thanks to its location between the nation's media capital, New York City, and its political capital, Washington, D.C., as well as the timing of the opening of the movie *The China Syndrome*, Three Mile Island was America's best-publicized nuclear accident. However, it was not the largest such accident.

The biggest expulsion of radioactive material in the United States occurred on July 16, 1978, at 5 A.M. on the Navajo Reservation, less than twelve hours after President Carter had proposed plans to use more nuclear power and fossil fuels. On that morning, more than 1,100 tons of uranium mining wastes—tailings—gushed through a mud-packed dam near Church Rock, New Mexico. With the tailings, 100 million gallons of radioactive water gushed through the dam before the crack was repaired.

By 8 A.M., radioactivity was monitored in Gallup, New Mexico, nearly fifty miles away. The contaminated river, the Rio Puerco, showed 6,000 times the allowable standard of radioactivity below the broken dam shortly after the breach was repaired, according to the Nuclear Regulatory Commission. The few newspaper stories about the spill outside of the immediate area noted that the region was "sparsely populated" and that the spill "poses no immediate health hazard."[9]

While no one in New York or Washington, D.C., had much to worry about, the Navajo and white residents of the area did. The area is high desert, and the Rio Puerco is a major source of water.

The Los Angeles *Times* sent a reporter, Sandra Blakeslee, to the area a month after the spill occurred. By that time, United Nuclear Corporation, which owns the dam, had cleaned up only 50 of the 1,100 tons of spilled waste. Workers were using pails and shovels because heavy machinery could not negotiate the steep terrain around the Rio Puerco.

Along the river, officials issued press releases telling people not to drink the water, but they had a few problems: many of the Navajo residents could not read English and had no electricity to power television sets and radios while other consumers of the water—cattle—don't read.

John Bartlitt, of New Mexico Citizens for Clean Air and Water, expressed perplexity over the lack of attention paid to the accident. About 80 percent of the radioactivity in uranium ore remains in the tailings, he said. "The radioactivity which remains in a pile of tailings after 600 years is greater than that remaining in [nuclear] power-plant water after 600 years," Bartlitt said.[10]

This enormous spill of nuclear waste into the area's water supply was but one incident in a distinctly nuclear way of life on Navajo lands. The nuclear-mining legacy of thirty years blows through the outlying districts of Shiprock, New Mexico, the Navajos' largest city, on windy days. The hot, dry winds shave radioactive dust from the tops and sides of large tailings piles around the city. One of them is seventy feet high and a mile long. Until the mid-1970s, the Atomic Energy Commission assured the Navajos of Shiprock that the tailings were harmless.

In early 1978, however, the Department of Energy released a Nuclear Waste Management Task Force report which said that persons living near the tailings piles had twice the expected rate of lung cancer. By 1978, the Navajos were beginning to trace the roots of a lung cancer epidemic which had perplexed many of them, since the disease was very rare among Navajos before World War II. In addition to exposure from the tailings piles, many of the miners who started America's nuclear stockpile had died of lung cancer.

*Cleanup of a spill of a nuclear uranium waste spill along the Rio Puerco,
on the Navajo Nation, 1979. Photograph by Dan Budnick © 1979.*

Although health and safety measures have improved in the mines since the 1950s, due to governmental and popular pressure, present practices still expose workers to unhealthy amounts of radon. As for Kerr-McGee, in whose mines many of the Navajos worked, a company statement maintained as late as mid-1979 that uranium-related deaths among miners were mere allegations.

Lung cancer is believed to result from inhalation of radon gas, a by-product of uranium's decay into radium. Tom Barry, in an investigative series for the *Navajo Times*, found documentation that miners who worked for Kerr- Mc-Gee during the 1940s were exposed to between one hundred and one thousand times the dosage of radon now considered safe by the federal government. Harris Charley, who worked in the mines for fifteen years, told a U. S. Senate hearing in 1979, "We were treated like dogs. There was no ventilation in the mines." Pearl Nakai, daughter of a deceased miner, told the same hearing that "No one ever told us about the dangers of uranium."[11] The Senate hearings were convened by Sen. Pete Domenici, New Mexico Repub-lican, who is seeking compensation for disabled uranium miners and for the families of the deceased. "The miners who extracted uranium from the Colorado Plateau are paying the price today for the inadequate health and safety standards that were then in force," Domenici told the hearing, held at a Holiday Inn near the uranium boomtown of Grants, New Mexico.

The 1979 Senate hearings were part of a proposal to compensate the miners for what investigators called deliberate negligence. Radioactivity in uranium mines was linked to lung cancer by tests in Europe by 1930. Scientific evidence linking radon gas to radioactive illness existed after 1949, but measures to ventilate the Navajo mines were never taken, as the government pressured Kerr-McGee and other producers to increase the amount of uranium they were mining. The Public Health Service (PHS) recommended ventilation in 1952, but the Atomic Energy Commission said it bore no responsibility for the mines, despite the fact that it bought more than 3 million pounds of uranium from them in 1954 alone.[12] The PHS monitored the health of more than 4,000

Tony Light, uranium dog hole mine shaft at Oak Spring, Arizona. The early uranium mines allowed no ventilation. Miners handled radioactive rock and breathed air laced with radon. Photograph by Dan Budnick © 1979.

*George Tutt, a retired Navajo uranium miner, points to sev-
eral uranium mines near Red Valley, on the Navajo Reservation, which were abandoned by 1993. Courtesy of
AP/Wide World Photos.*

miners between 1954 and 1960 without telling them of the threat to their health.

Dr. Joseph Wagoner, special assistant for occupational carcinogens at the Occupational Safety and Health Administration, a federal agency, said that of 3,500 persons who mined uranium in New Mexico, about 200 had died of cancer by the late 1970s. In an average population of 3,500 persons, 40 such deaths could be expected. The 160 extra deaths were not the measure of ignorance, he said. Published data regarding the dangers of radon was widely available to scientists in the 1950s, according to Wagoner. But health and safety precautions in the mines were not cost-effective for the companies, he said. "Thirty years from now we'll have the hidden legacy of the whole thing," Wagoner told Molly Ivins of the *New York Times.*

Bills that would compensate the miners were introduced, discussed, and died in Congress for a dozen years. By 1990, the death toll among former miners had risen to 450 and was still rising.[13] Relatives of the dead recalled how the miners had eaten their lunches in the mines, washing them down with radioactive water, never having been told that it was dangerous. Many of the men did not even speak English. And the Navajo language contains no indigenous word for "radio-activity."

In 1990, after years of failed attempts, the U.S. Congress passed a compensation for Navajo uranium miners. By the early 1990s, about 1,100 Navajo miners or members of their families had applied for compensation related to uranium exposure. The bureaucracy had approved 328 cases, denied 121, and withheld action on 663, an approval rate which Rep. George Miller, chairman of the House Natural Resources Committee, characterized as "significantly lower than in other cases of radiation compensation."[14] Representative Miller said that awards of compensation were being delayed by "a burdensome application system developed by the Department of Justice."[15]

Miller's committee was investigating not only the Navajo death toll from radiation poisoning but many other reports that indigenous peoples were willfully and recklessly exposed to radiation during the Cold War. The geographic range of purported radiation poisonings spans half the globe—from the Navajos in the Southwest United States, to Alaskan natives whose lives were endangered when atomic waste products from Nevada were secretly buried near their villages, to residents of the Marshall Islands in the South Pacific, an area in which the United States tested atomic and hydrogen bombs in the atmosphere between 1946 and 1958. As investigations deepened, it appeared that the treatment of Navajos was not the exception but only one example of a deadly pattern of reckless disregard for indigenous life—human and otherwise—in colonized places.

Notes

1. Leonard Peltier, statement at extradition hearing, Vancouver, B.C., May 13, 1976. Mimeographed.
2. *Navajo Times*, June 22, 1978; Bruce E. Johansen, "The Great Uranium Rush," *Baltimore Sun*, May 13, 1979, K-1.
3. Tom Barry and Beth Wood, "Uranium on the Checkerboard: Crisis at Checkpoint," *American Indian Journal* (June 1978): 10.
4. *Navajo Times*, June 15, 1978.
5. Ibid.
6. *Navajo Times*, June 22, 1978.
7. *Navajo Times*, June 29, 1978.
8. Bruce E. Johansen, "Uranium Rush in the Black Hills, *The Nation*, April 14, 1979, 396.
9. Bruce E. Johansen, "Native American's Future: Half-Life in the Tailings?," University of Washington *Daily*, October 17, 1979, 14.
10. Ibid.
11. University of Washington *Daily*, October 17, 1979, 14.
12. James N. Baker, "Keeping a Deadly Secret: The Feds Knew the Mines Were Radioactive," *Newsweek*, June 18, 1990, 20.
13. Ibid.
14. Bunty Anquoe, "House Begins Investigating Possible Radiation Exposure," *Indian Country Today*, June 9, 1993, A-8.
15. Ibid.

Native Americans march across the George Washington Bridge into New York City November 11, 1980. They had marched from San Francisco to place the mining of uranium, the sterilization of Native American women, and problems with nuclear power on the agenda of the United Nations. Courtesy of UPI/Bettmann.

Larry Anderson of the American Indian Movement points to sign saying radiation area at Church Rock Dam, Arizona. Photograph by © Dan Budnick.

Chapter Nine

Native American
Environmental Testimonies:
The Last Frontiers of Ecocide

In the late twentieth century, technological society is moving into the last "wild" areas of the world. In eastern Canada, the sweeping forests and undulating grasslands bordering James Bay are targeted for development of the world's largest hydroelectric project, while in southern Mexico, the tendrils of industrial capitalism are reaching the Lacandon Mayas, one of very few peoples on the continent who had been able to evade a way of life they see as undesirable. In the Arctic, "civilization" has come to the bands of Inuits (Eskimos) and other hunting peoples in the form of thinning herds and fish containing residues of PCBs and other industrial chemicals, which are being carried thousands of miles from their sources.

The Largest Earth-moving Project in History

Hydro-Quebec's "James Bay II" proposes to dam eight major rivers that flow into James Bay in northern Quebec at a cost of up to $170 billion to provide electricity for urban Canada and several states in the northeastern United States. The area is virtually unknown to most Euro-Americans but has been home for thousands of years to roughly ten thousand Crees, many of whom would be forced from their homelands by flooding and toxic contamination. The Crees maintain that the second phase of the project (James Bay II) should be stopped, based on hardships they have encountered from its first phase, completed in 1985 at a cost of $20 billion.

James Bay I dammed or diverted five large rivers and flooded four thousand square miles of forest. Rotting vegeta-

A small section of the massive James Bay hydro-electric complex in northern Quebec. Courtesy of UPI/ Bettmann.

tion in the area had released about 184 million tons of carbon dioxide and methane gas into the atmosphere by 1990,
possibly accelerating global warming around the world,
meanwhile saddling Quebec electric rate payers with a debt
of $3,500 per person.[1] Rotting vegetation also was causing an
acceleration in microbial activity converting elemental mercury in submerged glacial rock to toxic methyl mercury,
which was rapidly diffusing through the food chain. Methyl
mercury poisoning can cause loss of vision, numbness of
limbs, uncontrollable shaking, and chronic neurological disease. By 1990, some Cree elders had twenty times the level of
methyl mercury in their bodies that the World Health
Organization considers safe. A 1984 survey of people residing
in Chisasibi showed that 64 percent of its people had elevated levels of this toxin in their bodies. The Quebec government responded to these findings by telling the Crees not to
eat fish, one of their main sources of protein, just as the
Mohawks of Akwesasne had been told to quit eating fish from
the rivers of their polluted homeland.[2]

The human problems brought on by James Bay I are not
limited to the flooding of forest land and increasing discharge
of toxins. The large-scale construction in the area (including
road building) brought in large numbers of non-Indians and
is linked by Cree leaders with rising levels of alcoholism (as
well as abuse of other drugs), violence, and suicide in their
communities. Traditional family patterns and ways of making
a living have been breaking down; one quarter of the Crees'
caribou herds, about twelve thousand animals, drowned in
the first phase of the project.[3] The Crees believe that the
demise of their environment will kill them. The entire culture
and cosmology of the Crees revolves around seasonal activities
associated with the land and its waters.

The Crees fought Phase I of the James Bay project through
the Canadian courts but lost. In their efforts to stop Phase II,
the Crees have been forging alliances with environmental
groups around the world, with special emphasis on the northeastern United States, where a large proportion of the power
generated by the project would be sold. By 1992, there were
signs that New York State might withdraw from agreements

*James Bay. First of three power plants under construction. First phase of
La Grande Complex to be completed by 1995. Courtesy of UPI/Bettmann.*

to purchase power from Hydro-Quebec. The Crees fear not only that flooding and construction of roads and dams will compound all the problems developing from Phase I, but also that the impact will be worse if Hydro-Quebec lures aluminum smelters and other heavy industry to the James Bay area with promises of electricity at discount rates.

In addition to the negative impact on other wildlife, the advance guard of industrialization is marching into a land that hosts hundreds of thousands of geese which migrate to the area each year. The geese nest in the reeds along the banks of shallow lakes that are being flooded by the dams and choked by construction run-off. The rivers which Hydro-Quebec has dammed or plans to dam feed the home waters of beluga whales in James and Hudson bays. The rivers also support large populations of a number of fish species that have been poisoned out of existence in other waterways to the south.

It is important to understand that the James Bay projects are not single dams across single rivers that flood valleys between mountains. They are massive earth-moving projects across an area as large as the state of Oregon. According to Matthew Coon-Come, grand chief of the Crees:

A project of this kind involves the destruction and rearrangement of a vast landscape, literally reshaping the geography of the land. This is what I want you to understand: it is not a dam. It is a terrible and vast reduction of our entire world. *It is the assignment of vast territories to a permanent and final flood. The burial of trees, valleys, animals, and even the graves [of the Crees] beneath tons of contaminated soil. All of this serves only one purpose: the generation of more electricity to get more revenue and more temporary jobs and to gain political power.*[4]

James Bay I was built without considering environmental impacts because of a Quebec law which says that no environmental impact assessments must be done for projects north of the 49th parallel. Yet, in connection with James Bay I, two

As early as 1973, Native Americans occupied the Canadian Department of Indian Affairs building in an attempt to stop destruction of their land and cultures by the first phase of the James Bay projects. Courtesy of UPI/Bettmann.

thousand Crees were moved from their ancestral lands at the mouth of the La Grande River to a totally new town inland. The town was constructed on a French Canadian model unsuited to the Crees, who live in small villages whose people meet only in the summer for exchange of stories and the carrying on of traditions. Hydro-Quebec has extended some monetary compensation for damage already incurred, but money is of little use to the Crees whose land has been destroyed.

The plans of Hydro-Quebec are but one part of energy development in the Canadian north. In the early 1970s, a series of dams was built on the Nelson and Churchill river systems in Manitoba, which also empty into James Bay. Existing dams provide 2,600 megawatts of power. Expansion plans in Manitoba may add another 6,000 megawatts. The plans are going forward despite major problems with silting behind existing dams; this is the first construction project of its type to take place on permafrost, which melts because of contact with encroaching water. The impact on the environment and the wildlife has been alarming. In some parts of the dammed area, the shoreline has been retreating 130 to 140 feet a year. According to the Canadian Freshwater Institute, based in Winnipeg, "shoreline retreat" may continue for eighty years. The melting of the permafrost and associated silting chokes reservoirs, causes widespread mercury poisoning, and has killed up to 98 percent of wildlife in some areas. Native moose hunters have reported finding the animals sinking up to their necks in silt. One in six people living on the Nelson River suffer some degree of mercury poisoning. In addition, several hundred native people whose lands were flooded have been moved to settlements where they are no longer allowed (or able) to wrest a living from the land. Alcoholism and other forms of social disorientation are occurring. Up to 90 percent of adults have abused alcohol and other drugs, and juveniles frequently engage in fights. Jim Tobacco, a member of the Moose Lake Band, said:

There is a very hostile attitude in the community. Our

young people are always beating each other up. My
people don't know who the hell they are. They live
month to month on welfare. Our way of life and
resources have been destroyed. We were promised bene-
fits from the hydro project. Today, we are poor and
Hydro-Manitoba is rich.[5]

In Tobacco's village, a settlement of fewer than a thousand
people, there were an average of fifteen suicide at-tempts per
month in the 1980s. At nearby Cross Lake, another small village, suicide attempts averaged twenty a month, ten times the
provincial average.[6]

Reacting to the Crees' commitment to their land, Hydro-
Quebec composed plans to hire nearly two hundred extra
security personnel to concentrate on what it regarded as
potential terrorism. A Hydro-Quebec report cited the violent
confrontation over land rights in 1990 at Oka. In two decades of opposition to Hydro-Quebec, the Crees have never
used violence, and their leaders said that the Hydro-Quebec
report and plans to hire a small army of "Hydro police"
were an affront to their dignity. The real terrorists, to the
Crees, are those who would destroy the earth that sustains
them.

The totality of the prospective destruction is conveyed by
the following statement by Matthew Coon-Come given at a
conference in Seattle organized by the Lummi Tribe in
1991. Coon-Come has served as president of Canada's
Assembly of First Nations. This statement is followed by two
others, also delivered at that conference, which indicate the
magnitude of environmental crises on the peripheries of the
industrial world. The third statement, "The Time Before the
End of Time," which deals with the Lacandon Mayas, is
authored by Kurt Russo and Lisa Dabek; and the final statement, "Ecocide and Genocide," is by Jewell Praying Wolf
James, Lummi elder and spiritual leader. The authors are
grateful to the Lummi Tribe, the Florence Kluckhohn Center
of Bellingham, Washington, and Kurt Russo, editor of the
proceedings of the 1991 conference in Seattle, from which
these remarks are excerpted.[7]

Testimony: "This Is a Terrible and Vast Reduction of Our Entire World"
—MATTHEW COON-COME, *Grand Chief, Crees of Northern Quebec (Canada)*

My name is Matthew Coon-Come, I am the Grand Chief of the Grand Councils of the Crees of Quebec. There are nine Cree communities. Each Cree community has its own chief and its own elected council. There are ten thousand of us. I am elected at large to be the chief spokesman for the Crees of James Bay.

We are the only permanent inhabitants of our territory. We hunt and fish in the vast region of northern Quebec that borders the coast of Hudson Bay and James Bay. We occupy a territory of 144,000 square kilometers of land, and we use every inch of it. Our territory is larger than France, and we have lived in it for tens of thousands of years.

Further north there is another community of indigenous people, the Inuit, who live on the coast of Hudson Bay. They are also the only inhabitants of their territory. Our territory is very beautiful. It is quite flat and is traversed by several large rivers full of thousands of small lakes and ponds. The southern part of our territory is forest, but hundreds of miles to the north the forest disappears except in river valleys which are rich with life.

My people live in and use every inch of that land. We have lived here for so long that everything has a name: every stream, every hill, almost every rock. The Cree people have an intimate relationship with the land. It is very difficult to describe, but I think "intimate" is very close to describ[ing] how close we are to the land; how we care for it and how we know it. I will attempt to give you a picture of the area that we live in and come back to why we oppose the hydro-electric project that the government of Quebec plans for our territory.

Every year, thousands and thousands of geese come to nest and raise their young in the rich and grassy reed lands that are a natural part of the shallow lakes. It is a place like no other in the world. The waters of Hudson Bay and James Bay are the home territory of the beluga whales and many kinds of seals. The waters are shallow and are fed by numerous small streams and several large rivers which produce the perfect mix of fresh and salt water to form the ideal habitat for those large marine mammals. The waters abound in fish which migrate between the fresh waters of the streams and the salt water of Hudson Bay. There are several species of trout in addition to Arctic char, pickerel, pike, and several species of white fish and sturgeon. Our sturgeon are huge, and our rivers support populations of fish which have now become extinct in other places.

My people have depended for untold generations on the bear, the moose, the caribou, and beaver, and they are animals which have always fed our people. We protect and respect them and know them well. We watch them all year long, and we are very careful to allow them to survive and multiply. The lives of our people and the lives of these animals have been related for a very long time, for we live together. Many other animals live in this land, like the martin, the mink otter, foxes, wolves, and muskrat. And there are many kinds of birds like eagles, hawks, falcons, and many, many sea birds. It is full of life.

Our land and our lives have remained largely unchanged for thousands of years. We are very far north, and the climate is very cold in the winter and still today there are very few roads. In short, we were very much left alone and our lives as hunters, fishers, and trappers was not easy but our people survived and flourished. That is why we are here now. Contact with the Europeans began in the late 1600s. We contributed to the European economy for hundreds of years but, nevertheless, we managed to carry on our lives, and our culture survived with us.

I have told you all of this because it will help you to understand our situation now. I suppose we have been very fortunate. Sometimes, when I look at a new place, when I see a place where there is now a city, or a highway, or farms, I try to imagine what it must have been like before people started changing it. What did it look like when the Creator made it?

In our territory, we are fortunate enough to see the land

and the animals in much the same way as our parents did. We have not seen change in everything. We can see through our own eyes what our people saw thousands and thousands of years ago. Nothing or only very little has been spoiled. There is great value in this. We need to know what the natural world looks like and how it seemed through the eyes of our old people. We need to maintain some sense of order of life. Some part of this earth shouldn't be violated, and must be set aside so that future generations will know what the earth really is.

I am not against development or all construction or economic activity and all the rest. That is not the position of the Crees of northern Quebec. We know that some development is necessary, and we understand that there is value in progress and advancement. Neither are we trying to prevent the expression of modern lifestyles. We are not trying to live in some distant past. We are not attempting to avoid high technology, machinery, electricity, and other signs of progress. But I must ask if every project, if every new structure, every new highway, if every dam is really "development."

I see so much that was considered development at one time that was being promoted and is now considered harmful. For a while, the Corps of Engineers was straightening rivers in various parts of the United States. Swamps were being drained to create new farmland. Dams were built to control floods. Anyone who opposed these things was called a fool. People rallied around these projects. They thought flood control was a good thing. The influx of new capital would benefit everyone. But people are beginning to realize that they did not know as much as they needed to know. It turns out that the wetlands are filters and moderators of water flow. The drained swamps led to contamination of the water. The land became poisoned. The water tables dropped and the fish died. It all turned out to be wrong. Scientists and engineers who were "right" a few years before were now proven wrong.

I have great respect for science and technology. I hunt and live off the land and work the traplines. I find that most development projects are not driven by wisdom and intelli-

gence: They are driven by greed. Governments decide what they want to do primarily because of the economics and politics and the scientists and engineers are called in to produce the plans and justify the impacts. They say, "We need jobs," or "We must not let the water go to the sea and be wasted." Arguments like this are dangerous and are made every day. The Province of Quebec decided the water in our rivers was going to waste. Quebec said we would all become rich and prosperous if all the rivers flowing into the Hudson and James bays were dammed to produce electricity. They said the way to what they called "stimulate the economy" was for Quebec to develop this mega-project.

One day, after we have lived in our land for thousands of years, a decision was made to block our rivers, cut down our forests, and flood our lands. No one came to talk to us. We were not told of these plans. All of this just happened. Our permission was not requested. The government of Quebec thinks that we have no legal title to our land, that we must live there. We were squatters, they think, squatters in our own land.

Then someone heard about what they are doing to our people on the radio soon after the first construction started. There was no talk, then, about the environment. There was no environmental impact assessment or ecological audit. Suddenly, there were roads being built across our traplines and heavy machinery tearing up our land. I could be here all day and night telling you how outraged we were. How we tried, then, to talk to the government, how we took legal action to try to stop this project, but that is another story.

I want to explain something else. When we think of hydroelectric dams, we usually think of some kind of structure blocking a river canyon. The water is backed up for several miles behind the dam and the river valley is partially flooded. There are dams like this on the Columbia River, in Washington State in the United States and on the Colorado. Beautiful and productive valleys are flooded, river flow is altered and serious destruction takes place. Fish runs are disrupted or destroyed.

The James Bay project was not like this at all. The Proj-

ect La Grande is not a dam on the La Grande River. This is a project like no other and is the biggest hydroelectric complex in the world. A project of this kind involves the destruction and rearrangement of a vast landscape, literally reshaping the geography of the land. This is what I want you to understand: it is not a dam. It is a terrible and vast reduction of our entire world. *It is the assignment of vast territories to a permanent and final flood. The burial of trees, valleys, animals, and even graves beneath tons of contaminated water.*

All of this serves only one purpose: the generation of more electricity to get more revenue and more temporary jobs and to gain political power. La Grande is not a dam. It is the diversion of six beautiful and mighty rivers. Two of the rivers are now almost completely dry and dead because of what they have done. We have an east main river that was once about 200 yards wide and now is a small creek. The fish are gone. The wetlands are gone and so are the geese and the wildfowl.

The other four rivers have had their flow cut by half. The waters from these destroyed rivers cannot be contained without the construction of hundreds of miles of dikes and diversion channels. The diversion channels alone cover over 2,229 square kilometers of our land. Nine dams and 212 dikes are required to force the redistribution of water. Almost 14,000 square kilometers of territory are under water. You can see why I say this is not a dam.

All of this was done on our land against our will and our efforts to prevent it. We did manage, at the very last minute, after most of the destruction had already been accomplished, to negotiate a treaty. But even that treaty, the James Bay Northern Quebec Agreement, has already been broken by Canada and by Quebec. How can money compensate the poisoning of the earth, the loss of the heritage, and the permanent destruction of an economy?

James Bay I was built without a single environmental hearing, without an environmental assessment, without the least accommodation to environmental considerations. Special laws were passed which permit every kind of expedient to avoid compliance with existing laws. All this for whom? For Hydro-Quebec.

The government of Quebec neatly passed legislation exempting any mega-project north of the 49th parallel from a study of environmental impacts. The government must have realized from the beginning that the James Bay Project would be a disaster because they decided to block any and all social and environmental assessments. The project has proved to be worse than we could ever have anticipated.

Shortly after the project was completed, a high mercury level was discovered in the fish that live in the lakes and rivers connected to the reservoirs. This has been described as the equivalent of a massive industrial spill of mercury. The mercury levels are so dangerous that the Crees are now warned to stop eating fish, a major source of our protein. There are no supermarkets up there. We are miles away from any accessible road.

They have moved 2,000 people [inland] from the mouth of the La Grande River. . . . They have created a totally new community. We are not used to being close together. We were scattered over 144,000 square miles of land. We only come together in the summer to exchange stories, to carry on certain traditions, and have our ceremonial dances. But Hydro-Quebec says, "We have carried out a study." They want to be the evaluators, the assessors, the judge and jury. They say there is no environmental damage in James Bay I, but their dream for us has become a nightmare. Our fish are poisoned with mercury.

They have rerouted the migration patterns of all the animals. Because of the mismanagement of the reservoirs, Hydro-Quebec has drowned 10,000 caribou and who do they blame it on? They blame it on God! Next, they couldn't control the dikes in one of their reservoirs. Do you know what their excuse was? It's the sun, they said! My people take their children out of school and teach them a way of life they can be proud of. Everyone wants that. But now, our graves are under water, there is mercury in our fish. The geese and ducks are fewer every year.

Hydro-Quebec and the government of Quebec have decid-

ed to build two new hydroelectric projects in our territory. One is to the north of the Project La Grande, and this is called the Great Whale Project. The other is to the south and will dam three other rivers. These are called, respectively, the Great Whale and NBR projects. James Bay I is already built. We are now trying to stop the second phase that will consist of five dams and 133 dikes. It will have four diversion channels, and over 4,000 square kilometers of our territory will be covered with water.

Great Whale will require three river diversions and flow reversal in flood conditions on two other rivers. [It] will require that two of the major rivers flowing into James Bay be permanently cut off. God only knows what all this will do. How is it possible with our present state of knowledge to do these things?

Hydro-Quebec is drowning our territory, a territory the size of the state of Oregon. Our homelands are being destroyed [along with] the protection provided in our treaty. The treaty is a fiction without the fish. What good is compensation if our people are sick and drunk?

Again, five years down the line, they will talk about those lazy, good-for-nothing Indians. They will say, "Why are we paying taxes to pay for their education, health and social services? Why can't they support themselves?" Meanwhile, we are, today, self-sufficient. We don't need the government hand-out. But they are destroying us. We will be destroyed through James Bay II. We want to protect the land and the animals and our way of life. If you destroy, if you clearcut, if you kill the small and big game, if you drive that away, you, in essence, drive us off the land.

You will kill our culture. You will kill my people and our way of life that depends upon the rivers continuing to flow and upon the forests and the animals that continue to thrive. This is our Amazon but, unlike the Amazon, we can prevent a major ecological disaster before it happens.

They haven't started building yet. But they plan to build roads. They plan to sell the energy in New York and Vermont. They plan to continue this environmental racism. Together, we can save James Bay. We can tell the governors

*of the Northeast United States they must not have energy
taken off the back of Native peoples. We can tell the Province
of Quebec they must practice what they preach about distinct
societies. We must live and learn together. The Crees of northern Quebec have a unique heritage and way of life. We know
the land. We love the land. We share the land in harmony. We
need your help and for everyone to realize [that] the holocaust of "discovery" is still going on in James Bay.*

The Arctic as Global Dump

During the late twentieth century, the Arctic has become the
"last frontier" in North America for environmental contamination. The problems of the Crees are being matched elsewhere in the far north.

As if to illustrate just how pervasive pollution of the
entire earth has become, studies of Inuit (Eskimo) women's
breast milk in the late twentieth century reveal abnormally
high levels of PCBs. Toxic levels of the carcinogenic chemical
have spread from emissions sources in the lower latitudes
(such as Akwesasne, see Chapter Seven), into the oceanic food
chain of the Arctic. The Inuits are being poisoned by eating
fish and marine mammals, their major source of protein for
thousands of years. Still more PCBs were dumped into the
Arctic environment by military installations.

Studies around the rim of Hudson's Bay, conducted by
Dr. Eric Dewailly of Laval University in 1988, found that
nursing mothers' milk contained more than twice the level of
PCBs (3.5 parts per million) considered "safe" by the Canadian government. The fish that most Inuits eat act as "con-
centrators" of PCBs and other toxic materials in the food
chain. By eating the fish, people take part in the same diffu-
sion of the chemicals. In addition to PCBs, scientists have
found other contaminants in Inuit mothers' milk. According
to Winona LaDuke, "Related contaminants include radioactive cesium, DDT, toxophene, and other pesticides," most of
which have been banned for use in North America but are
still used in many other countries.[8]

The Inuits' bodies are collecting toxins because the Arctic itself is becoming a global atmospheric dump. Dr. Lyle Lockhart, an employee of the Canadian government's Fisheries and Oceans Department in Winnipeg, Manitoba, says that toxic materials emitted in the warmer regions of the atmosphere sometimes circulate in the air for years, collecting and descending in the air over the Arctic and Antarctic. Lockhart cited toxophene, which is used in cotton fields thousands of miles from the Mackenzie River in Canada's northwest territories. The Canadian government has caught fish in the Mackenzie with toxophene in their livers.[9] Larger animals, including human beings, concentrate the toxins in their bodies. Worst hit may be the polar bear, which eats almost nothing except fish. One study indicates that the polar bear may become extinct by the year 2006 due to sterility caused by PCBs.[10]

On the far northwest coast of Alaska, Inuit people have been fighting the U.S. Atomic Energy Commission (AEC) since the late 1950s, when the agency proposed to demonstrate the peaceful uses of atomic energy by blowing open a new harbor at Point Hope with an atomic blast. The government shelved the plan, which was called Operation Chariot, in 1962. Then, without telling the Inuits, the U.S. government turned parts of their homeland into a nuclear dump. The dump contained debris gathered from within a mile of "ground zero" at a Nevada atomic test site. The purpose of the experiment was to test the toxicity of radiation in an Arctic environment. The dump experiment was carried out by the U.S. Geological Survey under license from the AEC. The fact that the area was occupied by native people seemed superfluous to the government.[11]

The Inuits did not learn of the nuclear dump until Dan O'Neill, a researcher at the University of Alaska, made public documents he had found describing it as he researched a book on the abandoned plan to blow a nuclear harbor in the coast. For many years, the Inuits in the area have suffered a cancer rate "that far exceeds the national average."[12] The government acknowledges that soil in the area contains "trace amounts" of radiation but denies that its experiment is causing the Inuits' increased cancer rate. According to O'Neill, the nuclear dump was clearly illegal and contained "a thousand times . . . the allowable standard for this kind of nuclear burial."[13]

Point Hope, the closest settlement to the dump, is an Inuit village of seven hundred people, most of whom make a living as whalers. It is one of the oldest continuously occupied town sites in North America. Mayor David Stone, a leader in the fight against the dump, said, "We feel betrayed."[14] Jeslie Kaleak, mayor of North Slope Borough, which includes Point Hope and seven other settlements, added: "I can't tell you how angry I am that they considered our home to be nothing but a big wasteland. . . . They didn't give a damn about people who live up here."[15]

The environmental devastation of remote areas in the Arctic is wrenching, but one must realize that whole societies of native people are crumbling along with the environment on which they depend. When the land dies, people do, too. In 1960, before widespread energy development on Alaska's North Slope, the suicide rate among native people there was 13 per 100,000, comparable to averages in the United States as a whole. By 1970, the rate had risen to 25 per 100,000; by 1986, the rate had risen to 67.6 per 100,000. Homicide rates by the middle 1980s were three times the average in the United States as a whole, between 22.9 and 26.6 per 100,000 people, depending on which study is used. Death rates from homicide and suicide appear linked to rising alcoholism. In the mid-1980s, 79 percent of native suicide victims had some alcohol in their blood at the time of death. Slightly more than half (54 percent) were legally intoxicated.[16]

Personal stories illustrate just how pervasive environmental pollution has become. The following anecdote from Cree Glen Cooper was first published in *Akwe:kon Journal*'s special issue on James Bay:[17]

> *I have a story to tell about my father and the situation that occurred when he killed a moose in early April. I remember this very vividly because it struck me very hard and personally. This was the first time that I had*

ever realized the direct impact that the hydroelectric de-velopment and the massive environmental destruction had on me.

I went out to visit my parents in the woods. Early that day my father went moose hunting. He was gone all day. Usually, he comes home around 5 P.M., when the sun begins to set. That evening he came home around 9:30 P.M. Everybody was gone; my brother Alan and I were the only ones there. My father walked through the door, totally silent, and didn't say anything. I was standing in the kitchen and I asked him if he had killed a moose. He did not respond to my question right away. I could tell my Dad was hurt. He gave my brother a hug, and said: "We can't eat it." He said that he had killed a moose, but as he cut it open, he saw that the insides were full of mucous, the pancreas had white spots, the kidneys were very small, and the heart had water on it.

He had tears in his eyes, although he did not cry bit-terly. I remember a story that I was told which says that an elderly man never cries because he must stay strong for the young. My father, who was going to be sixty, wept before my eyes because he had killed a moose which he could not eat and feed his family. These are some of the social impacts that hydroelectric develop-ment have on the Cree people and the Cree way of life.

The Lacandon Mayas: "Without the Forest, the Sky Will Fall"

"All the roots of the stars are the roots of the trees of heaven. When a tree falls, in heaven . . . a star falls."
—CHAN K'IN VIEJO, *Mayan Lacandon*

At the end of the twentieth century, farming, mining, road building, and other forms of development are encroaching on the last "wild" areas of Central America's tropical rain-forests. The people inhabiting these shrinking wild areas are facing forms of disease, alcoholism, and other forms of social dysfunction that sound familiar to any student of indigenous American history.

At least 2 million descendants of the Mayas live in present-day Central America. Most have been absorbed to varying degrees by the Hispanic cultures of Guatemala and Mexico. An exception has been the Lacandon Mayas, who have elected to remain outside the ambit of modern world culture, living in the rainforest of Mexico's Chiapas state along the border with Guatemala. In that rainforest, with its towering mahogany trees and date palms, this last fragment of the independent, self-sufficient Mayas is fighting a losing battle with encroaching logging, cattle ranching, and other activities which are deforesting the land they have inhabited since at least the third century A.D. By 1990, the population of the Lacandon Mayas had declined to about five hundred people in two principal villages, Naja and Lacanja Chansayab. More than half of the Lacandons' original rainforest habitat has been logged. In the 1980s, the rainforest also became the site of several refugee camps housing people who escaped a bloody civil war in Guatemala. The camps, maintained by the Mexican government, housed roughly one hundred thousand people throughout southern Mexico in 1992.[18]

Logging on the Lacandons' land was officially banned by Patricino Gonzalez Garrido, governor of Chiapas, in 1988. In the early 1990s the ban was being evaded. For 150,000 pesos (about $60 in 1992), government agents could be bribed to let loggers take out a mahogany tree.[19] Logging initiates a natural destructive process that can lead to erosion, pollution of streams, and desertification of the fragile tropical soils. Ranching often speeds the destruction of the rainforest, in which most of the soil is very poor.

The Lacandons' rainforest also has become range to hunters, many of whom capture tropical birds for export to the United States and other countries. The World Wildlife Fund estimates that for every bird that is eventually sold, ten die being hunted or in captivity.[20] Poachers also have been killing jaguars, ocelots, jararundis, and margays to sell their skins. Many of these animals are becoming extinct even with-

Kin Garcia, a Lacandon Maya, paddles a mahogany dugout canoe on Lake Naja. He wears a traditional Mayan haircut and tunic, with pants manufactured outside his homeland. Courtesy of AP/Wide World Photos.

out being hunted because their habitat has been so severely diminished.

In addition to logging, ranching, and hunting, the area has become a site for limited oil exploration. The Mexican government also has talked of initiating hydroelectric projects in the area (none had been started by 1990), even as it urges landless Mayas from other parts of Mexico to settle in the rapidly shrinking rainforest.

Despite their isolation, in recent years the Lacandon Mayas have united with native peoples around the Western Hemisphere in an attempt to stop the destruction of their rainforest homeland. The Lummi Indian Nation of Western Washington has established a liaison project with the Lacandones and called on tribal leaders in the United States and Canada to support their cause. A statement on the Lacandon rainforest and the Mayas signed by a number of tribal representatives concluded:

> *It is now the time before the end of time and we must tie the bonds, as children of the earth, or suffer the loss of all things given to us by the Creator. Without the forest, the sky will fall. The destiny of one is the destiny of all. We stand together in this, the final struggle that will determine the common destiny of all peoples of this, our Mother Earth.*[21]

Testimony: "The Time Before the End of Time"
—KURT RUSSO AND LISA DABEK

[The following is excerpted from a Lummi report on the conditions of the Lacandones. A longer version of this report appeared as Kurt Russo and Lisa Dabek, "Common Cause and Common Destiny: The Lacandon Rainforest Project."[22]]

The Lacandon is the northernmost tropical rainforest in the Americas. It is filled with indigenous plants and animals, including mahogany trees, date palms, scarlet macaws, and jaguars. Since at least the third century A.D., this rich habitat has been home to many groups of indigenous Mayan people, including the Mayan Lacandones. The Lacandones remained relatively isolated in the forest until the late 19th century, when logging companies began to extract timber. This was the start of the irreversible invasion and the destruction of the forest. Between 1875 and 1982, over half the original rainforest area was logged and the population of Lacandones reduced to just over 500 people distributed between the two main villages of Naja and Lacanja Chansayab.

Five principal forces have contributed to the deforestation: logging, cattle ranching, legal and illegal trade in plants and animals, oil exploration, and government-sponsored resettlement projects. In the 1980s, the rainforest became a sanctuary from the bloody civil war now raging in Guatemala. Logging in the Lacandon rainforest continued until a ban was declared by Patricino Gonzalez Garrido, governor of Chiapas, in 1988.

At this point it is debatable how well the ban is enforced. There is evidence that some illegal logging is occurring. For example, a Lacandon man told project staff that the protection of the forest is ineffective. He claimed that for a bribe of 150,000 pesos (about $60 at that time) to a government agent, people can cut down a mahogany tree. Cattle ranching began in the 1940s and increased as logging-road construction brought more people into the area. Presently most beef from the Lacandon rainforest goes to domestic markets in Mexico City, Tabasco, and Villehermosa. The government has encouraged cattle production through programs of credit and loans to ranchers, and recently to the Lacandones themselves.

Ranching is not ecologically sustainable and continual, extensive grazing depletes the soil of nutrients and makes it impossible for the land to regenerate. The conversion of forest to pasture also causes widespread erosion because the soil has no protection from the rain which eventually may lead to desertification.

Legal and illegal trade in plant and animal products of the Lacandon rainforest has seriously threatened certain species. Live tropical birds are exported to the United States and other countries. The World Wildlife Fund estimates that ten die for every bird that survives to be sold in the developed nations. Poachers are killing jaguars, ocelots, jagarundis, and margays to sell the skins in markets within Mexico and abroad. Turtle shells and snake skins are also sold illegally. Species such as the jaguar, tapir, spider and black howler monkeys, scarlet macaw, and harpy eagle face the double threat of poaching and habitat destruction.

Oil exploration in the Lacandon rainforest and neighboring Peten in Guatemala is destroying the forest because of road building and clearing for test areas. The Mexican government also plans hydroelectric dam projects on the nearby Usumacinta River. . . . The result of development projects is the introduction of more roads, more people, and increased pollution of soil, water, and air.

Resettlements of landless people also have created a major problem in this region. Starting in the 1940s, the government urged Mayas from other parts of Mexico to move to the rainforest, in response to increasing pressure for land elsewhere. The impact of thousands of people settling in a rainforest environment unfamiliar to them radically altered the face of the forest. Much of the forest was cleared for farms and ranches as settlers attempted to support their families. These resettlements have created conflict between the Lacandones and the newcomers.

The Lacandones are deeply concerned about the loss of their forest. K'in Bor, a Lacandon Maya, spoke passionately of their need to protect what is left of their land from outsiders. As he walked through the forest, he remarked that although there are still mahogany trees left, there are no more very large, very red ones. The forest is fast disappearing.

"What's happening to them has happened to us," said Hazel Umtuch, a Yakima Indian elder, shortly before departing San Cristobal de las Casas for the rainforest. "I hope they will know that we are all brothers and sisters." "It's like being back in history," said Ken Cooper, a Lummi traditional leader, after arriving in the village. "The Lacandones have no conception of the modern world. I see some innocent people that are going to get used. I see people who have no idea what's coming their way. But they are very, very powerful

people, the Mayan Lacandon." *Their hosts in the village were K'in Bor Panagua and Manuel Chan Bor who, just six months before, had traveled to the United States.*

During their first few days in the village, Mrs. Umtuch and Mr. Cooper met with different families. They also were taken to see the milpas *where up to 79 different varieties of crops are cultivated. They were shown medicinal plants that abound in the forest; they also visited a number of ruins, or godhouses, of the* nukuck winik *(the ancient ones), predecessors of the* hach winik, *the Mayan Lacandones.*

Meeting with the families had a special meaning for Mrs. Umtuch. "*I couldn't help but think of how our people were once this way,*" *she said,* "*and I could see the destruction that is coming and what it will mean to these people. Our ancestors went through hell . . . much like we've learned they are doing to the Indian people, down here.*"

The Lacandones' cosmology includes belief in an afterlife, heaven and an underworld, in the concept of human souls and the onen *(the animistic spirits in nature), the premonitory power of dreams. They believe that Hachakyum, the principal god of the Lacandones, who created the world, is overlord of the lowest of three heavens, and walks the realm of the night sky.*

"*I thought and thought about what K'in Bor said there, up in the ruins,*" *Mr. Cooper said.* "*Here are all these outsiders saying the Lacandones don't have their traditions or don't use those places for ceremony. It's just like it was with us. We'd been suppressed for so long that we didn't tell anyone what we did. It's the same with them here, now.*"

Mrs. Umtuch told the villagers through an interpreter at one of their gatherings: "*We've had to organize ourselves to protect our resources and our culture. We had to learn how to work with other tribes . . . because what happens to one happens to all of us . . . I want to say that we bring with us a message that we support you in your efforts to preserve the forest and protect your culture.*" *Cooper added a note of warning, looking out at the clearing littered with utility poles that would soon bring electricity to the village:* "*The government brought us electricity and paved the road with broken promises. They told us they would respect and protect the land . . . but they are cutting down the last of the ancient forests. When they do that, they cut out our culture. They don't listen. Or don't care. Or don't believe us. Or can't afford to. . . ."*

In another meeting with the community, the Lacandones identified what they felt to be their most pressing needs. Of utmost importance was the need for doctors and medical assistance. Later, a medical team visited the area, coordinated by Norman Shaifer of the Lacandon Rainforest Project. Team members, which included a specialist in tropical rainforest diseases, paid their own way and volunteered their time and resources to the project. Over a period of five days, and in consultation with the heads of the families, they examined many men, women, and children of the village. They also distributed medicines and collected numerous blood and stool samples. Diagnoses of the samples at Henry M. Ford Memorial Hospital revealed that 90 percent of the villagers suffered from intestinal parasites, over half tested positive for tuberculosis, and none of the villagers had developed an immunity to the deadly measles virus.

"I think about those kids," Mr. Cooper said "and see them. . . . I think about how the Lacandones still speak their own tongue and wear their traditional clothes. It's important that we try to understand them and respect their ways and learn from them, and share what we know with them. It's something cultural and spiritual that we, as Indian people, do for each other."

Testimony: Ecocide and Genocide
—JEWELL PRAYING WOLF JAMES *("Se-Sealth")*

[Jewell Praying Wolf James, a lineal descendant of Chief Seal'th (after whom the city of Seattle was named), coordinates the Lummi tribe's Treaty Protection Task Force. He has extensive experience in law, environment, and politics at the state, national, and international levels. He is the chairman of the board of the Florence R. Kluckhohn Center, founder and director of the Indian-in-the-Moon Foundation, and treasurer of the newly formed National Tribal Environmental Council.]

From the northernmost to the southernmost tips of the Americas [when] we were found [by Europeans], we were living under the teachings of the Mother Earth spirituality. Our cultures lived with respect for creation. We had a form of government known as tribalism which included the individual freedoms of democracy and the social responsibilities of communalism.

Our people have been colonized by foreign governments. We speak and practice vestiges of our own language, culture, and spiritualism; but, the non-Indian language, religions, mode of living, cultural values, concepts of individualism, greed, private property, and the nuclear family system have been forced upon our societies through governmental and church programs and policies of extermination, termination, assimilation, acculturation, and enculturation. Most recently, in line with the United Nations declarations, the Indian peoples are learning of the possibility that the colonial governments may open the path to self-determination and self-government.

Amongst the Indian nations, we find that many of the colonial governments of the Western Hemisphere (whether of British, Portuguese, Spanish, Russian, or French background) have practiced the very same policies and programs as the United States invented to keep our people under control. They instituted laws that took the land, the air, the water, the foods, the minerals of their indigenous peoples. They restricted the indigenous people to limited geographical boundaries called reservations that are not large enough to sustain current populations let alone future generations.

Indigenous participation in the economic development of the few remaining natural resources has been limited by law, since indigenous peoples are usually defined as legally incompetent and non-competent, like wards to their guardians. For the American Indians, commerce and trade with non-Indian governments and society is restricted so that revenues and benefits are taken out of our communities, rather than multiply within. Non-Indian governments claim superior powers to tax business, industry, and natural resources over and above our own government's rights.

Non-Indian governments grant their citizens immunity from tribal laws and are not held accountable to tribal justice, while the Indians are held totally accountable to all non-Indian laws and make up a high percentage of prison populations. Jurisdiction within our reserved territories is exercised by non-Indian governments, although their laws and constitutions forbid such actions. As Professor [Milnar] Ball stated, "There are two constitutions in America," one with honor and the other dishonorable. The first applies to the non-Indians and the second applies to the Indians.

It is with irony we note that the U.S. Congress has finally recognized that the American Indian confederacies and societies were a great influence in the formation of America's form of constitutional democracy, the bill of individual rights and freedoms, the systems of checks and balances upon leadership, the advocation of the use of the caucus for consensus building, and the teaching of respect for speakers when addressing each other. This modeling influence is commemorated in the U.S. congressional hearings held for House Resolution #331 of 1988 and Senate Concurrent Resolution #76 of 1987, both passed during the 200th year of the U.S. Constitution.

The next irony of world government is the motivating influence Indian concepts of communalism had upon the evolution of Communism as a form of government and the duty of society to care for the old, the weak, and the war-injured, and the idea of collective (communal) ownership of property into the next generations. In this society there was no police, no nobles, no kings or queens, no regents, no prefects, no prisons, and no state. There existed a socialist form of economics and marketing.

While the world looks upon the superpowers of the United States and Russia, we wonder why each chose to take the Indian forms of governance and society beyond what the Indian models advocated. The U.S. Constitution has been used to justify the constant taking of Indian rights, natural resources, and lands. The Bill of Rights does not apply to the

Indian race. And the treaty-committed word of the United States is changed whenever it is popular amongst the greedy of non-Indian society to demand it. While the U.S.S.R dismantled itself, governmentally and economically collapsing, the majority of the U.S. citizens do not even know the contents of the Bill of Rights of their own Constitution.

Today, it is corporate and industrial greed that demands more from the government, more exploitation of individual rights and the natural resources. The rich get richer and the poor die in toxic contamination caused by mass production, the fever of consumerism, and rampaging materialism. Multinational, transnational, and international corporations and industry owe loyalty to profit-making and not humanity. [When] national governments . . . impose stricter laws to protect the poor, the environment, the wilderness, or to force conservation measures to be implemented, these corporations and industries—with "good conscience for high profits"—transplant themselves amongst the Third or Fourth world peoples. They then tell their own people that they are "unproductive" and export their exploitation and toxic wastes to Third World and "underdeveloped" countries.

The people may be treated as pawns in this "global economy" but nobody is fooled. The whole process is driven by a work ethic that is oriented toward domination over nature, individualism, self-interest, and greed. The quest for a higher standard of living as defined by most Americans in the United States is the nightmare of the rest of the world. This standard has placed America at the top of the list as users of natural resources and producers of toxic contamination.

Technology and science have "objectively" separated care and consideration of the cumulative impacts of humankind's collective behavior away from social responsibility. The global community must discover an orientation that teaches the world to do with the minimal and not the maximum. We have to address our levels of consumption before the whole global community dies from ecocide. America's standard cannot be the standard of the world. It is too demanding of the world's scarce resources.

It has been very difficult for the U.S. Indian nations and societies to adjust to the non-Indian values, society, and governmental system. The American Indians have the highest infant mortality, shortest life-expectancy, highest unemployment and underemployment, lowest educational and vocational attainment, highest poverty, and the poorest housing. They have been deprived of their traditional foods and medicines, [and] have been forced to convert to religions that oppose the Mother Earth spirituality of indigenous peoples. Their parents and grandparents have been forced out of the traditional roles, and family institutions have been destroyed. Our traditional forms of government have been destroyed and non-Indian governmental structure instituted. Our people suffer great amounts of alcohol and drug abuse, and psychological and sociological depression and dysfunctionality.

At one time our plains, plateaus, and ancient forests were respected and not considered a wilderness. The skies were darkened with migrating fowl. The plains were blanketed with massive herds of buffalo. Our mountains teemed with elk, deer, bear, beaver, and other fur-bearing animals. All the rivers were full of salmon and fish—so much that you could walk across their backs to get to the other side. The plants and trees were medicines or food for us.

We knew neither hunger nor diseases until contact came in 1492, then our holocaust began and that of the plants, animals, and environment. Our oral traditions, teachings, and spirituality taught respect for all things. From one generation to the next we were taught the glorification of respecting nature and creation. All things were once spiritual and transformed to provide the human children the gifts of the creating spirit. The Earth was our mother, the sky was our father, and our prayers brought the two together to form one unified spirit. Our ceremonies and traditions were like the umbilical cord that attaches the mother and child, and bonded the father to children.

Without this connection we would forget respect and die. Without Mother Earth we would not be nurtured. Without Father Sky we would have no air to breathe or life-giving rains to cleanse our souls.

Arlecho Creek basin, shown in this composite photograph, was recently clear-cut by Mutual Life Insurance Company of New York. Clear-cuts such as this have pushed salmon to the brink of extinction in the Northwest, causing severe hardship in native communities such as the Lummi Indian tribe. Courtesy of the Lummi Indian Nation.

Respect connected the youngest to the oldest, the strongest to the weakest, the wisest to the most humble. We were a part of the circle. Indian leaders have been documented as making speeches to the non-Indian governments and churches time and time again, since 1492. Each time the advocation of love and respect for the earth and sky was well noted. It became romantic for the world governments and societies to think of the "noble savage" that loved creation as its own life force. Still, today, the world believes the Indian to represent the true concept of living in "harmony" with all things.

This concept must be the focus of change for the global community of nations and societies. The whole world is being confronted with the death of the future generations due to the conditions the recent generations have superimposed upon our progeny. Our "gift" to the future is death through ecocide. We may destroy the world by toxic wastes, solid wastes, air pollution, water pollution, destruction of the forests, destruction of the plants and animals, destruction of the ecosystems, destruction by nuclear holocaust, or some other derivative of "civilized societies." Whichever causes it, [the result] is still the same: the death of our world.

This concern for the survival of nature, and therefore human and cultural survival, has been expressed by many different groups and organizations, not only by Indian tribes and nations. It was recently discussed by representatives from throughout the world in Mexico in a meeting organized by Homero Aridjis and the Group of One Hundred. I had the opportunity to attend the meeting along with writers, artists, intellectuals, scientists, and environmentalists from throughout the world. The participants drafted and signed the Morelia Declaration (see below) that calls for the creation of an International Court of the Environment in which "environmentally criminal activity can be brought to the attention of the entire world."

We, as Indian peoples, can feel sorry for ourselves. We can sit back and join movements that demand justice. But, it will not matter what we demanded if the world dies.

We know . . . the gifts of the Western Hemisphere. Indigenous peoples and societies to the white, black, and yel-

low brother and sister societies. As the red race, we owe a duty to try to influence the others. At one time all races were close to creation. They had institutionalized the Mother Earth Spirituality. This kept them in balance with their environment and was the source of trans-generational teachings. . . . Our white, black, and yellow brothers and sisters have fallen off the path of respect for creation. We must bring them back for they make up the other three directions of the worldly compass, and the earth and sky make up the other two. Therefore, we must challenge the others to think about living in harmony with creation rather then dominating it, exploiting it.

We must change path. We know that it is difficult to remember to follow these teachings. So, we have chosen to plant thoughts for changing the global society by showing everyone a monthly reminder that nature has already phenomenally provided the whole world. The Mother Earth Spirituality is cognizant of the special place the Moon has in cycles and ceremony. We reawaken this acknowledgement by introducing the Indian-in-the-Moon to the world. We are dedicated to preserving the Indian environmental legacy by teaching all observers how to see the Indian-in-the-Moon image created by the full moon's craters and crater shadows.

The Indian people have a deep cultural respect and love for all creation. This is known worldwide, but the world needs a reminder. When the full moon (full circle) rises on the eastern horizon, it is then one can see the image of an Indian, sitting, legs crossed, hands in lap, head bowed, and two feathers draped over the forehead (one represents Father Sky, the other Mother Earth). The best time to observe the image is early evening. As the moon moves across the sky it rotates 180 degrees and goes down head first in the west.

Throughout the world there are remnants of the "Mother Earth" ceremonies and traditions that taught respect for creation. The world was considered spiritual, and societies developed methods to maintain this respect from one generation to another. Most often legends, myths, and creation stories were handed down with each new generation of children. American Indian folklore still teaches this basic respect through creation myths and ceremonials. Recognition of this image is a call to reflect upon how each and every one of us may do our part to save Father Sky and Mother Earth.

Native Americans are famous for seeking through vision quests the power to live in balance and harmony with creation. The concept of harmony is root to ceremony and tradition. There are seven basic harmonies:

①Mental Harmony (questing to create strength and balance within one's mind);

② Physical Harmony (questing to create inner physical balance of strength and purity);

③ Social Harmony (questing to find societal balance with all of humankind);

④ Environmental Harmony (questing to find balance with all of creation and the environment);

⑤ Space-Time Harmony (questing to understand our place in space and time of creation);

⑥ Cosmological Harmony (questing to understand our place of balance in the microcosm and macrocosm beyond our earthly environment);

⑦ Spiritual Harmony (questing to find the strength to fulfill the above).

To live these harmonies is to fulfill the respect needed to preserve the world.

These harmonies are root to the institutionalized laws and theories of human understanding of their place in existence. We forget [that] we are only a part of a much bigger and more divine plan for creation. Each month, if we can take the time to pause and look at the full moon as it rises in the eastern sky and see the Indian-in-the-Moon, then perhaps we can remember the message the indigenous peoples of the Western Hemisphere have for the world. In order to make a true difference for the future, then all races, governments, and churches need to cooperate.

We must be willing to instill in the next generation a greater vision beyond personal profit and greed. We must reawaken the values of respect and ceremony. We must keep the concepts of harmony constantly within our minds and those of our children and the next seven generations. The only way to avoid ecocide or some other worldwide catastrophe or holocaust is to reawaken the world to a global commonality of earthly spirituality.

We are all citizens of the world. We are all dependent upon the earth and sky. All of our children deserve a better life. To design a better future we have to see a better vision. Our vision is for the world to see this image and remember to keep in harmony with creation. This becomes a catalytic setting for action, consciousness, and conscience building. In closing, we ask you to look for the next Full Moon and remember the Moon's Prayer: "O, Mighty Spirit, Great Father, Forgive us for not loving Mother Earth; but save her for the Children."

The Morelia Declaration

A unique exchange has taken place. For the first time environmentalists, scientists, representatives from the native tribes of North and South America, political activists, and writers from 20 countries have spent a week in Mexico discussing the state of the world as we approach the end of the millennium. Independently, but without exception, each participant expressed concern that life on our planet is in grave danger.

• 24 billion tons of topsoil from cropland are being lost every year. If deforestation and other forms of land erosion continue at the current rate, the scientists present stated that by the end of the decade the earth will have no additional farmland, but nearly a billion new mouths to feed.

• The nuclear disaster of Chernobyl in 1986, which in varying degrees has subjected over 35 million people to radioactive assault, was only one of more than a hundred nuclear accidents which took place over the last decade. At the conference the scientist responsible for the clean-up of Chernobyl stated his belief that at least three nuclear catastrophes on the scale of Chernobyl are likely to take place by the year 2000 A.D.

• *70% of the world's population lives within 100 miles of the sea. The profligate use of fossil fuels by the industrialized world is rapidly and irreversibly changing our climate. Experts stressed that continued rising sea levels and global warming will lead to massive flooding of coastal areas, creating millions of new environmental refugees on an even greater scale than we witness annually in countries like Bangladesh.*

• *Human survival depends on biological diversity. At current rates of environmental destruction, especially the wanton destruction of tropical forests in the Americas, Asia, and Africa, we will lose at least a million species within the next ten years and a quarter of all living species within the next fifty years.*

I. *We, the participants of the Morelia Symposium, urge the leaders of the world at the Earth Summit to be held in June 1992 in Brazil to commit themselves to ending ecocide and ethnocide, and we propose the creation of an International Court of the Environment modeled on the International Court of Justice at The Hague.*

II. *20% of the world's population consumes 80% of its wealth and is responsible for 75% of its pollution. We believe there is sufficient knowledge and technology available to reduce the obscene disparity of wealth. We demand a genuine transfer of knowledge and resources from North to South, not the dumping of obsolescent and inefficient technologies and products. There must be an immediate end to the international traffic in toxic waste, urgent reduction of the pollution of rivers and oceans by industrial waste and human sewage, an end to the unprincipled export of banned pesticides and other chemicals to the economically desperate countries of the Third World, and the immediate availability of information and means to allow people to individually and voluntarily pursue the goal of population stabilization.*

III. *Traditionally, societies are generally the best managers of biodiversity. For the last 500 years the knowledge and the rights of the Native American peoples have been ignored. We believe that respecting the interests of indigenous peoples, both in the Americas and throughout the rest of the world, who have become exploited minorities in their countries is crucial for the preservation of biological and cultural diversity. We deplore the cultural pollution and loss of tradition which have led to global rootlessness, leaving humans, through the intensity of mass-marketing, vulnerable to the pressures of economic and political totalitarianism and habits of mass-consumption and waste which imperil the earth.*

IV. At the Earth Summit of June 1992 we demand that world leaders sign a Global Climate Change Convention. Industrialized countries must make a minimum commitment to a 20% reduction of their carbon dioxide emissions by the year 2000 A.D. We insist on rigorous implementation of the Montreal Protocol on Protection of the Ozone Layer. We also demand the signing of a convention to protect biological diversity, and the evidence of concrete progress in negotiations for a global forests treaty.

V. The proven economic folly of nuclear power coupled to the probability of environmental catastrophe necessitate the urgent substitution for nuclear energy of clean, safe, and efficient energy systems. The military establishment must cease the proliferation of nuclear, biological, and chemical weapons and convert a significant proportion of military expenditure to expenditure on environmental security. To ensure this, we demand an end to secrecy and a right to freedom of information in all matters concerning the world's environment.

The participants at this conference wish to stress that environmental destruction cannot be confined within the boundaries of any nation state.

We urge our fellow writers, environmentalists, scientists, members of indigenous minorities, and all concerned people to join us in demanding the creation of an International Court of the Environment at which environmentally criminal activity can be brought to the attention of the entire world.

If the latter half of the 20th century has been marked by human liberation movements, the final decade of the second millennium will be characterized by liberation movements among species, so that one day we can attain genuine equality among all living things.

Homero Aridjis (Mexico)
F. Sherwood Rowland (United States)
Peter Matthiessen (United States)
Vladimir Chernousenko (Soviet Union)
Gita Mehta (India)
Evaristo Nugkuag (Peru)
Kjell Espmark (Sweden)
Thomas Lovejoy (United States)
Augusto Ron Bastos (Paraguay)
Margarita Marino de Botero (Colombia)
J. M. G. LeClezio (France)
Amory Lovins (United States)
Yuco Tsushima (Japan)
Gert Bastian (Germany)
Nellda Pinon (Brazil)
Betty Ferber de Aridjis (United States)
Roberto Juarroz (Argentina)
Vikram Seth (India)
Monika van Paemel (Belgium)
Miguel Alvarez del Toro (Mexico)
Hans van de Waarsenburg (Netherlands)
Lester Brown (United States)
Octavio Paz (Mexico)
Petra Kelly (Germany)
Mirosiav Holub (Czechoslovakia)
Alvaro Umaha (Costa Rica)
W. S. Merwin (United States)
Adam Markham (Great Britain)
Vassily Aksyonov (Soviet Union)
Arturo Gomez-Pompa (Mexico)
Kirkpatrick Sale (United States)
Alan Durning (United States)
Agneta Pleifel (Sweden)
Jewell James (Lummi Tribe)
Miguel Grinberg (Argentina)
Jeffery Wilkerson (United States)
Carmen Boullosa (Mexico)
Fernando Cesarman (Mexico)
Sandra Cisneros (United States)

Mechael Ondaatje (Canada)
Folke Isaksson (Sweden)

Notes

1. Mary Fadden, "The James Bay Hydro-electric Project, *Northeast Indian Quarterly* 8, no. 2 (Summer 1991): 28.
2. P. Gorrie, "The James Bay Power Project—The environmental Cost of Reshaping the Geography of Northern Quebec," *Canadian Geographic* (February/March 1990): 20-31; cited in Fadden, "James Bay," 28.
3. J. Rosenthal and J. Beyea, *The Long-term Threats to Canada's James Bay from Human Development*, Washington, D.C.: National Audubon Society Environmental Policy Analysis Report No. 29 (1989).
4. Matthew Coone-Come, "A Reduction of Our World," in *Our People, Our Land: Perspectives on the Columbus Quincentenary*, ed. Kurt Russo (Bellingham, Wash.: Lummi Tribe and Kluckhohn Center, 1992), 82. Emphasis added.
5. Winona LaDuke, "Tribal Coalition Damns Hydro-Quebec Project," *Indian Country Today*, July 21, 1993, A-3. See also: Winona LaDuke, "Indigenous Environmental Perspectives: A North American Primer," in *Indigenous Economics: Toward a Natural World Order*, ed. José Barreiro. *Akwe:kon Journal* 9, no. 2 (Summer 1992), 66.
6. LaDuke, "Tribal Coalition," A-3.
7. Russo, ed. *Our People, Our Land.*
8. LaDuke, "Environmental Perspectives," 66.
9. Ibid.
10. Lea Foushee, "Acid Rain Research Paper," Indigenous Women's Network, testimony before the International Council of Indigenous Women, Samiland, Norway, August 1990; cited in LaDuke, "Environmental Perspectives," 66, 71.
11. Timothy Egan, "Eskimos Learn They've Been Living Amid Secret Pits of Radioactive Soil," *New York Times*, December 6, 1992.
12. Ibid.
13. Ibid.
14. Ibid.
15. Ibid.
16. Paul A. Kettl, "Suicide and Homicide: The Other Costs of Development," *Akwe:kon Journal* 8, no. 4 (Winter 1991): 58-61.
17. Glen Cooper, *Akwe:kon Journal* 8, no. 4 (Winter 1991): 30.
18. Interview, Richard Flamer with Bruce E. Johansen, Omaha,

Nebraska, June 13, 1992.

19. Kurt Russo and Lisa Dabek, "Common Cause and Common Destiny: The Lacandon Rainforest Project," in *Our People, Our Land*, ed. Russo, 77.

20. Ibid.

21. Ibid., 79.

22. In *Our People, Our Land*, ed. Russo.

Chapter Ten
Conclusion: Toward Liberation of the Natural World

Although the destruction of American Indian peoples is well understood, the profound sorrow that American Indian people have for the resulting degradation of the environment and landscape is less well known. Three generations ago, an old Omaha voiced a profound sense of loss about environmental change in Nebraska:

> *When I was a youth the country was very beautiful. Along the rivers were belts of timberland, where grew cottonwood, maple, elm, ash, hickory, and walnut trees, and many other shrubs. And under these grew many good herbs and beautiful flowering plants. In both the woodland and the prairies I could see the trails of many animals and could hear the cheerful songs of many kinds of birds. When I walked abroad I could see many forms of life, beautiful living creatures which Wakanda had placed here; and these were, after their manner, walking, flying, leaping, running, playing all about. But now the face of the land is all changed and sad. The living creatures are all gone. I see the land desolate and I suffer an unspeakable sadness. Sometimes I wake in the night and I feel as though I should suffocate from the pressure of this awful feeling of loneliness.*[1]

This poignant statement preceded the environmental calamity of the Dust Bowl on the Great Plains in the 1930s. The Dust Bowl was not only created by overgrazing and intensive cereal crop agriculture but by the disappearance of the buffalo. As long as buffalo roamed the Great Plains, their enormous weight on their hooves turned the hard topsoil so that deeply rooted grasses like the buffalo grass could take hold and thus curb wind and water erosion on the Great Plains, especially in dry years.[2] Thus, plowing the Plains for agricultural use might have resulted in short-term economic benefits but profound long-term ecological consequences.

"Managing" the environment to increase productivity or even to maintain current environmental norms may have enormous future consequences. Although the complexity of creation is incomprehensible to the human mind, we can respect creation and its rhythms as native people have done for centuries. Perhaps this is the key to an environmental ethic for the future. In essence, as long as Western man feels that he is a demigod above creation and pretends to make environmental management decisions that allegedly preserve or "improve" the environment, then each generation will swap one set of environmental problems for another. But that is not all that happens; as time goes by a reductionist environmental problem (the disappearance of species and fragile environments) emerges that further limits a return to historical environments and confines our future environmental options.

Yet, many Native Americans understand that ultimately the Creator will reclaim the environment, and balance will be restored. It is only a question of how harsh this process will be in the resultant reclamation of creation. Indeed, Chief Smohalla, a Wanapum Indian, believed that

> God . . . commanded that the lands and the fisheries should be common to all who lived upon them; that they were never to be marked off or divided, but that the people should enjoy the fruits that God planted in the land, and the animals that lived upon it, and the fishes in the water. God said he was the father and the earth was the mother of mankind; that nature was the law; that the animals, and fish, and plants obeyed nature, and that man only was sinful. This is the old law. . . . Those [people] who cut up the lands or sign papers for lands will be defrauded of their rights and be punished by God's anger.[3]

As human beings drift away from the processes of creation and develop a more indirect, engineered relationship with the environment, they will become increasingly vulnerable to the awesome powers of the natural world (fires, earthquakes, storms, drought, flooding, and climatic changes). Those human groups closer to nature experientially will adapt as best they can in order to survive, and those groups that suffer under the illusion of living outside or above nature will experience increasing difficulties in maintaining their economies and environments—if environmental degradation continues unimpeded. For traditional Native American medicine people like Bull Lodge (Sioux), "humbling [oneself] . . . with resignation to the will of [the] . . . Maker" will be the key to survival for both indigenous and industrial peoples.[4]

A few generations ago, statements lamenting environmental change and preparation for survival in an altered world were treated as the idealistic and unprogressive actions of "vanishing Americans," but today such statements resonate sympathetically with many non-native peoples. The attack on the environment is no longer just an attack on the indigenous peoples of the United States but also an assault on all the peoples of North America and the world. Environmental destruction and degradation can no longer be "contained" through technological fixes or shunted aside as the quaint musings of American Indian traditionalists.

Native Americans maintain this environmental "memory" of times past because their spirituality and philosophy reflect the centrality of nature in its orientation. Animals are to be venerated and respected as well as plants and all of creation. Often, American Indian spiritual communications are directed through the animal brothers, and the Creator often speaks to American Indian people through visions and stories that involve animals. To many Native Americans, animals and the whole spectrum of life-forms in the natural environment give insights into the nature of the cosmic creative force. Through environmentally specific rites, Native Americans hand down to future generations the knowledge of their cultural realities. The environment is a mirror that reflects

cultural values. The sweat lodge, the drum, thanksgiving ceremonies, pipe ceremonies, the Sun Dance, and many other
rites reinforce the cyclical rhythms of creation and one's individual and collective connectedness to the immediate environment.[5]

In the Native American world, time becomes a continu-
um connected to place; linear time is viewed as an invention
outside the reality of the processes of creation. The sacredness of time and place among Native Americans is reinforced
through mythic realities. Experiencing local natural land-
marks as a group and as individuals contributes to the identities of the people. Similarly, oral traditions of animal beings
clarify, sanctify, and identify the myriad forms of the environment. Chief Oren Lyons (Onondaga Nation) summarizes
this Native American valuing of the natural world and the
living forms of creation in this way:

> *We see it as our duty to speak as caretakers for the nat-
> ural world . . . the principle being that all life is equal,
> including the four-legged and the winged things. The
> principle has been lost; the two-legged walks about
> thinking he is supreme with his manmade laws. But
> there are universal laws of all living things. We come
> here and we say they too have rights.*[6]

Thus, each land form as well as the flora and fauna is an
experience that places the group and the individual in a
unique natural and mythic environment that sanctifies and
imparts meaning to all facets of creation. By localizing meaning in places, Native Americans cannot conceive of themselves
as being separate from the land and local environment. An
old road man in the Native American Church summarized
the concept succinctly when he said that "the white man
thinks he owns the earth while the American Indian knows
the earth owns him."[7]

In essence, those native societies and people that sanctify
time and place, free humanity from the mundane, concrete,
and profane manifestations of space and time. People that
are constrained by the profaning of time and space often feel

nostalgia for past historical environments or indulge in day-dreams about outer space explorations. But such flights of fantasy cannot escape the limitations of time and space in the concrete world. Only the shaman can transcend time and space in a sacred manner and thus experience the world in its totality albeit fleetingly.[8]

The answer to the ecological crisis lies in ourselves. The capitalist restructuring of agriculture that began in the fifteenth century transformed the old subsistence agroecosystems throughout the world from a mosaic of forest lands, pasture lands, and intensive croplands into a landscape of intensive specialized croplands that produced commodities (tobacco, sugar, rice, wheat, maize, and so forth) for a market outside the place that it was produced. Old subsistence practices maintained much of the diversity and complexity of creation while maintaining social stability.[9] But while the old subsistence practices retained much of the wisdom of nature, capitalist land utilization practices became less responsible to the web of creation and more oriented to the price structure of the global market.

The capitalist mode of production commoditized goods and people. Plantation economies arose that sold not only cotton but people. In this new economic order, people like American Indians who did not fit were either killed or removed. Karl Marx's analysis of economic restructuring under capitalism largely ignores its environmental impact since he chose to emphasize the reconfiguration of human relations in industrial societies.[10]

And yet it is in agricultural capitalism that we see how clearly environmental degradation works. The most profound innovation of capitalism that changes the way human groups relate to nature is the selling of land. By creating a market for land, all the complex interactions of plants, animals, and minerals were reduced to one simple word, *land*. However, in reality, land is not a commodity (something produced by humans for sale in a market), but it was made to look as though it were a commodity. Once regarded as a commodity, it was traded without restraint. Traditional forms of meaning and identity that were invested in the land by native peoples were ridiculed as "savage" or suppressed so that the marketing of land could proceed. The results of this new mindset about land are not easily fathomed. Essentially, once nature was reduced to land it disappeared until the end of the nineteenth century when the American frontier closed and it was apparent that quantities of land as a commodity were quite fixed.[11] This realization has compelled some Americans to turn to science and economics to deal with the notion of a limited land base and its consequent consumption problems.

Native people such as Glen Morris (Shawnee) believe that faith in the abilities of science and technology to deliver us from ecological disaster will only result in variations of "fascism."[12] Morris asserts that the population of North America presently exceeds the carrying capacity by a factor of ten and that this human "overshoot" in population is presently sustained through the destruction of forests to create agricultural lands.[13]

As a result of the exploding population in the nineteenth century, vast areas of land were devoured to produce raw materials for the industrializing process. Energy consumption and the resulting toxic emissions were increased geometrically to maintain an ever-expanding industrial life support system. Indeed, the entire aquasystem of the North American continent was reoriented to support the burgeoning needs of the agricultural and industrial sectors of the new industrial economy.[14] The dominant society in North America saw this commoditization of land as a "civilizing" process for native peoples. In the nineteenth century, the powerful forces of capitalism felt that

> *in integrating the native's resources (whether these be land or valuable ores or timber or water or labor) into an expanding industrial empire they were dragging native peoples from savagery into "higher" and "better" ways of life. Towards such worthy and constructive ends no measure of brutality was foreclosed.*[15]

Essentially, Native American people have experienced the problems of reducing nature to a marketable item for a long time. The Haudenosaunee (Iroquois) summarized the resulting environmental problems at the end of the twentieth century in this way:

In the beginning we were told that the human beings who walk about on the Earth have been provided with all the things necessary for life. We were instructed to carry a love for one another, and to show a great respect for all beings on this Earth. We were shown that our life exists with the tree of life, that our well-being depends on the well-being of the Vegetable Life, that we are close relatives of the four-legged beings.

The original instructions direct that we who walk about on the Earth are to express a great respect, an affection and a gratitude toward all spirits which create and support Life. When people cease to respect and express gratitude for all these many things, then all life will be destroyed, and human life on this planet will come to an end.

To this day the territories we still hold are filled with trees, animals, and the other gifts from the Creation. In these places we still receive our nourishment from our Mother Earth.

The Indo-European people who have colonized our lands have shown very little respect for the things that create and support Life. We believe that these people ceased their respect for the world a long time ago. Many thousands of years ago, all the people of the world believed in the same Way of Life, that of harmony with the Universe. All lived according to the Natural Ways.

Today the species of Man is facing a question of [its] very survival. The way of life known as Western Civilization is on a death path on which their own culture has no viable answers. When faced with the reality of their own destructiveness, they can only go forward into new areas of more efficient destruction.

The air is foul, the waters poisoned, the trees dying, the animals are disappearing. We think even the systems of weather are changing. Our ancient teaching warned us that if Man interfered with the Natural laws, these things would come to be. When the last of the Natural Way of Life is gone, all hope for human survival will be gone with it. And our Way of Life is fast disappearing, a victim of the destructive process.

The technologies and social systems which destroyed the animal and plant life are destroying the Native people. We know there are many people in the world who can quickly grasp the intent of our message. But our experience has taught us that there are few who are willing to seek out a method for moving to any real change.

The majority of the world does not find its roots in Western culture or tradition. The majority of the world finds its roots in the Natural World, and it is the Natural World, and the traditions of the Natural World, which must prevail.

We all must consciously and continuously challenge every model, every program, and every process that the West tries to force upon us. The people who are living on this planet need to break with the narrow concept of human liberation, and begin to see liberation as something that needs to be extended to the whole of the Natural World. What is needed is the liberation of all things that support life—the air, the waters, the trees—all things which support the sacred web of Life.

The Native peoples of the Western Hemisphere can contribute to the survival potential of the human species. The majority of our peoples still live in accordance with the traditions which find their roots in the Mother Earth. But the Native people have need of a forum in which our voice can be heard. And we need alliances with the other people of the world to assist in our struggle to regain and maintain our ancestral lands and protect the Way of Life we follow.

The traditional Native people hold the key to the reversal of the processes of Western Civilization, which hold the promise of unimaginable future suffering and destruction. Spiritualism is the highest form of political consciousness. Our culture is among the world's surviv-

ing proprietors of that kind of consciousness. Our cul-
ture is among the most ancient continuously existing
cultures in the world. We are the spiritual guardians of
this place. We are here to impart that message.[16]

Land, and the culture that is connected with it, is what
the Iroquois and other native peoples consider most important. It is central to understanding North American politics
of the last five hundred years. Control of land, and the resources contained in it and on it, colors the course of the ecological juggernaut of post-1492 North America.

No discussion of American Indian ecology of the last five
hundred years could end without the realization that resource development, land ownership, social control, and other
configurations of European power are inextricably tied
together to create an environmental ideology that is distinctly
Eurocentric in its orientations. This makes substantive ecological change in North America decidedly difficult since
decisions about the environment have been made by non-
natives for so long a time. This Eurocentric theorizing about
the North American environment assumes that European-
developed theories about the environment are universal and
that native peoples outside of Europe have little to teach the
"civilized" world about environmental perspectives. Indeed,
Calvin Martin has postulated that the American Indian cannot teach Europeans anything about the environment and
that Native Americans were elevated intentionally and inap-
propriately to the high priesthood of the "ecology cult" in the
late 1960s.[17] Martin believes that the conservationists needed
a spiritual leader in the post-World War II era and that the
American Indian served conveniently to flesh out the theology of environmentalism. Although he fails to make a convinc-
ing case concerning the idealization of Native Americans as
the first ecologists, Martin nevertheless believes that

[t]he Indian still remains a misfit guru. Even if he were
capable of leading us, we could never follow him. The
Indian's was a profoundly different cosmic vision when
it came to interpreting Nature—a vision Western man

could never adjust to. There can be no salvation in the
Indian's traditional conception of Nature for the trou-
bled environmentalist. Some day, perhaps, he will real-
ize that he must look to someone else other than the
American Indian for realistic spiritual inspiration.[18]

From the Native American viewpoint, Martin's pessimis-
tic and deterministic musings about the viability of American
Indian environmental perspectives in today's world work
against the liberation of native and non-native lands and
peoples alike. In accepting the hegemony of European
thought, he categorizes and isolates the wisdom of American
Indian people as though it were unfathomable or at least
inscrutable to European people. Martin's discussion of the
commoditization of the fur trade in North America and his
implication that Native American spiritualism was fractured
by the ensuing market economy is a simplistic overgeneral-
ization that cannot withstand scrutiny when factored into a
complex and interrelated ecosystem.

Moreover, contemporary Native American intellectuals
like Ward Churchill are diametrically opposed to Martin's
opinion on American Indian environmentalism. In essence,
Churchill charges that the Eurocentric intellectual isolation
of American Indian environmental spirituality and thought
is a form of monocultural orthodoxy that excludes Native
American wisdom not for its message but because it fails to
live up to European norms which involve assumptions about
"savages" and other universalizing concepts inherent in the
discourse of Eurocentric scholars.[19] Furthermore, Churchill
maintains that the great majority of non-Indians in America
have nothing to lose and a great deal to gain in returning
American Indian lands to native peoples so that they can use
the land in traditional ways. In fact, he states that liberation
of the land must precede human liberation. Indeed, he maintains that most human liberation movements stand in the
way of land liberation and thus implies that nothing can be
accomplished until we restore the land (nature) to its rightful
place as a central factor in human existence.[20]

The concept of liberation has been a very important

part of the discourse of empire during the last two hundred years. As the problems of urban poverty arose as a by-product of industrialization in the nineteenth century, liberal caretakers evolved to "help" the poor; but control of the client people (like control of the land) remained a dominant force in poverty programs. But once the poor became increasingly restive under this control, many liberal caretakers switched to helping racial minorities, which also became vocal about the control exercised over them. Finally, the liberal caretakers focused on the environment, which did not talk back; but control rather than harmony was still the watchword. This emphasis on environmental control (such as the maintenance of "wilderness" and "recreation" areas) runs counter to an ethic of harmony and interrelatedness, and as such environmental control is as exclusive in its practices as any timber or railroad baron of olden times. In any discourse on environmentalism, the Eurocentric thinker focuses on control while the native thinker focuses on harmony.[21] This is an impasse that must be overcome so that the earth and its peoples can survive without excessive depletion of natural resources.

The Native American world of participative harmony is aptly summarized by the astronomer and anthropologist Anthony Aveni in the following passage on the intellectual life of the pre-Columbian Mayas:

> These people did not react to the flow of natural events by struggling to harness and control them. Nor did they conceive of themselves as totally passive observers in the essentially neutral world of nature. Instead, they believed that they were active participants and intermediaries in a great cosmic drama. The people had a stake in all temporal enactments. By participating in the rituals, they helped the gods of nature to carry their burdens along their arduous course, for they believed firmly that the rituals served formally to close time's cycles. Without their life's work the universe could not function properly. Here was an enviable balance, a harmony in the partnership between humanity and nature, each with a purposeful role to play.[22]

Another commentator elaborates on these spiritual and natural perceptions in a more comparative way:

> *[Among the] . . . Andeans, . . . [t]he land surrounding one told the story of one's first ancestors as much as it told one's own story and the story of those yet to come. It was right that the familiar dead were seen walking through the fields they had once cultivated, thus sharing them with both the living and with the original ancestors who raised the first crops in the very same fields. Death was thus the great leveler not because, as in Christian thought, it reduced all human beings to equality in relation to each other and before God. Rather, death was a leveler because by means of it humans were reintegrated into a network of parents and offspring that embraced the entire natural order.*[23]

In the Judeo-Christian world, soul is divorced from nature, and as a consequence humans place the existential maintenance of their individual souls above the collective maintenance of the environment. Scholars like Calvin Martin believe that such European philosophical differences from the holistic and participative views of Native Americans render the environmental ideas of American Indians useless to the Eurocentric peoples of North America. However, few North Americans go to Europe today for any length of time, and when they do they seem to achieve a profound sense of their identity as Americans. Indeed, Americans have an identity that involves something greater than Europe, one that has a Native American dimension to it. Perhaps that is why environmentalism is so deeply rooted in the American public discourse as the twentieth century ends. At the beginning of the twentieth century, it seems to have been mostly American Indians like the old Omaha who felt the "unspeakable sadness" and "loneliness" of environmental degradation. By the end of the twentieth century, it appears that many non-natives are experiencing the same spiritual malaise.

In the late twentieth century, it seems certain that multiple perspectives on the environmental dilemma are preferable to an exclusively Eurocentric approach. New and diverse ecological and spiritual views emerge to meet the demands of the human endeavor. These emerging worldviews and ways of life transform the human experience in the myriad environments that they function in. Such transformations help cultures (Native American, Eurocentric, and new syntheses) to deal with the changes that are encountered. And these changing paradigms (conservative or accommodating) seek to resolve the dilemmas of constancy and change through a process called "tradition."

Although we tend to learn about appropriate human behavior through example, we usually get most of our education about the environment from our local surroundings. In the modern world, we like to think that we get most of our knowledge from libraries, universities, and complex data bases. But how do we internalize such vast amounts of information into a meaningful whole? Unfortunately, the European mentality has abstracted today's natural world so much that many people are currently residing in an intellectually and artificially constructed universe that is self-threatening and self-defeating. In a world where people get their knowledge of birds, animals, and natural forces from the media, the natural world appears to be one of cuddly felines, comical coyotes, or cartoon ducks. Increasingly, people experience the animal forms of creation through zoos, domesticated animals that are dependent on us, and/or chance encounters with animals while driving along the freeway.

In the postmodern world configured and reconfigured through the electronic superhighway, the theoretical universe created by academic, corporate, and governmental authority in the past is crumbling. Abstract all-encompassing theories that explain and rationalize the *status quo* regardless of the realities of a given situation are giving way to electronic conversations, publications and information sharing that approach reality in a much more "tentative" and experiential way. Thus, the electronic information networks make knowledge more process oriented and less factual through the very technique through which they are distributed. Essentially in the Native American world, finding out what is going on is more important than "explaining" what happened. This "tentativeness" and process orientation in the information superhighway is more akin to Native American perceptions of the world and its workings. After several centuries of technologies that foster control and manipulation through military might, we may be entering into an era in which modern information technology liberates rather than controls situations. Of course, universal access remains a problem just as universal access to today's environment remains problematic. In the past, corporations, railroads, and governmental agencies sought to increase their control over the American people's access to the environment (that is, corporate and railroad development of the American West versus westward movement of squatters and frontiersmen). By making land a commodity at the beginning of the development of the United States, access to land and the fruits of the environment were controlled and distributed not so much on the basis of direct and obvious need for every member of the society, as it was in most indigenous societies, but rather on the basis of wealth and power that was vested in an elite. In essence, the very process of developing the environment industrially alienates the common people from the environment even before they are alienated from the factory work processes. This attentuation and alienation of the great mass of industrial humanity from the environment paves the way for those in power to attack the environment for short-term full employment goals and material profit.

In contrast to these attentuated industrially constructed experiences with creation, Native Americans perceived themselves as participating in a natural structure of life that deeply involved all other species. Since human beings were regarded as latecomers to creation, it was important to respect every other form of life so that we could learn lessons from animal beings necessary for survival and prosperity. Since it was recognized that they had detailed knowledge of the universe and how to live in it, the observation of animals was a very serious matter for American Indians. Clans and social systems were patterned after native perceptions of animal behavior with clan totems (bear, deer, turtle, and so forth) reflecting this process. Some American Indian nations even had a psychology of birds and animals that emphasized the parallels between human and animal behavioral traits; the accuracy of these psychological descriptions have surprised many European observers.

Technical skills could also be learned from animals to ensure continued prosperity. Native Americans could often determine the best materials for constructing houses in specific locales by observing bird nests, or learn the shortest routes over mountains through forests, or through deserts by observing game animals. Information about water sources and quality as well as edible plants could be obtained by observing beaver dams and by watching other animal brothers. Methods of gathering plants as well as hunting techniques were also gleaned from the habits of animals. For instance, a surplus rodent population might mean a declining coyote and/or cougar population. Watching animal behavior might also indicate the sites of medicinal plants useful to humans. As Native Americans collected such knowledge by observing the animals that inhabited the places they lived, they developed a pharmacology to treat animals as well as human maladies.

Observation of the natural process was also reflected in spiritual ceremonies and rituals. In the Hopi Snake Dance or Rain Dance the snake people were asked to bring water to the Hopis while, according to the Navajos, it was Coyote that brought fire to them. Some rituals involved the sacrificing of an eagle or some other animal to ensure that the animal was incorporated into the process. In these rituals, the animals participated as partners in the process of living and dying.

For many Native Americans, the relationship with the animal kingdom was so close that it was thought that humans could take the shape of birds or animals after their death. Hence, the circling of a hawk, owl, or woodpecker over a village after the death of a loved one was not an uncommon site. Professor Grinde was personally visited by a bear shortly after the death of his brother-in-law. Such visitations in the native world are considered common and are to be taken literally not symbolically.

Many tribes classified birds and animals in order to explain complicated relationships. The Plains Indians made an important distinction between two-legged and four-legged animals. The two-legged animals were birds, bears, and humans. According to many native peoples, the knowledge of these creatures was concerned with healing, and it is the two-legged creatures that were responsible for putting the world back in harmony when it became unbalanced. In native societies certain animals and certain humans were often grouped together, and the animals often gave warnings of impending danger to the humans and to the environment in general. Thus, the disappearance or sufferings of a certain species might be a warning to human beings to restore harmony to the world. In today's world, many native peoples feel that they are the only ones who see the warning signs of an environment in trouble. Obviously, people lose their ability to sense subtle changes when their relation with the environment becomes attentuated and less direct, as it has in industrialized society.[24]

Thus, the means for comprehending the processes of creation, their meaning for human existence, and threats to such processes cannot be easily grasped in the abstract constructions of the European world. American society still has much to learn from the native peoples of America, just as the native peoples of the Americas have learned much from the Europeans. Today, ideas can mix freely between cultures and ethnic groups aided by modern communication and transportation. The notion of exclusivity in the pursuit of human awareness and knowledge narrows the diversity of our options and produces less joy in relating to the human and environmental condition. In the final analysis, the achievement of wisdom concerning environmental conditions should not be associated with any particular race or territory. Our feet all rest on the same earth.

As a result of the mass destruction of human life in World Wars I and II through the techniques of mechanized and nuclear war, the surviving European ideologies (democratic capitalism and Communism) turned away from the wholesale and physical destruction of people and instead developed policies that led to the wholesale exploitation and destruction of environments. From a pragmatic point of view, this decision produced some semblance of a lasting peace for a couple of generations since the physical environment neither reads nor comprehends the works of Karl Marx or Adam Smith. Unlike humanity, the environment could not register its disapproval of these policy decisions through rebellions and revolutions at the initial stages of its implementation. Since 1945, the world's populations enjoyed some material gains and respite from cataclysmic wars that destroyed people by the tens of millions. But the uneasy peace borne on accelerated environmental degradation is now coming to an end. Today, the environment is sending us a clear message that the partial shifting of exploitation from the masses of humanity to the physical environment in the quest for peace and stability cannot be sustained. Obviously, it would not be humane to return to the wholesale exploitation and destruction of human populations that occurred in the first half of the twentieth century. Conversely, we should not continue, willy nilly, to pursue policies that sacrifice our environment in the name of promoting economic stability and moderating international and national, as well as race, class, and gender tensions. What is to be feared is the path of least resistance—where the environment is allowed continually to deteriorate and the resulting mass destruction of populations will "appear" to be by the hand of "God." The Christian notion of the Apocalypse easily sanctifies this process as does Adam Smith's notion of the "invisible hand" (equivalent to the hand of God), when it really is a result of a lack of political courage, vision, and leadership. Such a destructive set of circumstances—if allowed to work itself out—would represent a resurfacing of fascism in advanced industrialized societies, but this time around the destruction would appear to be done through the environment and not through human hands and war machines. Given the horrors of such a scenario, a positive and affirming spiritual path must evolve that explains and harmonizes the conflicting forces of environmental destruction, human "progress," and human freedom. In the framing and implementation of this new path, Native Americans and other indigenous peoples must play a crucial and central role—unfettered by the economic and intellectual tenets of empire and modernization.

At the same time that access to diverse modes of consciousness has become more widespread, the ecological crisis facing modern capitalist society has become more omnipresent, and more obvious. As we researched this book, we were consistently amazed at how far-reaching the environmental crisis has become—extending even to the most remote regions. At a time when PCBs are being found in mothers' milk above the Arctic Circle, the pervasiveness of the ecological crisis has spawned a search by many peoples, in many cultures, for alternative ways of thinking, living, and making a living. The popularity of Native American perspectives on the environment in the late twentieth century is no accident, but part of a species-wide search for modes of living that will address the number one problem everyone now faces: the survival of a sustaining earth.

More than a century and a half ago Chief Seal'th said, "We may be brothers after all"—at a time when most Euro-Americans looked at the bounty of America as free and nearly endless. Today, the perspective is much different, and there is widespread realization that time is short. More people of all cultures are realizing that the only way out of this dilemma is to think and act to sustain a viable earth. This is one issue that connects us all and on which our common survival has come to depend. Liberating "mother earth" from totally Eurocentric conceptions of the environment will allow for a wider range of choices and solutions that will hopefully serve a broader group of peoples and cultures in the future. Since most American Indian communities are ecocentric, liberation of the environment involves liberation of Native American people.

Notes

1. Quoted in Melvin R. Gilmore, *Prairie Smoke* (New York: Columbia University Press, 1929), 36.
2. For a good example of Plains Indian respect for the buffalo and admonitions to not overhunt the herds, see George Bird Grinnell, *Pawnee Hero Stories and Folk Tales* (New York: Forest and Stream Publishing Company, 1889), 132-44.
3. Chief Smohalla's speech in *Fourteenth Annual Report of the Bureau of American Ethnology* (Washington, D.C.: Government Printing Office, 1896), part 2, 220-21.
4. George Horse Capture, ed., *The Seven Visions of Bull Lodge* (Lincoln: University of Nebraska Press, 1980), 120.
5. Horse Capture, ed., *Visions of Bull Lodge*, passim.
6. Quoted in Matthew Fox, *A Spirituality Named Compassion and the Healing of the Global Village, Humpty Dumpty and Us* (Minneapolis, Minn.: Winston Press, 1979), 164.
7. Conversation with Donald A. Grinde, Jr., and Elwood Koshiway (Otoe), April 4, 1983.
8. Joseph Epes Brown, *The Spiritual Legacy of the American Indian* (New York: Crossroad Publishing Co., 1982), 51-52.
9. See Ward Churchill and Elizabeth R. Lloyd, *Culture versus Economism: Essays on Marxism in the Multicultural Arena* (Denver, Colo.: Fourth World Center for the Study of Indigenous Law and Politics, 1989) for a fuller discussion of these issues.
10. Ibid.
11. For a more intensive discussion of these themes, see Donald Worster, "Transformations of the Earth: Toward an Agroecological Perspective in History," *Journal of American History* 76, no. 4 (March 1990): 1087-106.
12. Churchill and Lloyd, *Culture versus Economism*; see the introduction by Glen Morris, 4.
13. Ibid., 2. Morris gets his analysis in part from William Catton, *Overshoot: The Ecological Basis for Revolutionary Change* (Urbana: University of Illinois Press, 1980).
14. Churchill and Lloyd, *Culture versus Economism*, 3.
15. Ibid., 5.
16. Excerpted from Editors, *A Basic Call to Consciousness, Akwesasne Notes* (New York: Mohawk Nation via Rooseveltown, 1978).
17. Oddly enough, a survey of the environmental textbooks of the period Martin discusses contain little or no mention of American Indians as environmental gurus. In fact, mass-marketed texts such as Richard Wagner, *Environment and Man* (New York: W. W. Norton, 1974) contain no mention of American Indians at all.

18. Calvin Martin, *Keepers of the Game: Indian-Animal Relationships and the Fur Trade* (Berkeley: University of California Press, 1978), 188.

19. Churchill and Lloyd, *Culture versus Economism*, 29.

20. Ward Churchill, "The Earth Is Our Mother: Struggles for American Indian Land and Liberation in the Contemporary United States," in *The State of Native America*, ed. M. Annette Jaimes (Boston: South End Press, 1992), 177.

21. For some new approaches and perspectives with regard to environmental alliances between native peoples and environmentalists, see Al Gedicks, *The New Resource Wars: Native and Environmental Struggles Against Multinational Corporations* (Boston: South End Press, 1993).

22. Anthony Aveni, *Empires of Time* (New York: Basic Books, 1989), 252.

23. Sabine MacCormack, "Demons, Imagination and the Incas," *Representations* 33 (1991): 134.

24. Vine Deloria, Jr., *God Is Red* (New York: Dell Publishing Company, 1973), 73. See also Dennis Tedlock and Barbara Tedlock, eds., *Teachings from the American Earth* (New York: Liverwright, 1975) for a fuller discussion of the nature of American Indian spirituality and the environment.

Bibliography

Introduction

Barnouw, Victor. *Wisconsin Chippewa Myths and Tales and Their Relation to Chippewa Life.* Madison: University of Wisconsin Press, 1977.

Bryan, Kirk. "PreColumbian Agriculture in the Southwest, as Conditioned by Periods of Alluviation." *Annals of the Association of American Geographers* 31, no. 4 (1941).

Codman, Hislop. *The Mohawk.* New York: Rinehart and Company, 1948.

Deloria, Vine Jr. *God Is Red.* New York: Dell Publishing Company, 1973.

Drucker, Philip. *Cultures of the North Pacific Coast.* New York: Chandler Publishing Company, 1902.

Hallowell, A. I. "Ojibwa Metaphysics of Being and the Perception of Persons." In *Person Perception and Interpersonal Behavior,* eds. Renato Taquiri and Luigi Petrullo. Palo Alto, Calif.: Stanford University Press, 1958.

———."Some Empirical Aspects of Northern Saulteaux Religion." *American Anthropologist* 36 (1934).

Interpress Columnists Service, ed. *Story Earth: Native Voices on the Environment.* San Francisco: Mercury House, 1993.

Lee, Dorothy. "Linguistic Reflection of Wintu Thought." In *Freedom and Culture.* Prospect Heights, Ill.: Waveland Press, 1987.

Merchant, Carolyn, ed. *Major Problems in American Environmental History.* Lexington, Mass.: Heath, 1993.

Milfort, Louis LeClerc. *Memoirs or, a Quick Glance at My Various Travels and My Sojourn in the Creek Nation.* Savannah, Ga.: Beehive Press, 1972.

North, Douglass C. *Growth and Welfare in the American Past: A New Economic History.* Englewood Cliffs, N.J.: Prentice-Hall, 1966.

Reichard, Gladys A. *Navajo Religion: A Study of Symbolism.* 2d ed. Princeton, N.J.: Princeton University Press, 1950.

Stannard, David. *American Holocaust: Columbus and the Conquest of the New World.* New York: Oxford University Press, 1992.

Toynbee, Arnold J. *A Study of History.* 12 vols. London: Oxford University Press, 1935–1962.

Trennert, Robert A. *Alternative to Extinction: Federal Indian Policy*

and the Beginning of the Reservation System, 1846-1851.
Philadelphia: Temple University Press, 1975.

Trigger, Bruce. Review of Axtell's *After 1492* in *Ethnohistory* 40, no. 3 (Summer 1993): 466–68.

Vivian, R. Gwinn. "An Inquiry into Prehistoric Social Organization in Chaco Canyon, New Mexico." In *Reconstructing Prehistoric Pueblo Societies*, ed. William Longacre. Albuquerque: University of New Mexico Press, 1970.

Waters, Frank. *Brave Are My People: Indian Heroes Not Forgotten.* Santa Fe, N.M.: Clear Light Publishers, 1993.

Native Ecology and Worldviews

Barnouw, Victor. *Wisconsin Chippewa Myths and Tales and Their Relation to Chippewa Life.* Madison: University of Wisconsin Press, 1977.

Barreiro, José, ed. "Indigenous Economics: Toward a Natural World Order." *Akwe:kon Journal* 9, no. 2 (Summer 1992).

Benedict, Ruth Fulton. "The Concept of the Guardian Spirit in North America." *Memoirs of the American Anthropological Association.* Menasha, Wisc.: The American Anthropological Association, 1923.

Bennett, John W. *The Ecological Transition: Cultural Anthropology and Human Adaptation.* New York: Pergamon Press, 1976.

Black, Mary Bartholomew. "An Ethnoscience Investigation of Ojibwa Ontology and World View." Ph.D. diss., Stanford University, 1967.

Black Elk. *The Sacred Pipe*, ed. Joseph Epes Brown. New York: Penguin Books, 1973.

Boaz, Franz. *Contributions to the Ethnology of the Kwakiutl.* Columbia University Contributions to Anthropology, 3. New York: Columbia University Press, 1925.

Borah, Woodrow. "The Historical Demography of Aboriginal and Colonial America: An Attempt at Perspective." In *The Native American Population of the Americas in 1492*, ed. William M. Denevan. Madison: University of Wisconsin Press, 1976.

Brandon, William. *American Heritage Book of Indians.* New York: Dell, 1961.

Bryan, Kirk. "PreColumbian Agriculture in the Southwest, as Conditioned by Periods of Alluviation." *Annals of the Association of American Geographers* 31, no. 4 (1941).

Capps, Walter Holden, ed. *Seeing with a Native Eye: Essays on Native American Religion.* New York: Harper Forum Books, 1976.

Casas, Bartolomé de las. *The Devastation of the Indies* [1542]. New York: Seabury Press, 1974.

Cook, Sherburne F., and Leslie B. Simpson. "The Population of Central Mexico in the Sixteenth Century." In *Ibero-Americana*, no. 31. Berkeley and Los Angeles: University of California Press, 1948.

Coon-Come, Matthew. "A Reduction of Our World." In *Our People, Our Land: Perspectives on the Columbus Quincentenary*, ed. Kurt Russo. Bellingham, Wash.: Lummi Tribe and Kluckhohn Center, 1992.

Cornell, George. "Native American Perceptions of the Environment." *Northeast Indian Quarterly* 7, no. 2 (Summer 1990): 3-13.

Cronon, William. *Changes in the Land: Indians, Colonists and the Ecology of New England.* New York: Hill & Wang, 1983.

Day, Gordon. "The Indian as an Ecological Factor in the Northeastern Forest." *Ecology* 34 (April 1953).

Deloria, Vine Jr. *God Is Red: A Native View of Religion.* 2d ed. Golden, Colo.: North American Press/Fulcrum, 1992.

———."Comfortable Fictions and the Struggle for Turf: An Essay Review of James Clifton, *The Invented Indian . . . .*" *American Indian Quarterly* 16, no. 3: 397-410.

Denevan, William M., ed. *The Native Populations of the Americas in 1492.* Madison: University of Wisconsin Press, 1976.

Dobyns, Henry F. "More Methodological Perspectives on Historical Demography." *Ethnohistory* 36, no. 3 (Summer 1989): 285-98.

———."Estimating Aboriginal American Population." *Current Anthropology* 7 (October 1966): 395-416.

———.*Their Numbers Became Thinned.* Knoxville: University of Tennessee Press, 1983.

Drucker, Philip. *Cultures of the North Pacific Coast.* New York: Chandler Publishing Company, 1902.

Engelbrecht, William. "Factors Maintaining Low Population Density among the Prehistoric New York Iroquois." *American Antiquity* 52 (January 1987): 13-27.

Fadden, Mary. "The James Bay Hydro-electric Project." *Northeast Indian Quarterly* 8, no. 2 (Summer 1991): 28-30.

Ford, Paul L., ed. *The Writings of Thomas Jefferson.* New York: G. P. Putnam Sons, 1892-1899.

Gill, Sam. *Mother Earth.* Chicago: University of Chicago Press, 1987.

Ginther, Erna. "Analysis of the First Salmon Ceremony." *American Anthropologist* 38 (1926).

Gorrie, P. "The James Bay Power Project—The Environmental Cost of Reshaping the Geography of Northern Quebec." *Canadian Geographic* (February/March 1990): 20-31.

Hallowell, A. I. "Ojibwa Ontology, Behavior, and World View." In *Contributions to Anthropology: Selected Papers of A. Irving Hallowell.* Chicago: University of Chicago Press, 1976.

———."Ojibwa Metaphysics of Being and the Perception of Persons." In *Person Perception and Interpersonal Behavior,* eds. Renato Taquiri and Luigi Petrullo. Palo Alto, Calif.: Stanford University Press, 1958.

———.*Culture and Experience.* Philadelphia: University of Pennsylvania Press, 1955.

———."Some Empirical Aspects of Northern Saulteaux Religion." *American Anthropologist* 36 (1934).

Haury, Emil W. *The Hohokam, Desert Farmers and Craftsmen: Excavations at Snaketown, 1964-65.* Tucson: University of Arizona Press, 1976.

Henige, David. "On the Current Devaluation of the Notion of Evidence: A Rejoinder to Dobyns." *Ethnohistory* 36, no. 3 (Summer 1989): 304-7.

Hudson, Charles. "Cherokee Concept of Natural Balance." *Indian Historian* 3.

Hughes, J. Donald. *American Indian Ecology.* El Paso: Texas Western Press, 1983.

Interpress Columnists Service, ed. *Story Earth: Native Voices on the Environment.* San Francisco: Mercury House, 1993.

Isaacs, Hope L. "Orenda: An Ethnographic Cognitive Study of Seneca Medicine and Politics." Ph.D. diss., State University of New York at Buffalo, 1973.

Iverson, Peter. "Taking Care of the Earth and Sky." In *America in 1492: The World of the Indian Peoples Before the Arrival of Columbus,* ed. Alvin Josephy. New York: Alfred A. Knopf, 1992.

James, Jewell Praying Wolf. "Nations, Treaties, Tribes." In *Our People, Our Land: Perspectives on the Columbus Quincentary,* ed. Kurt Russo. Bellingham, Wash.: Lummi Tribe and Kluckhohn Center, 1992.

Johansen, Bruce E. "Black Hills Uranium Rush." In *America's Energy,* ed. Robert Engler. New York: Pantheon, 1980.

Jones, Jeff. "A Nation Divided." *Metroland,* June 7-13, 1990.

Jones, Malcolm. "Just Too Good to Be True: Another Reason to Beware of False Eco-Prophets." *Newsweek,* May 4, 1992.

Josephy, Alvin, ed. *America in 1492: The World of the Indian Peoples Before the Arrival of Columbus.* New York: Alfred A. Knopf, 1992.

Kroeber, A. L. *Cultural and Natural Areas of Native North America.* University of California Publications in American Archaeology and Ethnology 38. Berkeley: University of California Press, 1939.

Lee, Dorothy. "Linguistic Reflection of Wintu Thought." In *Freedom and Culture*. Englewood Cliffs, N.J.: Prentice-Hall, 1959.

Lewis, Henry T. "Patterns of Indian Burning in California: Ecology and Ethnohistory." *Ballena Press Anthropological Papers* 1 (1973).

Lord, Lewis, and Sarah Burke. "America Before Columbus." *U.S. News & World Report*, July 8, 1991.

MacDonald, Peter. "Technology and Indigenous Thought." *Akwe:kon Journal* (Spring 1992): 35–38.

Mander, Jerry. *In the Absence of the Sacred: The Failure of Technology and the Survival of the Indian Nations*. San Francisco: Sierra Club Books, 1991.

Martin, Calvin. *Keepers of the Game: Indian-Animal Relationships and the Fur Trade*. Los Angeles: University of California Press, 1978.

Matthews, Washington. "The Night Chant: A Navajo Ceremony." *Memoirs of the American Museum of Natural History* 6 (1902).

McDowell, Bart. "The Aztecs." *National Geographic*, December 1980.

McGaa, Ed. *Mother Earth Spirituality*. San Francisco: HarperCollins, 1991.

Mooney, James. *The Aboriginal Population of North America North of Mexico*. In *Smithsonian Miscellaneous Collections*, ed. J. R. Swanton, 80, no. 7. Washington, D.C.: Smithsonian Institution, 1928.

———."Population." In *Handbook of American Indians North of Mexico*, ed. F. W. Hodge. Bureau of American Ethnology Bulletin 30, no. 2. Washington, D.C.: Government Printing Office, 1910.

Nabokov, Peter, ed. *Native American Testimony*. New York: Harper & Row, 1978.

Nabokov, Peter, and Dean Snow. "Farmers of the Woodlands." In *America in 1492: The World of the Indian Peoples Before the Arrival of Columbus*, ed. Alvin Josephy. New York: Alfred A. Knopf, 1992.

New York State Assembly Hearings. *Crisis at Akwesasne*. Day 1 (Ft. Covington, N.Y.), July 24, 1990; Day 2 (Albany, N.Y.) August 2, 1990. Transcript in files of New York State Assembly Environmental Conservation Committee.

Oliver, Symmes C. *Ecology and Cultural Continuity as Contributing Factors in the Social Organization of the Plains Indians*. Berkeley: University of California Press, 1962.

Ortiz, Alfonso. *The Tewa World: Space, Time, Being and Becoming in a Pueblo Society*. Chicago: University of Chicago Press, 1969.

Persons, Elsie Clews. *Pueblo Indian Religion*. 2 vols. Chicago: University of Chicago Press, 1939.

Picard, A. "James Bay II." *The Amicus Journal* (Fall 1990): 10–17.

Porter, Tom. New York State Assembly Hearings. *Crisis at Akwesasne.* Day 1 (Ft. Covington, N.Y.), July 24, 1990, transcript.

Portilla, Miguel Leon. *The Broken Spears: The Aztec Account of the Conquest of Mexico.* Boston: Beacon Press, 1962.

Ramenofsky, Ann F. *Vectors of Death: The Archaeology of European Contact.* Albuquerque: University of New Mexico Press, 1987.

Reichard, Gladys A. *Navajo Religion: A Study of Symbolism.* 2d ed. Princeton, N.J.: Princeton University Press, 1950.

Rosenthal, J., and J. Beyea. *The Long-term Threats to Canada's James Bay from Human Development.* National Audubon Society Environmental Policy Analysis Report No. 29 (1989).

Russo, Kurt, ed. *Our People, Our Land: Perspectives on the Columbus Quincentenary.* Bellingham, Wash.: Lummi Tribe and Kluckhohn Center, 1992.

Sauer, Carl O. "Grassland, Climax, Fire and Man." *Journal of Range Management* 3 (1950).

Snow, Dean R., and Kim M. Lanphear. "'More Methodological Perspectives': A Rejoinder to Dobyns." *Ethnohistory* 36, no. 3 (Summer 1989): 299–303.

——."European Contact and Indian Depopulation in the Northeast: The Timing of the First Epidemics." *Ethnohistory* 35, no. 1 (Winter 1988): 15–33.

Standing Bear, Luther. *Land of the Spotted Eagle.* Lincoln: University of Nebraska Press, 1978.

Starna, William A. Review of *American Indian Environments.* In *American Anthropologist* 84, no. 2 (1982): 468–69.

Stuart, George E. "Maya Heartland under Siege." *National Geographic,* November 1992.

Swanton, John R. "Aboriginal Culture of the Southeast." *Forty-Second Annual Report of the Bureau of American Ethnology* [1924–1925]. Washington, D.C.: Government Printing Office, 1928.

Toelken, Barre. "Seeing with a Native Eye: How Many Sheep Will It Hold?" In *Seeing with a Native Eye: Essays on Native American Religion,* ed. Walter Holden Capps. New York: Harper Forum Books, 1976.

Toynbee, Arnold J. *A Study of History.* 12 vols. London: Oxford University Press, 1935–1962.

Ubelaker, Douglas. "The Sources of Methodology for Mooney's Estimates of North American Indian Populations." In *Native Population of the Americas in 1492,* ed. William M. Denevan. Madison: University of Wisconsin Press, 1972.

Underhill, Ruth. *Red Man's Religion: Beliefs and Practices of the Indians*

North of Mexico. Chicago: University of Chicago Press, 1965.

Vanderwerth, W. C. eds. *Indian Oratory: Famous Speeches by Noted Indian Chieftains.* Norman: University of Oklahoma Press, 1971.

Vecsey, Christopher, and Robert W. Veneables. *American Indian Environments: Ecological Issues in Native American History.* Syracuse, N.Y.: Syracuse University Press, 1980.

Vivian, R. Gwinn. "An Inquiry into Prehistoric Social Organization in Chaco Canyon, New Mexico." In *Reconstructing Prehistoric Pueblo Societies,* ed. William Longacre. Albuquerque: University of New Mexico Press, 1970.

Walker, J. R. *The Sun Dance and Other Ceremonials of the Oglala Division of the Teton Sioux.* New York: AMS Press, 1971.

Waters, Frank. *Brave Are My People: Indian Heroes Not Forgotten.* Santa Fe, N.M.: Clear Light Publishers, 1993.

Wedel, Waldo R. "Some Aspects of Human Ecology in the Central Plains." *American Anthropologist* 4 (1953).

White, Leslie A. *The Science of Culture: A Study of Man and Civilization.* New York: Farrar, Straus, and Giroux, 1969.

Wright, Ronald. *Stolen Continents: The Americas through Indian Eyes Since 1492.* Boston: Houghton-Mifflin, 1992.

Wyman, Leland C. *Blessingway.* Tucson: University of Arizona Press, 1970.

The Pueblo Revolt

Beck, Warren A. *New Mexico: A History of Four Centuries.* Norman: University of Oklahoma Press, 1969.

Bowden, Henry Warner. "Spanish Missions, Cultural Conflict, and the Pueblo Revolt of 1680." *Church History* 44 (Summer 1975).

Brandon, William. *American Heritage Book of Indians.* New York: Dell, 1969.

Dozier, Edward P. *The Pueblo Indians of North America.* New York: Holt, Rinehart and Winston, 1970.

Eliade, Mircea. *The Sacred and the Profane.* New York: Harcourt, Brace and World, 1957.

———.*Shamanism: Archaic Techniques of Ecstasy.* Bolingen Series, no. 76. New York: Pantheon, 1964.

Folsom, Franklin. *Red Power on the Rio Grande.* Chicago: Follett Publishing Co., 1973.

Hackett, Charles Edward, ed. and trans. *Historical Documents Relating to New Mexico, Nueva Vizcaya, and Approaches Thereto, to 1773.* Washington, D.C.: Carnegie Institute, 1923-1937.

Hackett, Charles Wilson, ed. *The Revolt of the Pueblo Indians of New Mexico and Otermin's Attempted Reconquest, 1680–1682.* Albuquerque: University of New Mexico Press, 1970.

Josephy, Alvin. *The Patriot Chiefs.* New York: Viking Press, 1969.

Levi-Strauss, Claude. *The Savage Mind.* Chicago: University of Chicago Press, 1966.

Ortiz, Alfonso. *New Perspectives on the Pueblos.* Albuquerque: University of New Mexico Press, 1972.

——.*The Tewa World.* Chicago: University of Chicago Press, 1969.

Ortiz, Roxanne D. "The Roots of Resistance: Pueblo Land Tenure and Spanish Colonization." *Journal of Ethnic Studies* 5 (Winter 1977).

Sando, Joe S. *The Pueblo Indians.* San Francisco: Indian Historian Press, 1976.

Silverburg, Robert. *The Pueblo Revolt.* New York: Weybright and Talley, 1970.

Spicer, Edward H. *Cycles of Conquest.* Tucson: University of Arizona Press, 1976.

Stember, Sol. *Heroes of the American Indian.* New York: Fleet Press Corp., 1971.

Twitchell, Ralph E. *The Leading Facts of New Mexico History.* Cedar Rapids, Iowa: Torch Press, 1912.

Yamasee Case Study

Andrews, Evangeline W., and Charles M. Andrews, eds. *Jonathan Dickensen's Journal or God's Protecting Providence.* New Haven, Conn.: Yale University Press, 1945.

Andrews, Mary P., Maragret M. Bubloz, and Beatrice Paolucci. "An Ecological Approach to the Family." *Marriage and Family Review* 3, no. 3 (Summer 1980).

Blair, Robert M. *White-tailed Deer in the Southern Forest Habitat.* Washington, D.C.: U.S. Department of Agriculture, 1969.

Bourne, Edward G., ed. *Narrative of the Career of Hernando de Soto.* New York: Allerton Books, 1904.

Bushnell, David I., Jr. *Native Villages and Village Sites East of the Mississippi.* Bureau of American Ethnology Bulletin No. 69. Washington, D.C.: U. S. Government Printing Office, 1919.

Caldwell, Joseph R., Catherine McCann, and Frederick S. Hulse. *Irene Mound Site, Chatham County, Georgia.* Athens: University of Georgia Press, 1941.

Chapman, H. H. "Is the Longleaf Type a Climax?" *Ecology* 4 (Winter 1932): 328–34.

Chicken, George. *Journal of George Chicken* [1715-1716]. In *Yearbook of the City of Charlestown*. Charleston, S.C.: City of Charleston, 1894.

Conner, Jeanette T., ed. *Colonial Records of Spanish Florida, 1570-1577*. Deland, Fla.: The Florida State Historical Society, 1925.

Crane, Verner. *The Southern Frontier*. Ann Arbor: University of Michigan Press, 1929.

Crosby, Alfred, Jr. *The Columbian Exchange*. Greenwich, Conn.: Greenwood Press, 1972.

Denevan, William M., ed. *The Native Population of the Americas in 1492*. Madison: University of Wisconsin Press, 1972.

Dixon, Hollingsworth. *Indians of the Savannah River*. Sylvania, Ga: Partridge Pond Press, 1976.

Dobyns, Henry F. *Native American Historical Demography*. Bloomington: Indiana University Press, 1976.

Fairbanks, Charles H. "Gulf Complex Subsistence Economy." *Southeastern Archaeological Conference Bulletin* 3.

Ferguson, Robert. *The Present State of Carolina with Advice to the Settlers*. London: John Bringhurst, 1682.

Fernandez de Oviedo, Gonzalo. *Historia General y Natural de las Indias*. Vols. 117-121 of Bibloteca de Autores Españoles. Madrid: Graficas Orbe, 1959.

Flannery, Regina. "Some Notes on a Few Sites in Beaufort County, South Carolina." Bureau of American Ethnology Bulletin No. 133. Washington, D.C.: Government Printing Office, 1943.

Foucault, Michel. "Truth and Power." In *The Foucault Reader*. New York: Pantheon Books, 1984.

Geronimo de Ore, Luis. *The Martyrs of Florida* [1612], trans. Maynard Geiger. Franciscan Studies No. 18. New York: Joseph F. Wagner, 1936.

Gibert, William H. *Surviving Indian Groups of the Eastern United States*. Washington, D.C.: Smithsonian Institution, 1948.

Gold, Robert. "Conflict in San Carlos: Indian Immigrants in Eighteenth Century Spain." *Ethnohistory* 17, no. 1 (Winter 1970): 1-10.

Gosting, Henry J. "Ecological Processes and Vegetation of the Maritime Strand in the Southeastern United States." *Botanical Review* 20, no. 3 (Summer 1954).

Griffin, James B. "An Analysis and Interpretation of the Ceramic Remains from Two Sites near Beaufort, South Carolina." Bureau of American Ethnology Bulletin No. 133. Washington, D.C.:

Government Printing Office, 1943.

Griffin, James B., ed. *Archaeology of the Eastern United States.* Chicago: University of Chicago Press, 1952.

Grinde, Donald A., Jr. "Native American Slavery in the Southern Colonies." *Indian Historian* 10, no. 2 (Spring 1975).

Haan, Richard L. "The Trade Does Not Flourish as Formerly: The Ecological Origins of the Yamasee War of 1715." *Ethnohistory* 28, no. 4 (Fall 1982).

Hanke, Lewis. *The Spanish Struggle for Justice in the Conquest of America.* Philadelphia: University of Pennsylvania Press, 1949.

Harper, Francis, ed. *The Travels of William Bartram, Naturalist's Edition.* New Haven, Conn.: Yale University Press, 1958.

Harper, Francis, annotator. "Diary of a Journey through the Carolinas, Georgia and Florida, from July 1, 1765, to April 10, 1766." In *Transactions of the American Philosophical Society* 23, no. 1.

Holder, Preston. "Excavations on Saint Simon's Island." (Winter 1936–1937). *Proceedings of the Society of Georgia Archaeology* 1, no. 1 (Spring 1938).

Hollingsworth, Dixon. *Indians of the Savannah River.* Sylvania, Ga.: Partridge Pond Press, 1976.

Howard, James H. "Yamasees." In *John Lawson: A New Voyage to Carolina, 1709*, ed. Hugh T. Lefler. Chapel Hill: University of North Carolina Press, 1967.

———."The Yamasee: A Supposedly Extinct Southeastern Tribe Rediscovered." *American Anthropologist* 62, no. 4. (August 1960).

———."Altamaha Cherokee Folklore and Customs." *Journal of American Folklore* 72, no. 284 (Spring 1959).

Hudson, Charles. *The Southeastern Indians.* Knoxville: University of Tennessee Press, 1976.

Lanning, John Tate. *The Spanish Missions of Georgia.* Chapel Hill: University of North Carolina Press, 1935.

Larson, Lewis H. *Aboriginal Subsistence Technology on the Southeastern Coastal Plain During the Late Prehistoric Period.* Gainesville: University of Florida Press, 1982.

Martyr D'Anghera, Peter. *De Orbe Novo* [1587]. New York: G. P. Putnam & Sons, 1912.

McDowell, W. L., ed. *Journals of the Comissioners of the Indian Trade, September 20–August 29, 1718.* In *Colonial Records of South Carolina*, series 2. Columbia: South Carolina Archives, 1955.

Milliken-Johnson, George. "A Short Description of the Province of South Carolina . . . ." London: John Hinton, 1763.

Milling, Chapman. *Red Carolinians.* Chapel Hill: University of North Carolina Press, 1966.

Oosting, Henry J. "Ecological Processes and Vegetation of the Maritime Strand in the Southeastern United States." *Botanical Review* 20, no. 3 (Summer 1954): 226-62.

Penford, William T., and M. E. O'Neil. "The Vegetation of Cat Island, Mississippi." *Ecology* 15, no. 1 (Spring 1934): 1-13.

Schaffer, James, and James H. Howard. "Medicine and Headdresses of the Yamasee." *American Indian Tradition* 8, no. 3 (1962).

Serrano y Sanz, M., ed. *Documentos Historicos de la Florida y la Luisiana, Siglos XVI al SVII.* Madrid: Libreria Generai de Victoriano Swarex, 1913.

Shelford, Victor E. *The Ecology of North America.* Urbana: University of Illinois Press, 1963.

Sirmons, M. Eugene. *Colonial South Carolina.* Chapel Hill: University of North Carolina Press, 1966.

Smyth, J. F. D. *A Tour of the United States.* London: G. Robinson, J. Robson, and J. Sewell, 1784.

———."Surviving Indian Groups of the Eastern United States." *Smithsonian Institute Annual Report.* Washington, D.C.: Smithsonian Institution, 1948.

Swanton, John R. *The Indian Tribes of North America.* Bureau of American Ethnology Bulletin No. 145. Washington, D.C.: Government Printing Office, 1952.

———. *Early History of the Creek Indians and Their Neighbors.* Bureau of American Ethnology Bulletin No. 73. Washington, D.C.: Government Printing Office, 1922.

Todd, Helen. *Tomochichi.* Covington, Kent: Cherokee Publishing Company, 1977.

Waddell, Gene. *Indians of the South Carolina Low Country, 1562-1757.* Columbia: University of South Carolina Press, 1980.

Wahlenberg, William G. *Longleaf Pine.* Washington, D.C.: U.S. Department of Agriculture, 1946.

Williams, Walter, ed. *Southeastern Indians Since the Removal Era.* Athens: University of Georgia Press, 1979.

Navajo Ecology and Government Policy

Aberle, David. *The Peyote Religion Among the Navaho.* Chicago: University of Chicago Press, 1966.

Billington, Roy A. *The Far Western Frontier 1830-1860.* New York: Harper and Row, 1956.

Capps, Walter H., ed. *Seeing with a Native Eye.* New York: Harper

Forum Books, 1976.

Churchill, Ward. "White Studies or Isolation: An Alternative Model for Native American Studies Programs." Unpublished paper at UCLA American Indian Studies Conference, May 1980.

Deloria, Vine Jr. *God Is Red.* New York: Dell Publishing Company, 1973. Reprinted by North American Press, Golden, Colo., 1993.

Iverson, Peter. "The Evolving Navajo Nation: Diné Continuity Within Change." Ph.D. diss., University of Wisconsin, 1975.

Jacobs, Wilbur P. "Indians as Ecologists . . . ." In *American Indian Environments,* ed. Christopher Vecsey and Robert W. Venables. Syracuse, N.Y.: Syracuse University Press, 1980.

Kammer, Jerry. *The Second Long Walk.* Albuquerque: University of New Mexico Press, 1980.

Martin, Calvin. *Keepers of the Game: Indian-Animal Relationships and the Fur Trade.* Berkeley: University of California Press, 1978.

Roessel, Ruth, ed. *Navajo Livestock Reduction.* Chinle, Ariz.: Navajo Community College, 1975.

Spicer, Edward, ed. *Human Problems in Technological Change.* New York: Russell Sage Foundation, 1952.

Taylor, Graham D. *The New Deal and American Indian Tribalism.* Lincoln: University of Nebraska Press, 1980.

Toelken, Barre. "Seeing with a Native Eye: How Many Sheep Will It Hold?" In *Seeing with a Native Eye,* ed. Walter H. Capps. New York: Harper Forum books, 1976.

Trennert, Robert Anthony. "The Far Western Indian Frontier and the Beginnings of the Reservation System, 1846–1851." Ph.D. diss., University of California, Santa Barbara, 1969.

U.S. Congress, House, Executive Document 263, 49th Cong., 1st sess., 15.

Vecsey, Christopher, and Robert W. Venables, eds. *American Indian Environments.* Syracuse, N.Y.: Syracuse University Press, 1980.

Wasburn, Wilcomb. *The Indian in America.* New York: Harper and Row, 1975.

Whorf, Benjamin Lee. "An American Indian Model of the Universe." In *Language, Thought, and Reality: Selected Writings of Benjamin Lee Whorf,* ed. John M. Carroll. Cambridge, Mass.: MIT Press, 1956.

Yazzie, Ethelou, ed. *Navajo History.* Chinle, Ariz.: Navajo Community College, 1971.

The Navajos and National Sacrifice

Abbey, Edward. *The Journey Home.* New York: Dutton, 1977.

Anquoe, Bunty. "House Begins Investigating Possible Radiation Exposure." *Indian Country Today*, June 9, 1993.

Box, Thadis, et al. *Rehabilitation Potential of Western Coal Lands.* Cambridge, Mass.: Ballinger Publishing Co., 1974.

Baker, James N. "Keeping a Deadly Secret: The Feds Knew the Mines Were Radioactive." *Newsweek*, June 18, 1990.

Barry, Tom, and Beth Wood. "Uranium on the Checkerboard: Crisis at Checkpoint." *American Indian Journal* (June 1978).

Cannon, James. *Leased and Lost: A Study of Public and Indian Coal Leasing in the West.* New York: Council on Economic Priorities, 1974.

——.*Capturing the Energy of the Sun.* Proceedings from the National Conference on Bioconversion as an Energy Resource, March 11–13, 1976.

Gordon, Suzanne. *Black Mesa: Angel of Death.* New York: John Day Co., 1973.

Johansen, Bruce E. "The Reservation Offensive." In *Essential Sociology*, eds. Robert L. Ellis and Marcia J. Lipetz. Glenview, Ill.: Scott, Foresman & Co., 1979.

Johansen, Bruce E., and Roberto F. Maestas. *Wasi'chu: The Continuing Indian Wars.* New York: Monthly Review Press, 1979.

National Indian Youth Council. *Annual Report.* Albuquerque, N.M.: NIYC, 1976.

National Indian Youth Council. *What Is Coal Gasification?* Albuquerque, N.M.: NIYC, 1976.

Reno, Philip. "The Navajos: High, Dry, and Penniless." *The Nation*, March 29, 1975.

U.S. Commission on Civil Rights. *The Farmington Report.* Washington, D.C.: Government Printing Office, July 1975.

U.S. Commission on Civil Rights. *The Navajo Nation: An American Colony.* Washington, D.C.: U.S. Commission on Civil Rights/Government Printing Office, 1975.

Fishing Rights

American Friends Service Committee, comp. *Uncommon Controversy: A Report on the Fishing Rights of the Muckleshoot, Puyallup and Nisqually Indians.* Seattle: University of Washington Press, 1970.

Barsh, Russel L. *The Washington Fishing Rights Controversy: An Economic Critique.* Seattle: University of Washington School of Business Administration, 1977.

Brack, Fred. "Fishing Rights: Who Is Entitled to Northwest Salmon?" *Seattle Post-Intelligencer Northwest Magazine*, January 16, 1977.

Brown, Bruce. *Mountain in the Clouds: A Search for the Wild Salmon.* New York: Simon & Schuster, 1982.

———."A Long Look at the Boldt Decision." *Argus* (Seattle), December 3, 1976.

A Guide to Understanding Chippewa Treaty Rights. Odanah, Wisc.: Great Lakes Indian Fish and Wildlife Commission, 1991.

Johansen, Bruce E. "The Klan in a Can." *The Progressive* (July 1988).

Johansen, Bruce E., and Roberto F. Maestas. *Wasi'chu: The Continuing Indian Wars.* New York: Monthly Review Press, 1979.

Keefe, Tom, Jr. "A Tribute to David Sohappy." *Native Nations* (June/July 1991) :4-7.

Lowman, Bill. *220 Million Custers.* Anacortes, Wash.: Anacortes Printing, 1978.

Meyer, William. *Native Americans: The New Indian Resistance.* New York: International Publishers, 1971.

Miller, Bruce J. "The Press, the Boldt Decision, and Indian-White Relations." *American Indian Culture and Research Journal* 17, no. 2: 75-98.

Netboy, Anthony. *The Atlantic Salmon: A Vanishing Species.* Boston: Houghton Mifflin, 1968.

U.S. Department of the Interior, Bureau of Reclamation. *Columbia River Comprehensive Report on Development.* Washington, D.C.: Government Printing Office, 1947.

U.S. Federal Task Force on Washington State Fisheries. *Settlement Plan for Washington State Salmon and Steelhead Fisheries.* June 1978.

U.S. Senate, Committee on Interior and Insular Affairs, Subcommittee on Indian Affairs. *Indian Fishing Rights: Hearings on S.J.R. 170 and 171.* 88th Cong., 2nd sess., August 5-6, 1964.

Williams, C. Herb, and Walt Neubrech. *Indian Treaties: American Nightmare.* Seattle: Outdoor Empire Publishing, 1976.

Akwesasne's Toxic Turtles

Bailey, Jeff. "EPA Complaint against Waste Haulers May Widen Responsibility in Disposal." *Wall Street Journal*, April 8, 1991.

Benedict, Lloyd. New York State Assembly Hearings. *Crisis at Akwesasne*, Day 1 (Ft. Covington, New York), July 24, 1990.

Churchill, Ward. "The Earth Is Our Mother: Struggles for American

Indian Land and Liberation in the Contemporary United States."
In *The State of Native America*, ed. M. Annette Jaimes. Boston:
South End Press, 1992.

Fenton, William, and Elisabeth Tooker. "Mohawk." In *Handbook of
North American Indians*, ed. William E. Sturtevant. Vol. 15.
Washington, D.C.: Smithsonian Institution, 1978.

Hamel, Peter. "Aborginal Land Rights: A National Crisis." Background
paper prepared for Archbishop Desmond Tutu and Archbishop
Michael Peer, August 3, 1990.

Hauptman, Laurence M. *The Iroquois Struggle for Survival: World War
II to Red Power*. Syracuse, N.Y.: Syracuse University Press, 1986.

Hill, Michael. "Pollution Ravages St. Regis Reservation." Syracuse
Herald-American, July 15, 1990.

Hornung, Rick. *One Nation Under the Gun: Inside the Mohawk Civil
War*. New York: Pantheon, 1991.

Johansen, Bruce E. *Life and Death in Mohawk Country*. Golden, Colo.:
North American Press/Fulcrum, 1993.

Jones, Jeff. "A Nation Divided." *Metroland*, June 7–13, 1990.

Landsman, Gail. *Sovereignty and Symbol: Indian-White Conflict at
Ganienkeh*. Albuquerque: University of New Mexico Press, 1988.

Matthiessen, Peter. *Indian Country*. New York: Viking Press, 1984.

Milich, John E. "Contaminant Cove: Where Polluters Defile Mohawk
Land." *The Progressive* (January 1989): 23–25.

Stone, Ward. New York State Assembly Hearings. *Crisis at Akwesasne*,
Day 2 (Albany, New York), August 2, 1990.

Tomsho, Rupert. "Dumping Grounds: Indian Tribes Contend with
Some of the Worst of America's Pollution." *Wall Street Journal*,
November 29, 1990.

Villan, Mane. "Man Who Remembers Good Days to Remain." Syracuse
Herald-American, June 30, 1991.

York, Geoffrey, and Loreen Pindera. *People of the Pines: The Warriors
and the Legacy of Oka*. Toronto: Little-Brown/Canada, 1992.

Pollution Case Studies

Anquo, Bunty. "House Begins Investigating Possible Radiation
Exposure." *Indian Country Today*, June 9, 1993.

Aranda, Marcelo, and Ignacio March. *Gula de los Mamiferos Silvestres
de Chiapas*. Veracruz, Mexico: INIREB, 1987.

Baker, James N. "Keeping a Deadly Secret: The Feds Knew the Mines
Were Radioactive." *Newsweek*, June 18, 1990.

Barry, Tom, and Beth Wood. "Uranium on the Checkerboard: Crisis at Checkpoint." *American Indian Journal* (June 1978): 10.

Blom, Gertrude D. *Bearing Witness*. Chapel Hill: University of North Carolina Press, 1984.

Bruce, Robert D. *Lacandon Dream Symbolism*. Mexico City: Ediciones Euroamericanas, 1979.

Caufield, Catherine. *In the Rainforest*. New York: Alfred A. Knopf, 1985.

Coon-Come, Matthew. "A Reduction of Our World." In *Our People, Our Land: Perspectives on the Columbus Quincentenary*, ed. Kurt Russo. Bellingham, Wash.: Lummi Tribe and Kluckhohn Center, 1992.

Egan, Timothy. "Eskimos Learn They've Been Living Amid Secret Pits of Radioactive Soil." *New York Times*, December 6, 1992.

Fadden, Mary. "The James Bay Hydro-electric Project." *Northeast Indian Quarterly* 8, no. 2 (Summer 1991).

Foushee, Lea. "Acid Rain Research Paper." Indigenous Women's Network, testimony before the International Council of Indigenous Women, Samiland, Norway, August 1990. Cited in LaDuke, "Indigenous Environmental Perspectives: A North American Primer." In *Indigenous Economics: Toward a Natural World Order*, ed. José Barreiro. *Akwe:kon Journal* 9, no. 2 (Summer 1992): 52–71.

Gil, Patricio Roble et al. *Tierra de Quetzal y del Jaguar*. Coleccion Editorial de Arte Chrysler.

Gorrie, P. "The James Bay Power Project—The Environmental Cost of Reshaping the Geography of Northern Quebec." *Canadian Geographic* (February/March 1990): 20–31.

Jones, Jeff. "A Nation Divided." *Metroland*, June 7–13, 1990.

Johansen, Bruce E. "The Great Uranium Rush." *Baltimore Sun*, May 13, 1979.

——."Uranium Rush in the Black Hills." *The Nation*, April 14, 1979.

——."Native America's Future: Half-Life in the Tailings?" University of Washington *Daily*, October 17, 1979.

Kettl, Paul A. "Suicide and Homicide: The Other Costs of Development." *Akwe:kon Journal* 8, no. 4 (Winter 1991): 58–61.

LaDuke, Winona. "Indigenous Environmental Perspectives: A North American Primer." In *Indigenous Economics: Toward a Natural World Order*, ed. José Barreiro. *Akwe:kon Journal* 9, no. 2 (Summer 1992): 52–71.

——."Tribal Coalition Damns Hydro-Quebec Project." *Indian Country Today*, July 21, 1993.

Leon-Portilla, Miguel. *Time and Reality in the Thought of the Maya*.

Norman: University of Oklahoma Press, 1990.

Myers, Norman. *The Primary Source: Tropical Forests and Our Future.* New York: W. W. Norton, 1984.

Nations, James D., and Ronald Nigh. "The Evolutionary Potential of Lacandon Maya Sustained-Yield Tropical Forest Agriculture." *Journal of Anthropological Research* 36, no. 1 (1980) 1–30.

Picard, A. "James Bay II." *The Amicus Journal* (Fall 1990): 10–17.

Price, T., and L. Hall. *Agricultural Development in the Mexican Tropics: Alternatives for the Selva Lacandona Region of Chiapas.* Cornell International Agricultural Economics Study. Ithaca, N.Y.: Cornell University, 1983.

Ramos, M. A., Gongora Lazcano, Romeo Dominguez, F. Gonzalez, and Ignacio March. *Inventorio Faunistico de la Reserva de la Biosfera Montes Azules.* Mexico: INIREB, 1983.

Rosenthal, J., and J. Beyea. "The Long-term Threats to Canada's James Bay from Human Development." National Audubon Society Environmental Policy Analysis Report No. 29. Washington, D.C.: National Audubon Society, 1989.

Russo, Kurt, and Lisa Dabek. "Common Cause and Common Destiny: The Lacandon Rainforest Project." In *Our People, Our Land: Perspectives of the Columbus Quincentenary*, ed. Kurt Russo. Bellingham, Wash.: Lummi Tribe and Kluckhohn Center, 1992.

———.*The Lacandon Rainforest Project Monitoring Program: A Meeting of Peoples.* Seattle: Kluckhohn Center, 1990.

Stone, Ward. New York State Assembly Hearings. *Crisis at Akwesasne,* Day 2 (Albany, New York), August 2, 1990.

Vos, Jan de. *La Paz de Dios y del Rey: Le Conquista de la Selva Lacandona por los Espanoles 1525-1812.* Primera edicion por el Gobierno del Estado de Chiapas, Tuxtla Gutierrez, 1980; segunda edicion por el Fondo de Cultura Economica, Mexico, D.F., 1988.

Conclusion: Toward Liberation of the Natural World

Aveni, Anthony. *Empires of Time.* New York: Basic Books, 1989.

A Basic Call to Consciousness. Akwesasne Notes. New York: Mohawk Nation via Rooseveltown, 1978.

Brown, Joseph Epes. *The Spiritual Legacy of the American Indian.* New York: Crossroad Publishing Co., 1982.

Catton, William. *Overshoot: The Ecological Basis for Revolutionary Change.* Urbana: University of Illinois Press, 1980.

Churchill, Ward. "The Earth Is Our Mother: Struggles for American

Indian Land and Liberation in the Contemporary United States." In *The State of Native America*, ed. M. Annette Jaimes. Boston: South End Press, 1992.

Churchill, Ward, and Elizabeth R. Lloyd. *Culture versus Economism: Essays on Marxism in the Multicultural Arena*. Denver, Colo.: Fourth World Center for the Study of Indigenous Law and Politics, 1989.

Fox, Matthew. *A Spirituality Named Compassion and the Healing of the Global Village, Humpty Dumpty and Us*. Minneapolis, Minn.: Winston Press, 1979.

Gedicks, Al. *The New Resource Wars: Native and Environmental Struggles Against Multinational Corporations*. Boston: South End Press, 1993.

Gilmore, Melvin R. *Prairie Smoke*. New York: Columbia University Press, 1929.

Grinnell, George Bird. *Pawnee Hero Stories and Folk Tales*. New York: Forest and Stream Publishing Company, 1889.

Horse Capture, George, ed. *The Seven Visions of Bull Lodge*. Lincoln: University of Nebraska Press, 1980.

MacCormack, Sabine. "Demons, Imagination and the Incas." *Representations* 33 (1991).

Martin, Calvin. *Keepers of the Game: Indian-Animal Relationships and the Fur Trade*. Berkeley: University of California Press, 1978.

Wagner, Richard. *Environment and Man*. New York: W. W. Norton, 1974.

Worster, Donald. "Transformations of the Earth: Toward an Agroecological Perspective in History." *Journal of American History* 76, no. 4 (March 1990): 1087–106.

Index

Mt. Sinai School of Medicine Environ-
mental Sciences Laboratory, PCB
contamination study by, 176, 178
Muir, John, 1
Muskogean, 88
Mutual Life Insurance Company, 251

Naja (Lacandon Maya village), 240, 243
Nakai, Pearl, 214
Namibia, 210
Narragansetts, 48
Narsisian, Mark, 196-97
National Academy of Sciences, 125, 131
National Aeronautics and Space
Administration (NASA), 133, 136
National Indian Youth Council (NIYC)
coal gasification and, 133, 137, 139
on harm of uncontrolled coal strip
mining, 135
opposition to uranium mining, 209, 210
support for fishing rights in the Pacific
Northwest, 150
"national sacrifice areas," 120, 125, 135
National Tribal Environment Council, 247
Native American Church, 264
Native Americans
concept of harmony and, 254-55
ecological and spiritual ethic of, 3-4,
261-78
European and Native American worldviews, 4-20
occupation of Canadian Department of
Indian Affairs building, 226
perspectives on the environment, 23-28
Native Australians, uranium poisoning
of, 1
natural gas, 136
Natural Resources Committee, House of
Representatives, U.S., 217
"nature trekkers," Nepal and, 1
Navajo
Pueblo slave raids against the, 61
reverance for corn, 42
treaty of 1868, 204-5
uranium mining on Navajo land, 206-11
uranium poisoning of, 1
use of range fires, 43
Navajo ecology
ecological perceptions, 107-8
and government policy, 105-7
ritual of apology, 108
sheepherding and "pacification," 111-12
stock reduction program, 113-16
U.S. bias in land-use patterns, 108-11
Navajo Election Board, 128
Navajo Irrigation Project, 133, 134
Navajo Service, 114
Navajo Times, 139, 208, 214
Navajo Tribal Council, 113, 114, 129, 139
Navajos and national sacrifice areas,
119-22
gasification, 137-41

mining the "Mother Mountain," 122-28
Navajo Liberation Front, 129-31
reclamation, 131-33
squandering water in an arid land,
34-37
Naval Undersea Center, 136
Nazis, 10
Nebraska, 261
Nelson, Ernest, 115
Nelson River, mercury poisoning in, 227
Nemo, South Dakota, 205
Nepal, and "nature trekkers," 1
Nevada, 218, 237
New Canaan, 5
New England, 5, 6, 50
land tenure in, 36, 37
New Jersey, 175
"New Life Lodge" (Cheyenne), 41
New Mexico, 12
uranium deposits in, 206-11
See also Pueblo Revolt (1680)
New Mexico Citizens for Clean Air and
Water, 212
New World, 45
New York, upstate, 175
New York Assembly Environmental
Conservation Committee, 199
New York City, population in 1770s, 49
New York Public Interest Research Group,
198
New York State
Department of Conservation, 185
Department of Environmental
Conservation, 173, 177-80, 187
Department of Health, 177, 178
frontier described, 7
New York Times, 217
Nez Perce, 31
Niehardt, John, 32
Nisqually (Indians), 150
Nisqually River, 144
noble savage, concept of, 36, 252
Nootka, 44
North America, 263
aquasystem of, 266
beavers in eastern, 5
land tenure in, 37
population before 1492, 45
Turtle Island, Iroquois symbol for, 25,
26, 27, 28, 185
North Slope, Alaska
alcoholism and Alaska natives, 238
suicide and homicide rates among
Alaska natives, 238
Northern Cheyennes
coal leases, 130
fishing rights, 154
Northwest coast, Native American peoples
of, 13, 40, 42
Northwest Indian Fish Commission, 150
Notes on the State of Virginia (Jefferson), 45
Nuclear Regulatory Commision, 211